Canada Under British Rule 1760-1900

Sir John G. Bourinot

Edited by G. W. Prothero

ESPRIOS DIGITAL PUBLISHING

CANADA UNDER BRITISH RULE 1760-1900

BY

SIR JOHN G. BOURINOT, K.C.M.G., LL.D., LITT.D.

Author of 'Parliamentary Procedure and Practice', 'Constitutional History of Canada,' 'The Story of Canada,' etc

1900

CAMBRIDGE HISTORICAL SERIES

EDITED BY G. W. PROTHERO, LITT.D., LL.D.

Honorary Fellow of King's College, Cambridge, and Late Professor of
History in the University of Edinburgh.

GENERAL PREFACE.

The aim of this series is to sketch the history of Modern Europe, with that of its chief colonies and conquests, from about the end of the fifteenth century down to the present time. In one or two cases the story commences at an earlier date: in the case of the colonies it generally begins later. The histories of the different countries are described, as a rule, separately, for it is believed that, except in epochs like that of the French Revolution and Napoleon I, the connection of events will thus be better understood and the continuity of historical development more clearly displayed.

The series is intended for the use of all persons anxious to understand the nature of existing political conditions. "The roots of the present lie deep in the past"; and the real significance of contemporary events cannot be grasped unless the historical causes which have led to them are known. The plan adopted makes it possible to treat the history of the last four centuries in considerable detail, and to embody the most important results of modern research. It is hoped therefore that the series will be useful not only to beginners but to students who have already acquired some general knowledge of European History. For those who wish to carry their studies further, the bibliography appended to each volume will act as a guide to original sources of information and works more detailed and authoritative.

Considerable attention is paid to political geography, and each volume is furnished with such maps and plans as may be requisite for the illustration of the text.

G.W. PROTHERO.

PREFACE.

I devote the first chapter of this short history to a brief review of the colonisation of the valley of the St. Lawrence by the French, and of their political and social conditions at the Conquest, so that a reader may be able to compare their weak and impoverished state under the repressive dominion of France with the prosperous and influential position they eventually attained under the liberal methods of British rule. In the succeeding chapters I have dwelt on those important events which have had the largest influence on the political development of the several provinces as British possessions.

We have, first, the Quebec Act, which gave permanent guarantees for the establishment of the Church of Rome and the maintenance of the language and civil law of France in her old colony. Next, we read of the coming of the United Empire Loyalists, and the consequent establishment of British institutions on a stable basis of loyal devotion to the parent state. Then ensued the war of 1812, to bind the provinces more closely to Great Britain, and create that national spirit which is the natural outcome of patriotic endeavour and individual self-sacrifice. Then followed for several decades a persistent popular struggle for larger political liberty, which was not successful until British statesmen awoke at last from their indifference, on the outbreak of a rebellion in the Canadas, and recognised the necessity of adopting a more liberal policy towards their North American dependencies. The union of the Canadas was succeeded by the concession of responsible government and the complete acknowledgment of the rights of the colonists to manage their provincial affairs without the constant interference of British officials. With this extension of political privileges, the people became still more ambitious, and established a confederation, which has not only had the effect of supplying a remarkable stimulus to their political, social and material development, but has given greater security to British interests on the continent of North America. At particular points of the historical narrative I have dwelt for a space on economic, social, and intellectual conditions, so that the reader may intelligently follow every phase to the development of the people from the close of the French régime to the beginning of the twentieth century In my summary of the most important political events for the last twenty-five years, I have avoided all comment on matters which are "as yet"—to quote the language of the epilogue to Mr. Green's "Short History"—"too near to us to admit of a cool and purely historical treatment." The closing chapter is a short review of the relations between Canada and the United States since the treaty of 1783—so conducive to international disputes concerning boundaries and fishing rights—until the present time, when the Alaskan and other international controversies are demanding adjustment.

I have thought, too, that it would be useful to students of political institutions to give in the appendix comparisons between the leading provisions of the federal systems of the Dominion of Canada and the Commonwealth of Australia. I must add that, in the revision of the historical narrative, I have been much aided by the judicious criticism and apt suggestions of the Editor of the Series, Dr. Prothero.

HOUSE OF COMMONS, OTTAWA, CANADA. 1st October, 1900

CONTENTS.

CHAPTER I.

THE FRENCH RÉGIME (1534—1760)

Section 1. Introduction

Section 2. Discovery and Settlement of Canada by France

Section 3. French exploration in the valleys of North America

Section 4. End of French Dominion in the valley of the St. Lawrence

Section 5. Political, Economic, and Social Conditions of Canada during French Rule

CHAPTER II.

BEGINNINGS OF BRITISH RULE (1749—1774)

Section 1. From the Conquest until the Quebec Act

Section 2. The Foundation of Nova Scotia (1749—1783)

CHAPTER III.

THE AMERICAN REVOLUTION AND THE UNITED EMPIRE LOYALISTS (1763—1784)

Section 1. The successful Revolution of the Thirteen Colonies in America

Section 2. Canada and Nova Scotia during the Revolution.

Section 3. The United Empire Loyalists

CHAPTER IV.

DEVELOPMENT OF REPRESENTATIVE INSTITUTIONS (1784-1812)

Section 1. Beginnings of the Provinces of New Brunswick, Lower Canada and Upper Canada.

Section 2. Twenty years of Political Development. (1792-1812)

CHAPTER V.

THE WAR OF 1812-1815

Section 1. Origin of the war between Great Britain and the United States

Section 2. Canada during the War

CHAPTER VI.

THE EVOLUTION OF RESPONSIBLE GOVERNMENT (1815-1839)

Section 1. The Rebellion in Lower Canada

Section 2. The Rebellion in Upper Canada

Section 3. Social and Economic Conditions of the Provinces in 1838

CHAPTER VII.

A NEW ERA OF COLONIAL GOVERNMENT (1839-1867)

Section 1. The Union of the Canadas and the establishment of Responsible Government

Section 2. Results of Self-government from 1841 to 1864

CHAPTER VIII.

THE EVOLUTION OF CONFEDERATION (1789-1867)

Section 1. The beginnings of Confederation

Section 2. The Quebec Convention of 1864

Section 3. Confederation accomplished

CHAPTER IX.

CONFEDERATION (1867—1900)

Section 1. The First Parliament of the Dominion of Canada (1867—1873)

Section 2. Extension of the Dominion from the Atlantic to the Pacific Ocean (1869—1873)

Section 3. Summary of Noteworthy Events from 1873 until 1900

Section 4. Political and Social Conditions of Canada under Confederation

CHAPTER X.

CANADA'S RELATIONS WITH THE UNITED STATES AND HER INFLUENCE IN IMPERIAL COUNCILS (1783—1900)

APPENDIX A: COMPARISONS BETWEEN CONSTITUTIONS OF THE CANADIAN DOMINION AND AUSTRALIAN COMMONWEALTH.

APPENDIX B: BIBLIOGRAPHICAL NOTES

INDEX

CHAPTER I.

THE FRENCH RÉGIME. 1534—1760.

SECTION I.—Introduction.

Though the principal object of this book is to review the political, economic and social progress of the provinces of Canada under British rule, yet it would be necessarily imperfect, and even unintelligible in certain important respects, were I to ignore the deeply interesting history of the sixteen hundred thousand French Canadians, about thirty per cent of the total population of the Dominion. To apply to Canada an aphorism of Carlyle, "The present is the living sum-total of the whole past"; the sum-total not simply of the hundred and thirty years that have elapsed since the commencement of British dominion, but primarily of the century and a half that began with the coming of Champlain to the heights of Quebec and ended with the death of Wolfe on the Plains of Abraham. The soldiers and sailors, the missionaries and pioneers of France, speak to us in eloquent tones, whether we linger in summer time on the shores of the noble gulf which washes the eastern portals of Canada; whether we ascend the St. Lawrence River and follow the route taken by the explorers, who discovered the great lakes, and gave to the world a knowledge of the West and the Mississippi, whether we walk on the grassy mounds that recall the ruins of the formidable fortress of Louisbourg, which once defended the eastern entrance to the St. Lawrence; whether we linger on the rocks of the ancient city of Quebec with its many memorials of the French régime; whether we travel over the rich prairies with their sluggish, tortuous rivers, and memories of the French Canadians who first found their way to that illimitable region. In fact, Canada has a rich heritage of associations that connect us with some of the most momentous epochs of the world's history. The victories of Louisbourg and Quebec belong to the same series of brilliant events that recall the famous names of Chatham, Clive, and Wolfe, and that gave to England a mighty empire in Asia and America. Wolfe's signal victory on the heights of the ancient capital was the prelude to the great drama of the American revolution. Freed from the fear of

France, the people of the Thirteen Colonies, so long hemmed in between the Atlantic Ocean and the Appalachian range, found full expression for their love of local self-government when England asserted her imperial supremacy. After a struggle of a few years they succeeded in laying the foundation of the remarkable federal republic, which now embraces forty-five states with a population of already seventy-five millions of souls, which owes its national stability and prosperity to the energy and enterprise of the Anglo-Norman race and the dominant influence of the common law, and the parliamentary institutions of England. At the same time, the American Revolution had an immediate and powerful effect upon the future of the communities that still remained in the possession of England after the acknowledgement of the independence of her old colonies. It drove to Canada a large body of men and women, who remained faithful to the crown and empire and became founders of provinces which are now comprised in a Dominion extending for over three thousand miles to the north and east of the federal republic.

The short review of the French régime, with which I am about to commence this history of Canada, will not give any evidence of political, economic, or intellectual development under the influence of French dominion, but it is interesting to the student of comparative politics on account of the comparisons which it enables us to make between the absolutism of old France which crushed every semblance of independent thought and action, and the political freedom which has been a consequence of the supremacy of England in the province once occupied by her ancient rival. It is quite true, as Professor Freeman has said, that in Canada, which is pre-eminently English in the development of its political institutions, French Canada is still "a distinct and visible element, which is not English,—an element older than anything English in the land,—and which shows no sign of being likely to be assimilated by anything English." As this book will show, though a hundred and forty years have nearly passed since the signing of the treaty of Paris, many of the institutions which the French Canadians inherited from France have become permanently established in the country, and we see constantly in the various political systems given to Canada from time to time—notably in the constitution of the federal union—the impress of these institutions and the influence of the people of the French section. Still, while the French Canadians by their adherence to their language, civil law and religion are decidedly "a distinct and visible element which is not English"—an element kept apart from the English by positive legal and constitutional guarantees or barriers of separation,—we shall see that it is the influence and operation of English institutions, which have made their province one of the most contented communities of the world. While their old institutions are inseparably associated with the social and spiritual conditions of their daily lives, it is after all their political constitution, which derives its strength from English, principles, that has made the French Canadians a free, self-governing people and developed the best elements of their character to a degree which was never possible under the depressing and enfeebling conditions of the French régime.

SECTION 2.—Discovery and settlement of Canada by France.

Much learning has been devoted to the elucidation of the Icelandic Sagas, or vague accounts of voyages which Bjorne Heriulfson and Lief Ericsson, sons of the first Norse settlers of Greenland, are supposed to have made at the end of the tenth century, to the eastern parts of what is now British North America, and, in the opinion of some writers, even as far as the shores of New England. It is just possible that such voyages were made, and that Norsemen were the first Europeans who saw the eastern shores of Canada. It is quite certain, however, that no permanent settlements were made by the Norsemen in any part of these countries; and their voyages do not appear to have been known to Columbus or other maritime adventurers of later times, when the veil of mystery was at last lifted from the western limits of what was so long truly described as the "sea of darkness." While the subject is undoubtedly full of interest, it is at the same time as illusive as the *fata morgana*, or the lakes and rivers that are created by the mists of a summer's eve on the great prairies of the Canadian west.

Five centuries later than the Norse voyagers, there appeared on the great field of western exploration an Italian sailor, Giovanni Caboto, through whose agency England took the first step in the direction of that remarkable maritime enterprise which, in later centuries, was to be the admiration and envy of all other nations. John Cabot was a Genoese by birth and a Venetian citizen by adoption, who came during the last decade of the fifteenth century, to the historic town of Bristol. Eventually he obtain from Henry VII letters-patent, granting to himself and his three sons, Louis, Sebastian, and Sancio, the right, "at their own cost and charges, to seek out and discover unknown lands," and to acquire for England the dominion over the countries they might discover. Early in May, 1497, John Cabot sailed from Bristol in "The Matthew," manned by English sailors. In all probability he was accompanied by Sebastian, then about 21 years of age, who, in later times, through the credulity of his friends and his own garrulity and vanity, took that place in the estimation of the world which his father now rightly fills. Some time toward the end of June, they made a land-fall on the north-eastern coast of North America. The actual site of the land-fall will always be a matter of controversy unless some document is found among musty archives of Europe to solve the question to the satisfaction of the disputants, who wax hot over the claims of a point near Cape Chidley on the coast of Labrador, of Bonavista, on the east shore of Newfoundland, of Cape North, or some other point, on the island of Cape Breton. Another expedition left Bristol in 1498, but while it is now generally believed that Cabot coasted the shores of North America from Labrador or Cape Breton as far as Cape Hatteras, we have no details of this famous voyage, and are even ignorant of the date when the fleet returned to England.

The Portuguese, Gaspar and Miguel Cortereal, in the beginning of the sixteenth century, were lost somewhere on the coast of Labrador or Newfoundland, but not before they gave to their country a claim to new lands. The Basques and Bretons, always noted for their love of the sea, frequented the same prolific waters and some of the latter gave a name to the picturesque island of Cape Breton. Giovanni da Verrazzano, a Florentine by birth, who had for years led a roving life on the sea, sailed in 1524 along the coasts of Nova Scotia and the present United States and gave a shadowy claim of first discovery of a great region to France under whose authority he sailed. Ten years later Jacques Cartier of St. Malo was authorised by Francis I to undertake a voyage to these new lands, but he did not venture beyond the Gulf of St. Lawrence, though he took possession of the picturesque Gaspé peninsula in the name of his royal master. In 1535 he made a second voyage, whose results were most important for France and the world at large. The great river of Canada was then discovered by the enterprising Breton, who established a post for some months at Stadacona, now Quebec, and also visited the Indian village of Hochelaga on the island of Montreal. Here he gave the appropriate name of Mount Royal to the beautiful height which dominates the picturesque country where enterprise has, in the course of centuries, built a noble city. Hochelaga was probably inhabited by Indians of the Huron-Iroquois family, who appear, from the best evidence before us, to have been dwelling at that time on the banks of the St. Lawrence, whilst the Algonquins, who took their place in later times, were living to the north of the river.

The name of Canada—obviously the Huron-Iroquois word for Kannata, a town—began to take a place on the maps soon after Cartier's voyages. It appears from his *Bref Récit* to have been applied at the time of his visit, to a kingdom, or district, extending from Ile-aux-Coudres, which he named on account of its hazel-nuts, on the lower St. Lawrence, to the Kingdom of Ochelay, west of Stadacona; east of Canada was Saguenay, and west of Ochelay was Hochelaga, to which the other communities were tributary. After a winter of much misery Cartier left Stadacona in the spring of 1536, and sailed into the Atlantic by the passage between Cape Breton and Newfoundland, now appropriately called Cabot's Straits on modern maps. He gave to France a positive claim to a great region, whose illimitable wealth and possibilities were never fully appreciated by the king and the people of France even in the later times of her dominion. Francis, in 1540, gave a commission to Jean François de la Roque, Sieur de Roberval, to act as his viceroy and lieutenant-general in the country discovered by Cartier, who was elevated to the position of captain general and master pilot of the new expedition. As the Viceroy was unable to complete his arrangements by 1541, Cartier was obliged to sail in advance, and again passed a winter on the St. Lawrence, not at Stadacona but at Cap Rouge, a few miles to the west, where he built a post which he named Charlesbourg-Royal. He appears to have returned to France some time during the summer of 1542, while Roberval was on his way to the St. Lawrence. Roberval found his way without his master pilot to

Charlesbourg-Royal, which he renamed France-Roy, and where he erected buildings of a very substantial character in the hope of establishing a permanent settlement. His selection of colonists—chiefly taken from jails and purlieus of towns—was most unhappy, and after a bitter experience he returned to France, probably in the autumn of 1543, and disappeared from Canadian history.

From the date of Cartier's last voyage until the beginning of the seventeenth century, a period of nearly sixty years, nothing was done to settle the lands of the new continent. Fishermen alone continued to frequent the great gulf, which was called for years the "Square gulf" or "Golfo quadrado," or "Quarré," on some European maps, until it assumed, by the end of the sixteenth century, the name it now bears. The name Saint-Laurens was first given by Cartier to the harbour known as Sainte-Geneviève (or sometimes Pillage Bay), on the northern shore of Canada, and gradually extended to the gulf and river. The name of Labrador, which was soon established on all maps, had its origin in the fact that Gaspar Cortereal brought back with him a number of natives who were considered to be "admirably calculated for labour."

In the reign of Queen Elizabeth, the English began to take a prominent part in that maritime enterprise which was to lead to such remarkable results in the course of three centuries. The names of the ambitious navigators, Frobisher and Davis, are connected with those arctic waters where so much money, energy, and heroism have been expended down to the present time. Under the influence of the great Ralegh, whose fertile imagination was conceiving plans of colonization in America, Sir Humphrey Gilbert, his brother-in-law, took possession of Newfoundland on a hill overlooking the harbour of St. John's. English enterprise, however, did not extend for many years to any other part of North Eastern America than Newfoundland, which is styled Baccalaos on the Hakluyt map of 1597, though the present name appeared from a very early date in English statutes and records. The island, however, for a century and longer, was practically little more than "a great ship moored near the banks during the fishing season, for the convenience of English fishermen," while English colonizing enterprise found a deeper interest in Virginia with its more favourable climate and southern products. It was England's great rival, France, that was the pioneer at the beginning of the seventeenth century in the work of exploring, and settling the countries now comprised within the Dominion of Canada.

France first attempted to settle the indefinite region, long known as *La Cadie* or *Acadie*[1]. The Sieur de Monts, Samuel Champlain, and the Baron de Poutrincourt were the pioneers in the exploration of this country. Their first post was erected on Dochet Island, within the mouth of the St. Croix River, the present boundary between the state of Maine and the province of New Brunswick; but this spot was very soon found unsuitable, and the hopes of the pioneers were immediately turned towards the beautiful basin, which was first named Port Royal by Champlain. The Baron de Poutrincourt obtained a grant of land around this basin, and determined to make his home in so beautiful a spot. De Monts, whose charter was revoked in 1607, gave up the project of colonizing Acadia, whose history from that time is associated for years with the misfortunes of the Biencourts, the family name of Baron de Poutrincourt; but the hopes of this adventurous nobleman were never realized. In 1613 an English expedition from Virginia, under the command of Captain Argall, destroyed the struggling settlement at Fort Royal, and also prevented the establishment of a Jesuit mission on the island of Monts-Déserts, which owes its name to Champlain. Acadia had henceforth a checquered history, chiefly noted for feuds between rival French leaders and for the efforts of the people of New England to obtain possession of Acadia. Port Royal was captured in 1710 by General Nicholson, at the head of an expedition composed of an English fleet and the militia of New England. Then it received the name of Annapolis Royal in honour of Queen Anne, and was formally ceded with all of Acadia "according to its ancient limits" to England by the treaty of Utrecht.

[1: This name is now generally admitted to belong to the language of the Micmac Indians of the Atlantic provinces. It means a place, or locality, and is always associated with another word descriptive of some special natural production; for instance, Shubenacadie, or Segubunakade, is the place where the ground-nut, or Indian potato, grows. We find the first official mention of the word in the commission given by Henry IV of France to the Sieur de Monts in 1604.]

It was not in Acadia, but in the valley of the St. Lawrence, that France made her great effort to establish her dominion in North America. Samuel Champlain, the most famous man in the history of French Canada, laid the foundation of the present city of Quebec in the month of June, 1608, or three years after the removal of the little Acadian colony from St. Croix Island to the basin of the Annapolis. The name Quebec is now generally admitted to be an adaptation of an Indian word, meaning a contraction of the river or strait, a distinguishing feature of the St. Lawrence at this important point. The first buildings were constructed by Champlain on a relatively level piece of ground, now occupied by a market-house and close to a famous old church erected in the days of Frontenac, in commemoration of the victorious repulse of the New England expedition led by Phipps. For twenty-seven years Champlain struggled against constantly accumulating difficulties to establish a colony on the St. Lawrence. He won the confidence of the Algonquin and Huron tubes of Canada, who then lived on the St. Lawrence and Ottawa rivers, and in the vicinity of Georgian Bay. Recognizing the necessity of an alliance with the Canadian Indians, who controlled all the principal avenues to the great fur-bearing regions, he led two expeditions, composed of Frenchmen, Hurons, and Algonquins, against the Iroquois or Confederacy of the Five Nations[2] — the Mohawks, the Oneidas, Onondagas, Cayugas, and Senecas — who inhabited the fertile country stretching from the Genesee to the Hudson River in the present state of New York. Champlain consequently excited against his own people the inveterate hostility of the bravest, cruellest and ablest Indians with whom Europeans have ever come in contact in America. Champlain probably had no other alternative open to him than to become the active ally of the Canadian Indians, on whose goodwill and friendship he was forced to rely; but it is also quite probable that he altogether underrated the ability and bravery of the Iroquois who, in later years, so often threatened the security of Canada, and more than once brought the infant colony to the very verge of ruin.

[2: In 1715 the confederacy was joined by the Tuscaroras, a southern branch of the same family, and was then called more properly the Six Nations.]

It was during Champlain's administration of affairs that the Company of the Hundred Associates was formed under the auspices of Cardinal Richelieu, with the express object of colonizing Canada and developing the fur-trade and other commercial enterprises on as large a scale as possible. The Company had ill-fortune from the outset. The first expedition it sent to the St. Lawrence was captured by a fleet commanded by David Kirk, a gentleman of Derbyshire, who in the following year also took Quebec, and carried Champlain and his followers to England. The English were already attempting settlements on the shores of Massachusetts Bay; and the poet and courtier, Sir William Alexander, afterwards known as the Earl of Stirling, obtained from the King of England all French Acadia, which he named Nova Scotia and offered to settlers in baronial giants. A Scotch colony was actually established for a short time at Port Royal under the auspices of Alexander, but in 1632, by the treaty of St. Germain-en-Laye, both Acadia and Canada were restored to France. Champlain returned to Quebec, but the Company of the Hundred Associates had been severely crippled by the ill-luck which attended its first venture, and was able to do very little for the struggling colony during the three remaining years of Champlain's life.

The Recollets or Franciscans, who had first come to the country in 1615, now disappeared, and the Jesuits assumed full control in the wide field of effort that Canada offered to the missionary. The Jesuits had, in fact, made their appearance in Canada as early as 1625, or fourteen years after two priests of their order, Ennemond Massé and Pierre Biard, had gone to Acadia to labour among the Micmacs or Souriquois. During the greater part of the seventeenth century, intrepid Jesuit priests are associated with some of the most heroic incidents of Canadian history.

When Champlain died, on Christmas-day, 1635, the French population of Canada did not exceed 150 souls, all dependent on the fur-trade. Canada so far showed none of the elements of prosperity; it was not a colony of settlers but of fur-traders. Still Champlain, by his indomitable will, gave to France a footing in America which she was to retain for a century and a quarter after his death. His courage amid the difficulties that surrounded him, his fidelity to his church and country, his ability to understand the Indian character, his pure unselfishness, are among the remarkable qualities of a man who stands foremost among the pioneers of European civilization in America.

From the day of Champlain's death until the arrival of the Marquis de Tracy, in 1665, Canada was often in a most dangerous and pitiable position. That period of thirty years was, however, also distinguished by the foundation of those great religious communities which have always exercised such an important influence upon the conditions of life throughout French Canada. In 1652 Montreal was founded under the name of Ville-Marie by Paul Chomedey, Sieur de Maisonneuve, and a number of other religious enthusiasts. In 1659, the Abbé de Montigny, better known to Canadians as Monseigneur de Laval, the first Roman Catholic bishop, arrived in the colony and assumed charge of ecclesiastical affairs under the titular name of Bishop of Petraea. Probably no single man has ever exercised such powerful and lasting influence on Canadian institutions as that famous divine. Possessed of great tenacity of purpose, most ascetic in his habits, regardless of all worldly considerations, always working for the welfare and extension of his church, Bishop Laval was eminently fitted to give it that predominance in civil as well as religious affairs which it so long possessed in Canada.

While the Church of Rome was perfecting its organization throughout Canada, the Iroquois were constantly making raids upon the unprotected settlements, especially in the vicinity of Montreal. The Hurons in the Georgian Bay district were eventually driven from their comfortable villages, and now the only remnants of a powerful nation are to be found in the community of mixed blood at Lorette, near Quebec, or on the banks of the Detroit River, where they are known as Wyandots. The Jesuit mission of Sainte-Marie in their country was broken up, and Jean de Brébeuf and Gabriel Lalemant suffered torture and death.

Such was the pitiable condition of things in 1663, when Louis XIV made of Canada a royal government. At this time the total population of the province did not exceed 2500 souls, grouped chiefly in and around Quebec, Three Rivers and Montreal. In 1665 the Marquis de Tracy and Governor de Courcelles, with a brilliant retinue of officers and a regiment of soldiers, arrived in the colony, and brought with them conditions of peace and prosperity. A small stream of immigration flowed steadily into the country for some years, as a result of the new policy adopted by the French government. The Mohawks, the most daring and dangerous nation of the Iroquois confederacy, were humbled by Tracy in 1667, and forced to sue for peace. Under the influence of Talon, the ablest intendant who ever administered Canadian affairs, the country enjoyed a moderate degree of prosperity, although trade continued entirely dependent on the orders and regulations of the King and his officials.

Among the ablest governors of Canada was undoubtedly Louis de la Buade, Count de Frontenac, who administered public affairs from 1672-1687 and from 1689-1698. He was certainly impatient, choleric and selfish whenever his pecuniary interests were concerned; but, despite his faults of character, he was a brave soldier, dignified and courteous on important occasions, a close student of the character of the Indians, always ready when the necessity arose to adapt himself to their foibles and at the same time able to win their confidence. He found Canada weak, and left it a power in the affairs of America. He infused his own never-failing confidence into the hearts of the struggling colonists on the St. Lawrence, repulsed Sir William Phipps and his New England expedition when they attacked Quebec in 1690, wisely erected a fort on Lake Ontario as a fur-trading post and a bulwark against the Iroquois, encouraged the fur-trade, and stimulated exploration in the west and in the valleys of the Ohio and the Mississippi. The settlements of New England trembled at his name, and its annals contain many a painful story of the misery inflicted by his cruel bands of Frenchmen and Indians.

Despite all the efforts of the French government for some years, the total immigration from 1663 until 1713, when the great war between France and the Grand Alliance came to an end by the treaty of Utrecht, did not exceed 6000 souls, and the whole population of the province in that year was only 20,000, a small number for a century of colonization. For some years after the formation of the royal government, a large number of marriageable women were brought to the country under the auspices of the religious communities, and marriages and births were encouraged by exhortations and bounties. A considerable number of the officers and soldiers of the Carignan-Salières regiment, who followed the Marquis de Tracy into Canada, were induced to remain and settle new seigniories, chiefly in palisaded villages in the Richelieu district for purposes of defence against Iroquois expeditions. Despite all the paternal efforts of the government to stimulate the growth of a large population, the natural increase was small during the seventeenth century. The disturbing influence, no doubt, was the fur-trade, which allured so many young men into the wilderness, made them unfit for a steady life, and destroyed their domestic habits. The emigrants from France came chiefly from Anjou, Saintonge, Paris and its suburbs, Normandy, Poitou, Beauce, Perche, and Picardy. The Carignan-Salières regiment brought men from all parts of the parent state. It does not appear that any number of persons ever came from Brittany. The larger proportion of the settlers were natives of the north-western provinces of France, especially from Perche and Normandy, and formed an excellent stock on which to build up a thrifty, moral people. The seigniorial tenure of French Canada was an adaptation of the feudal system of France to the conditions of a new country, and was calculated in some respects to stimulate settlement. Ambitious persons of limited means were able to form a class of colonial *noblesse*. But unless the seignior cleared a certain portion of his grant within a limited time, he would forfeit it all. The conditions by which the *censitaires* or tenants of the seigniorial domain held their grants of land were by no means burdensome, but they signified a dependency of tenure inconsistent with the free nature of American life. A large portion of the best lands of French Canada were granted under this seigniorial system to men whose names frequently occur in the records of the colony down to the present day: Rimouski, Bic and Métis, Kamouraska, Nicolet, Verchères, Lotbinière, Berthier, Beloeil, Rouville, Juliette, Terrebonne, Champlain, Sillery, Beaupré, Bellechasse, Portneuf, Chambly, Sorel, Longueuil, Boucherville, Chateauguay, Lachine, are memorials of the seigniorial grants of the seventeenth century.

The whole population of the Acadian Peninsula in 1710-13, was not more than 1500 souls, nearly all descendants of the people brought to the country by Poutrincourt and his successors Razilly and Charnisay. At no time did the French government interest itself in immigration to neglected Acadia. Of the total population, nearly 1000 persons were settled in the beautiful country which the industry and ingenuity of the Acadian peasants, in the course of many years, reclaimed from the restless tides of the Bay of Fundy at Grand Pré and Minas. The remaining settlements were at Beau Bassin, Annapolis, Piziquit (now Windsor), Cobequit (now Truro), and Cape Sable. Some small settlements were also founded on the banks of the St. John River and on the eastern bays of the present province of New Brunswick.

SECTION 3.—French exploration in the great valleys of North America.

The hope of finding a short route to the rich lands of Asia by the St. Lawrence River and its tributary lakes and streams, influenced French voyagers and explorers well into the middle of the eighteenth century. When Cartier stood on Mount Royal and saw the waters of the Ottawa there must have flashed across his mind the thought that perhaps by this river would be found that passage to the western sea of which he and other sailors often dreamed both in earlier and later times. L'Escarbot tells us that Champlain in his western explorations always hoped to reach Asia by a Canadian route. He was able, however, long before his death to make valuable contributions to the geography of Canada. He was the first Frenchman to ascend the River of the Iroquois, now the Richelieu, and to see the beautiful lake which still bears his name. In 1615 he found his way to Georgian Bay by the route of the Ottawa and Mattawa Rivers, Lake Nipissing and French River. Here he visited the Huron villages which were situated in the district now known as Simcoe county in the province of Ontario. Father le Caron, a Recollet, had preceded the French explorer, and was performing missionary duties among the Indians, who probably numbered 20,000 in all. This brave priest was the pioneer of an army of faithful missionaries—mostly of a different order—who lived for years among the Indians, suffered torture and death, and connected their names not only with the martyrs of their faith but also with the explorers of this continent. From this time forward we find the trader and the priest advancing in the wilderness; sometimes one is first, sometimes the other.

Champlain accompanied his Indian allies on an expedition against the Onondagas, one of the five nations who occupied the country immediately to the south of the upper St. Lawrence and Lake Ontario. The party reached Lake Ontario by the system of inland navigation which stretches from Lake Simcoe to the Bay of Quinté. The Onondagas repulsed the Canadian allies who returned to their settlements, where Champlain remained during the winter of 1616. It was during this expedition, which did much to weaken Champlain's prestige among the Indians, that Étienne Brulé an interpreter, was sent to the Andastes, who were then living about the headwaters of the Susquehanna, with the hope of bringing them to the support of the Canadian savages. He was not seen again until 1618, when he returned to Canada with a story, doubtless correct, of having found himself on the shores of a great lake where there were mines of copper, probably Lake Superior.

With the new era of peace that followed the coming of the Viceroy Tracy in 1665, and the establishment of a royal government, a fresh impulse was given to exploration and mission work in the west. Priests, fur-traders, gentlemen-adventurers, *coureurs de bois*, now appeared frequently on the lakes and rivers of the west, and gave in the course of years a vast region to the dominion of France. As early as 1665 Father Allouez established a mission at La Pointe, the modern Ashland, on the shores of Lake Superior. In 1668 one of the most interesting persons who ever appeared in early Canada, the missionary and explorer, Father Marquette, founded the mission of Sainte-Marie on the southern side of the Sault, which may be considered the oldest settlement of the north-west, as it alone has a continuous history to the present time.

In the record of those times we see strikingly displayed certain propensities of the Canadian people which seriously interfered with the settlement and industry of the country. The fur-trade had far more attractions for the young and adventurous than the regular and active life of farming on the seigniories. The French immigrant as well as the native Canadian adapted himself to the conditions of

Indian life. Wherever the Indian tribes were camped in the forest or by the river, and the fur-trade could be prosecuted to the best advantage, we see the *coureurs de bois*, not the least picturesque figures of these grand woods, then in the primeval sublimity of their solitude and vastness. Despite the vices and weaknesses of a large proportion of this class, not a few were most useful in the work of exploration and exercised a great influence among the Indians of the West. But for these forest-rangers the Michigan region would have fallen into the possession of the English who were always intriguing with the Iroquois and endeavouring to obtain a share of the fur-trade of the west. Joliet, the companion of Marquette, in his ever-memorable voyage to the Mississippi, was a type of the best class of the Canadian fur-trader.

In 1671 Sieur St. Lusson took formal possession of the Sault and the adjacent country in the name of Louis XIV. In 1673 Fort Frontenac was built at Cataraqui, now Kingston, as a barrier to the aggressive movements of the Iroquois and an *entrepôt* for the fur-trade on Lake Ontario. In the same year Joliet and Marquette solved a part of the problem which had so long perplexed the explorers of the West. The trader and priest reached the Mississippi by the way of Green Bay, the Fox and Wisconsin Rivers. They went down the Mississippi as far as the Arkansas. Though they were still many hundreds of miles from the mouth of the river, they grasped the fact that it must reach, not the western ocean, but the southern gulf first discovered by the Spaniards. Marquette died not long afterwards, worn out by his labours in the wilderness, and was buried beneath the little chapel at St. Ignace. Joliet's name henceforth disappears from the annals of the West.

Réné Robert Cavelier, better known as the Sieur de la Salle, completed the work commenced by the trader and missionary. In 1666 he obtained a grant of land at the head of the rapids above Montreal by the side of that beautiful expanse of the St. Lawrence, still called Lachine, a name first given in derisive allusion to his hope of finding a short route to China. In 1679 he saw the Niagara Falls for the first time, and the earliest sketch is to be found in *La Nouvelle Découverte* written or compiled by that garrulous, vain, and often mendacious Recollet Friar, Louis Hennepin, who accompanied La

Salle on this expedition. In the winter of 1681-82 this famous explorer reached the Mississippi, and for weeks followed its course through the novel and wondrous scenery of a southern land. On the 9th of April, 1682, at a point just above the mouth of the great river, La Salle took formal possession of the Mississippi valley in the name of Louis XIV, with the same imposing ceremonies that distinguished the claim asserted by St. Lusson at the Sault in the lake region. By the irony of fate, La Salle failed to discover the mouth of the river when he came direct from France to the Gulf of Mexico in 1685, but landed somewhere on Matagorda Bay on the Texan coast, where he built a fort for temporary protection. Finding his position untenable, he decided in 1687 to make an effort to reach the Illinois country, but when he had been a few days on this perilous journey he was treacherously murdered by some of his companions near the southern branch of Trinity River. His body was left to the beasts and birds of prey. Two of the murderers were themselves killed by their accomplices, none of whom appear ever to have been brought to justice for their participation in a crime by which France lost one of the bravest and ablest men who ever struggled for her dominion in North America.

Some years later the famous Canadians, Iberville and Bienville, founded a colony in the great valley, known by the name of Louisiana, which was first given to it by La Salle himself. By the possession of the Sault, Mackinac, and Detroit, the French were for many years supreme on the lakes, and had full control of Indian trade. The Iroquois and their English friends were effectively shut out of the west by the French posts and settlements which followed the explorations of Joliet, La Salle, Du Luth, and other adventurers. Plans continued to be formed for reaching the Western or Pacific ocean even in the middle of the eighteenth century. The Jesuit Charlevoix, the historian of New France, was sent out to Canada by the French government to enquire into the feasibility of a route which Frenchmen always hoped for. Nothing definite came out of this mission, but the Jesuit was soon followed by an enterprising native of Three Rivers, Pierre Gaultier de Varennes, generally called the Sieur de la Verendrye, who with his sons ventured into the region now known as the province of Manitoba and the north-west territory of Canada. He built several forts, including one on the site of the city of Winnipeg. Two of his sons are believed to have reached the Big Horn Range, an "outlying buttress" of the Rocky Mountains, in 1743, and to have taken possession of what is now territory of the United States. The youngest son, Chevalier de la Verendrye, who was the first to see the Rocky Mountains, subsequently discovered the Saskatchewan (Poskoiac) and even ascended it as far as the forks—the furthest western limits so far touched by a white man in America. A few years later, in 1751, M. de Niverville, under the orders of M. de St. Pierre, then acting in the interest of the infamous Intendant Bigot, who coveted the western fur-trade, reached the foot-hills of the Rocky Mountains and built a fort on the Saskatchewan not far from the present town of Calgary.

We have now followed the paths of French adventurers for nearly a century and a half, from the day Champlain landed on the rocks of Quebec until the Verendryes traversed the prairies and plains of the North-west. French explorers had discovered the three great waterways of this continent—the Mississippi, which pours its enormous volume of water, drawn from hundreds of tributaries, into a southern gulf; the St. Lawrence, which bears the tribute of the great lakes to the Atlantic Ocean; the Winnipeg, with its connecting rivers and lakes which stretch from the Rocky Mountains to the dreary Arctic sea. La Verendrye was the first Frenchman who stood on the height of land or elevated plateau of the continent, almost within sight of the sources of those great rivers which flow, after devious courses, north, south and east. It has been well said that if three men should ascend these three waterways to their farthest sources, they would find themselves in the heart of North America; and, so to speak, within a stone's throw of one another. Nearly all the vast territory, through which these great waterways flow, then belonged to France, so far as exploration, discovery and partial occupation gave her a right to exercise dominion. Only in the great North, where summer is a season of a very few weeks, where icebergs bar the way for many months, where the fur-trade and the whale-fishery alone offered an incentive to capital and enterprise, had England a right to an indefinite dominion. Here a "Company of Gentlemen-Adventurers trading into Hudson's Bay" occupied some fortified stations which, during the seventeenth century, had been seized by the daring French-Canadian corsair, Iberville, who ranks with the famous Englishman, Drake. On the Atlantic coast the prosperous English colonies occupied a narrow range of country bounded by the Atlantic Ocean and the Alleghanies. It was only in the middle of the eighteenth century—nearly three-quarters of a century after Joliet's and La Salle's explorations, and even later than the date at which Frenchmen had followed the Saskatchewan to the Rocky Mountains—that some enterprising Virginians and Pennsylvanians worked their way into the beautiful country watered by the affluents of the Ohio. New France may be said to have extended at that time from Cape Breton or Isle Royale west to the Rocky Mountains, and from the basin of the Great Lakes to the Gulf of Mexico.

SECTION 4.—End of French dominion in the valley of the St. Lawrence.

After the treaty of Utrecht, France recognized the mistake she had made in giving up Acadia, and devoted her attention to the island of Cape Breton, or Isle Royale, on whose southeastern coast soon rose the fortifications of Louisbourg. In the course of years this fortress became a menace to English interests in Acadia and New England. In 1745 the town was taken by a force of New England volunteers, led by General Pepperrell, a discreet and able colonist, and a small English squadron under the command of Commodore, afterwards Admiral, Warren, both of whom were rewarded by the British government for their distinguished services on this memorable occasion. France, however, appreciated the importance of Isle Royale, and obtained its restoration in exchange for Madras which at that time was the most important British settlement in the East Indies. England then decided to strengthen herself in Acadia, where France retained her hold of the French Acadian population through the secret influence of her emissaries, chiefly missionaries, and accordingly established a town on the Atlantic coast of Nova Scotia, ever since known as Halifax, in honour of a prominent statesman of those times. The French settlers, who by the middle of the eighteenth century numbered 12,000, a thrifty, industrious and simple-minded people, easily influenced by French agents, called themselves "Neutrals," and could not be forced to take the unqualified oath of allegiance which was demanded of them by the authorities of Halifax. The English Government was now determined to act with firmness in a province where British interests had been so long neglected, and where the French inhabitants had in the course of forty years shown no disposition to consider themselves British subjects and discharge their obligations to the British Crown. France had raised the contention that the Acadia ceded to England by the treaty of Utrecht comprised only the present province of Nova Scotia, and indeed only a portion of that peninsula according to some French authorities. Commissioners were appointed by the two Powers to settle the question of boundaries—of the meaning of "Acadie, with its ancient boundaries"—but their negotiations came to naught and the issue was only settled by the arbitrament of war. The French built the forts of Beauséjour and Gaspereau—the latter a mere palisade—on the Isthmus of Chignecto, which became the rendezvous of the French Acadians, whom the former persuaded by promises or threats to join their fortunes. In 1755 a force of English and Colonial troops, under the command of Colonels Moncton, Winslow and Scott, captured these forts, and this success was followed by the banishment of the Acadian French. This cruel act of Governor Lawrence and the English authorities at Halifax was no doubt largely influenced by the sentiment of leading men in New England, who were apprehensive of the neighbourhood of so large a number of an alien people, who could not be induced to prove their loyalty to Great Britain, and might, in case of continued French successes in America, become open and dangerous foes. But while there are writers who defend this sad incident of American history on the ground of stern national necessity at a critical period in the affairs of the continent, all humanity that listens to the dictates of the heart and tender feeling will ever deplore the exile of those hapless people.

Previous to the expulsion of the Acadians from their pleasant homes on the meadows of Grand Pré and Minas, England sustained a severe defeat in the valley of the Ohio, which created much alarm throughout the English colonies, and probably had some influence on the fortunes of those people. France had formally taken possession of the Ohio country and established forts in 1753 on French Creek, at its junction with the Alleghany, and also at the forks of the Ohio. Adventurous British pioneers were at last commencing to cross the Alleghanies, and a company had been formed with the express intention of stimulating settlement in the valley. George Washington, at the head of a small Colonial force, was defeated in his attempt to drive the French from the Ohio; and the English Government was compelled to send out a large body of regular troops under the command of General Braddock, who met defeat and death on the banks of the Monongahela, General Johnson, on the other hand, defeated a force of French regulars, Canadian Militia and Indians, under General Dieskau, at the southern end of Lake George.

In 1756 war was publicly proclaimed between France and England, although, as we have just seen, it had already broken out many months previously in the forests of America. During the first two years of the war the English forces sustained several disasters through the incompetency of the English commanders on land and sea. The French in Canada were now led by the Marquis de Montcalm, distinguished both as a soldier of great ability and as a man of varied intellectual accomplishments. In the early part of the Canadian campaign he was most fortunate. Fort William Henry, at the foot of Lake George, and Fort Oswego, on the south side of Lake Ontario, were captured, but his signal victory at the former place was sullied by the massacre of defenceless men, women and children by his Indian allies, although it is now admitted by all impartial writers that he did his utmost to prevent so sad a sequel to his triumph. The English Commander-in-Chief, Lord Loudoun, assembled a large military force at Halifax in 1757 for the purpose of making a descent on Louisbourg; but he returned to New York without accomplishing anything, when he heard of the disastrous affair of William Henry, for which he was largely responsible on account of having failed to give sufficient support to the defenders of the fort. Admiral Holbourne sailed to Louisbourg, but he did not succeed in coming to an engagement with the French fleet then anchored in the harbour, and the only result of his expedition was the loss of several of his ships on the reefs of that foggy, rocky coast.

In 1758 Pitt determined to enter on a vigorous campaign against France in Europe and America. For America he chose Amherst, Boscawen, Howe, Forbes, Wolfe, Lawrence and Whitman. Abercromby was unfortunately allowed to remain in place of Loudoun, but it was expected by Pitt and others that Lord Howe, one of the best soldiers in the British army, would make up for the military weakness of that commander. Louisbourg, Fort Duquesne, and the forts on Lake George, were the immediate objects of attack. Abercromby at the head of a large force failed ignominiously in his assault on Ticonderoga, and Lord Howe was one of the first to fall in that unhappy and ill-managed battle. Amherst and Boscawen, on the other hand, took Louisbourg, where Wolfe displayed great energy and contributed largely to the success of the enterprise. Forbes was able to occupy the important fort at the forks of the Ohio, now Pittsburg, which gave to the English control of the beautiful country to the west of the Alleghanies. Fort Frontenac was taken by Bradstreet, and Prince Edward Island, then called Isle St. Jean, was occupied by an English force as the necessary consequence of the fall of the Cape Breton fortress. The nation felt that its confidence in Pitt was fully justified, and that the power of France in America was soon to be effectually broken.

In 1759 and 1760 Pitt's designs were crowned with signal success. Wolfe proved at Quebec that the statesman had not overestimated his value as a soldier and leader. Wolfe was supported by Brigadiers Moncton, Townshend, Murray, and Guy Carleton—the latter a distinguished figure in the later annals of Canada. The fleet was commanded by Admirals Saunders, Durell and Holmes, all of whom rendered most effective service. The English occupied the Island of Orleans and the heights of Lévis, from which they were able to keep up a most destructive fire on the capital. The whole effective force under Wolfe did not reach 9000 men, or 5000 less than the regular and Colonial army under Montcalm, whose lines extended behind batteries and earthworks from the St. Charles River, which washes the base of the rocky heights of the town, as far as the falls of Montmorency. The French held an impregnable position which their general decided to maintain at all hazards, despite the constant efforts of Wolfe for weeks to force him to the issue of battle. Above the city for many miles there were steep heights, believed to be unapproachable, and guarded at all important points by detachments of soldiery. Wolfe failed in an attempt which he made at Beauport to force Montcalm from his defences, and suffered a considerable loss through the rashness of his grenadiers. He then resolved on a bold stroke which succeeded by its very audacity in deceiving his opponent, and giving the victory to the English. A rugged and dangerous path was used at night up those very heights which, Montcalm confidently believed, "a hundred men could easily defend against the whole British army." On the morning of the 13th September, 1759, Wolfe marshalled an army of four thousand five hundred men on the Plains of Abraham where he was soon face to face with the French army. Montcalm had lost no time in accepting the challenge of the English, in the hope that his superior numbers would make up for their inferiority in discipline and equipment compared with the smaller English force. His expectations were never realized. In a few minutes the French fell in hundreds before the steady deadly fire of the English lines, and Montcalm was forced to retreat precipitately with the beaten remnant of his army. Wolfe received several wounds, and died on the battlefield, but not before he was conscious of his victory. "God be praised," were his dying words, "I now die in peace." His brave adversary was mortally wounded while seeking the protection of Quebec, and was buried in a cavity which a shell had made in the floor of the chapel of the Ursuline Convent. A few days later Quebec capitulated. Wolfe's body was taken to England, where it was received with all the honours due to his great achievement. General Murray was left in command at Quebec, and was defeated in the following spring by Lévis in the battle of St. Foye, which raised the hopes of the French until the appearance of English ships in the river relieved the beleaguered garrison and decided for ever the fate of Quebec. A few weeks later Montreal capitulated to Amherst, whose extreme caution throughout the campaign was in remarkable contrast with the dash and energy of the hero of Quebec. The war in Canada was now at an end, and in 1763 the treaty of Paris closed the interesting chapter of French dominion on the banks of the St. Lawrence and in the valleys of the Ohio and the Mississippi.

SECTION 5.—Political, economic and social conditions of Canada during French ride.

France and England entered on the struggle for dominion in America about the same time, but long before the conquest of Canada the communities founded by the latter had exhibited a vigour and vitality which were never shown in the development of the relatively poor and struggling colonies of Canada and Louisiana. The total population of New France in 1759—that is, of all the French possessions in North America—did not exceed 70,000 souls, of whom 60,000 were inhabitants of the country of the St. Lawrence, chiefly of the Montreal and Quebec districts. France had a few struggling villages and posts in the very "garden of the North-west," as the Illinois country has been aptly called; but the total population of New France from the great lakes to the Gulf of Mexico did not exceed 10,000 souls, the greater number of whom dwelt on the lower banks of the Mississippi. At this time the British colonies in America, pent up between the Atlantic Ocean and the Appalachian mountains, had a population twenty times larger than that of Canada and Louisiana combined, and there was not any comparison whatever between these French and British colonies with respect to trade, wealth or any of the essentials of prosperity.

Under the system of government established by Louis XIV, under the advice of Colbert, the governor and intendant of Canada were, to all intents and purposes in point of authority, the same officials who presided over the affairs of a province of France. In Canada, as in France, governors-general had only such powers as were expressly given them by the king, who, jealous of all authority in others, kept them rigidly in check. In those days the king was supreme; "I am the state," said Louis Quatorze in the arrogance of his power; and it is thus easy to understand that there could be no such free government or representative institutions in Canada as were enjoyed from the very commencement of their history by the old English colonies.

The governor had command of the militia and troops, and was nominally superior in authority to the intendant, but in the course of time the latter became virtually the most influential officer in the colony and even presided at the council-board. This official, who had the right to report directly to the king on colonial affairs, had large civil, commercial and maritime jurisdiction, and could issue ordinances which had full legal effect in the country. Associated with the governor and intendant was a council comprising in the first instance five, and eventually twelve, persons, chosen from the leading people of the colony. The change of name, from the "Supreme Council" to the "Superior Council," is of itself some evidence of the determination of the king to restrain the pretensions of all official bodies throughout the kingdom and its dependencies. This body exercised legislative and judicial powers. The bishop was one of its most important members, and the history of the colony is full of the quarrels that arose between him and the governor on points of official etiquette or with respect to more important matters affecting the government of the country.

Protestantism was unknown in Canada under French rule, and the enterprise of the Huguenots was consequently lost to a country always suffering from a want of population. Even the merchants of La Rochelle, who traded with the country, found themselves invariably subject to restrictions which placed them at an enormous disadvantage in their competition with their Roman Catholic rivals. The Roman Catholic Church was all powerful at the council-board as well as in the parish. In the past as in the present century, a large Roman Catholic church rose, the most prominent building in every town and village, illustrating its dominating influence in the homes of every community of the province. The parishes were established at an early date for ecclesiastical purposes, and their extent was defined wherever necessary by the council at Quebec. They were practically territorial divisions for the administration of local affairs, and were conterminous, whenever practicable, with the seigniory. The curé, the seignior, the militia captain (often identical with the seignior), were the important functionaries in every parish. Even at the present time, when a canonical parish has been once formed by the proper ecclesiastical authority, it may be erected into a municipal or civil division after certain legal formalities by the government of the province. Tithes were first imposed by Bishop Laval, who practically established the basis of ecclesiastical authority in the province. It was only in church matters that the people had the right to meet and express their opinions, and even then the intendant alone could give the power of assembling for such purposes.

The civil law of French Canada relating to "property," inheritance, marriage, and the personal or civil rights of the community generally, had its origin, like all similar systems, in the Roman law, on which were engrafted, in the course of centuries, those customs and usages which were adapted to the social conditions of France.

The customary law of Paris became the fundamental law of French Canada, and despite the changes that it has necessarily undergone in the course of many years, its principles can still be traced throughout the present system as it has been modified under the influences of the British regime. The superior council of Canada gave judgment in civil and criminal cases according to the *coutume de Paris*, and below it there were inferior courts for the judicial districts of Quebec, Three Rivers and Montreal. The bishop had also special jurisdiction over ecclesiastical matters. The intendant had authority to deal with cases involving royal, or seigniorial, rights, and to call before him any case whatever for final review and judgment. In all cases appeals were allowable to the king himself, but the difficulty of communication with Europe in those days practically confined such references to a few special causes. The seigniors had also certain judicial or magisterial powers, but they never acted except in very trivial cases. Torture was sometimes applied to condemned felons as in France and other parts of the old world. On the whole justice appears to have been honestly and fairly administered.

Parkman, in a terse sentence, sums up the conditions which fettered all Canadian trade and industry, "A system of authority, monopoly and exclusion in which the government, and not the individual, acted always the foremost part." Whether it was a question of ship-building, of a brewery or a tannery, of iron works or a new fishery, appeals must be made in the first instance to the king for aid; and the people were never taught to depend exclusively on their individual or associated enterprise. At the time of the conquest, and in fact for many years previously, the principal products of the country were beaver skins, timber, agricultural products, fish, fish oil, ginseng (for some years only), beer, cider, rug carpets, homespun cloths—made chiefly by the inmates of the religious houses—soap, potash, leather, stoves, tools and other iron manufactures—made in the St. Maurice forges—never a profitable industry, whether carried on by companies or the government itself. All these industries were fostered by the state, but, despite all the encouragement they received, the total value of the exports, principally furs, seal and other oils, lumber, peas, grain and ginseng never exceeded 3,500,000 francs, or about one-tenth of the export trade of the English colonies to Great Britain. Two-thirds of this amount represented beaver skins, the profits on which were very fluctuating, on account of the unwise regulations by which, the trade was constantly crippled. This business was heavily taxed to meet the necessities of colonial government, which were always heavy, and could never have been met had it not been for the liberality of the king. In the year 1755 the amount of all exports did not reach 2,500,000 francs, while the imports were valued at 8,000,000 francs. These imports represented wines, brandies, hardware and various luxuries, but the bulk was made up of the supplies required for the use of the military and civil authorities. The whole trade of the country was carried in about thirty sea-going vessels, none of them of heavy tonnage. The royal government attempted to stimulate ship-building in the country, and a few war vessels were actually built in the course of many years, though it does not appear that this industry was ever conducted with energy or enterprise. During the last fifty years of French rule, in all probability, not a hundred sea-going vessels were launched in the valley of the St. Lawrence. Duties of import, before 1748, were only imposed on wines, brandies, and Brazilian tobacco; but after the commencement of the war with England, the king found it necessary to establish export and import duties: a special exception was however made in favour of the produce of the farm, forest and sea, which were allowed to enter or go out free. The whole amount of duties raised in ordinary years did not reach above 300,000 francs.

In the closing years of French dominion the total population of Quebec, Montreal and Three Rivers, the only towns in the province, did not exceed 13,000 souls—about the population of Boston. Quebec alone had 8000 inhabitants, Montreal 4000, and Three Rivers 1000. The architecture of these places was more remarkable for solidity than elegance or symmetry of proportions. The churches, religious and educational establishments, official buildings and residences—notably the intendant's palace at Quebec—were built of stone. The most pretentious edifice was the château of St. Louis—the residence of the governor-general—which was rebuilt by Count de Frontenac within the limits of the fort of St. Louis, first erected by Champlain on the historic height always associated with his name. The best buildings in the towns were generally of one story and constructed of stone. In the rural parishes, the villages, properly speaking, consisted of a church, presbytery, school, and tradesmen's houses, while the farms of the *habitants* stretched on either side. The size and shape of the farms were governed by the form of the seigniories throughout the province. M. Bourdon, the first Canadian surveyor-general, originally mapped out the seigniories in oblong shapes with very narrow frontage along the river—a frontage of two or three *arpents* against a depth of from forty to eighty *arpents*—and the same inconvenient oblong plan was followed in making sub-grants to the *censitaire* or *habitant*. The result was a disfigurement of a large portion of the country, as the civil law governing the succession of estates gradually cut up all the seigniories into a number of small farms, each in the form of the parallelogram originally given to the seigniorial grants. The houses of the *habitants*, then as now, were generally built of logs or sawn lumber, all whitewashed, with thatched or wooden roofs projecting over the front so as to form a sort of porch or verandah. The farm-houses were generally close together, especially in the best cultivated and most thickly settled districts between Quebec and Montreal. Travellers, just before the Seven Years' War, tell us that the farms in that district appeared to be well cultivated on the whole, and the homes of the *habitants* gave evidences of thrift and comfort. Some farmers had orchards from which cider was made, and patches of the coarse strong tobacco which they continue to use to this day, and which is now an important product of their province. Until the war the condition of the French Canadian *habitant* was one of rude comfort. He could never become rich, in a country where there was no enterprise or trade which encouraged him to strenuous efforts to make and save money. Gold and silver were to him curiosities, and paper promises to pay, paper or card money, were widely circulated from early times, and were never for the most part redeemed, though the British authorities after the peace of 1763 made every possible effort to induce the French government to discharge its obligations to the French Canadian people. The life of the *habitants* in peaceful times was far easier and happier than that of the peasants of old France. They had few direct taxes to bear, except the tithes required for the support of the church and such small contributions as were necessary for local purposes. They were, however, liable to be called out at any moment for military duties and were subject to *corvées* or forced labour for which they were never paid by the authorities.

The outbreak of the Seven Years' War was a serious blow to a people who had at last surmounted the greatest difficulties of pioneer life, and attained a moderate degree of comfort. The demands upon the people capable of bearing arms were necessarily fatal to steady farming occupations; indeed, in the towns of Quebec and Montreal there was more than once an insufficiency of food for the garrisons, and horse-flesh had to be served out, to the great disgust of the soldiers who at first refused to take it. Had it not been for the opportune arrival of a ship laden with provisions in the spring of 1759, the government would have been unable to feed the army or the inhabitants of Quebec. The gravity of the situation was aggravated for years by the jobbery and corruption of the men who had the fate of the country largely in their hands. A few French merchants, and monopolists in league with corrupt officials, controlled the markets and robbed a long-suffering and too patient people. The names of Bigot, Péan, and other officials of the last years of French administration, are justly execrated by French Canadians as robbers of the state and people in the days when the country was on the verge of war, and Montcalm, a brave, incorruptible man, was fighting against tremendous odds to save this unfortunate country to which he gave up his own life in vain.

So long as France governed Canada, education was entirely in the hands of the Roman Catholic Church. The Jesuits, Franciscans, and other religious orders, male and female, at an early date, commenced the establishment of those colleges and seminaries which have always had so important a share in the education of Lower Canada. The Jesuits founded a college at Quebec in 1635, or three years before the establishment of Harvard, and the Ursulines opened their convent in the same city four years later. Sister Bourgeoys of Troyes founded at Montreal in 1659 the Congrégation de Notre-Dame for the education of girls of humble rank; the commencement of an institution which has now its buildings in many parts of Canada. In the latter part of the seventeenth century Bishop Laval carried out a project for providing education for Canadian priests drawn from the people of the country. Consequently, in addition to the great seminary at Quebec, there was the lesser seminary where boys were taught in the hope that they would take orders. In the inception of education the French endeavoured in more than one of their institutions to combine industrial pursuits with the ordinary branches of an elementary education. But all accounts of the days of the French régime go to show that, despite the zealous efforts of the religious bodies to improve the education of the colonists, secular instruction was at a very low ebb and hardly reached the seigniories. One writer tells us that "even the children of officers and gentlemen scarcely knew how to read and write; they were ignorant of the first elements of geography and history." Still, dull and devoid of intellectual life as was the life of the Canadian, he had his place of worship where he received a moral training which elevated him immeasurably above the peasantry of England as well as of his old home. The clergy of Lower Canada confessedly did their best to relieve the ignorance of the people, but they were naturally unable to accomplish, by themselves, a task which properly devolved on the governing class. Under the French régime in Canada the civil authorities were as little anxious to enlighten the people by the establishment of public or common schools as they were to give them a voice in the government of the country.

Evidence of some culture and intellectual aspirations in social circles of the ancient capital attracted the surprise of travellers who visited the country before the close of the French dominion. "Science and the fine arts," wrote Charlevoix, in 1744, "have their turn and conversation does not fail. The Canadians breathe from their birth an air of liberty, which makes them very pleasant in the intercourse of life, and our language is nowhere more purely spoken." La Gallissonière, a highly cultured governor, spared no effort to encourage a sympathetic study of scientific pursuits. Dr. Michel Sarrasin, who was a practising physician in Quebec for nearly half a century, devoted himself most assiduously to the natural history of the colony, and made some valuable contributions to the French Academy. The Swedish botanist, Peter Kalm, was impressed with the liking for scientific study which he observed in the French colony. But such intellectual culture, as Kalm and Charlevoix mentioned, never showed itself beyond the walls of Quebec or Montreal. The province, as a whole, was in a state of mental sluggishness at the time of the conquest by England, under whose benign influence the French Canadian people were now to enter on a new career of political and intellectual development.

Canada Under British Rule 1760-1900

Pitt and Wolfe must take a high place among the makers of the Dominion of Canada. It was they who gave relief to French Canada from the absolutism of old France, and started her in a career of self-government and political liberty. When the great procession passed before the Queen of England on the day of the "Diamond Jubilee"—when delegates from all parts of a mighty, world-embracing empire gave her their loyal and heartfelt homage—Canada was represented by a Prime Minister who belonged to that race which has steadily gained in intellectual strength, political freedom, and material prosperity, since the memorable events of 1759 and 1760. In that imperial procession nearly half the American Continent was represented—Acadia and Canada first settled by France, the north-west prairies first traversed by French Canadian adventurers, the Pacific coast first seen by Cook and Vancouver. There, too, marched men from Bengal, Madras, Bombay, Jeypore, Haidarabad, Kashmir, Punjaub, from all sections of that great empire of India which was won for England by Clive and the men who, like Wolfe, became famous for their achievements in the days of Pitt. Perhaps there were in that imperial pageant some Canadians whose thoughts wandered from the Present to the Past, and recalled the memory of that illustrious statesman and of all he did for Canada and England, when they stood in Westminster Abbey, and looked on his expressive effigy, which, in the eloquent language of a great English historian, "seems still, with eagle face and outstretched arm, to bid England be of good cheer and to hurl defiance at her foes."

CHAPTER II.

BEGINNINGS OF BRITISH RULE. 1760-1774.

SECTION I.—From the Conquest until the Quebec Act.

For nearly four years after the surrender of Vaudreuil at Montreal, Canada was under a government of military men, whose headquarters were at Quebec, Three Rivers, and Montreal—the capitals of the old French districts of the same name. General Murray and the other commanders laboured to be just and considerate in all their relations with the new subjects of the Crown, who were permitted to prosecute their ordinary pursuits without the least interference on the part of the conquerors. The conditions of the capitulations of Quebec and Montreal, which allowed the free exercise of the Roman Catholic religion, were honourably kept. All that was required then, and for many years later, was that the priests and curés should confine themselves exclusively to their parochial duties, and not take part in public matters. It had been also stipulated at Montreal that the communities of nuns should not be disturbed in their convents; and while the same privileges were not granted by the articles of capitulation to the Jesuits, Recollets, and Sulpitians, they had every facility given to them to dispose of their property and remove to France. As a matter of fact there was practically no interference with any of the religious fraternities during the early years of British rule; and when in the course of time the Jesuits disappeared entirely from the country their estates passed by law into the possession of the government for the use of the people, while the Sulpitians were eventually allowed to continue their work and develope property which became of great value on the island of Montreal. (The French merchants and traders were allowed all the commercial and trading privileges that were enjoyed by the old subjects of the British Sovereign, not only in the valley of the St. Lawrence, but in the rich fur regions of the West and North-West.) The articles of capitulation did not give any guarantees or pledges for the continuance of the civil law under which French Canada had been governed for over a century, but while that was one of the questions dependent on the ultimate fate of Canada, the British military rulers took every possible care during the continuance of the military régime to respect so far as possible the old customs and laws by which the people had been previously governed. French writers of those days admit the generosity and justice of the administration of affairs during this military régime.

The treaty of Paris, signed on the 10th February, 1763, formally ceded to England Canada as well as Acadia, with all their dependencies. The French Canadians were allowed full liberty "to profess the worship of their religion according to the rites of the Romish Church, as far as the laws of Great Britain permit." The people had permission to retire from Canada with all their effects within eighteen months from the date of the ratification of the treaty. All the evidence before us goes to show that only a few officials and seigniors ever availed themselves of this permission to leave the country. At this time there was not a single French settlement beyond Vaudreuil until the traveller reached the banks of the Detroit between Lakes Erie and Huron. A chain of forts and posts connected Montreal with the basin of the great lakes and the country watered by the Ohio, Illinois, and other tributaries of the Mississippi. The forts on the Niagara, at Detroit, at Michillimackinac, at Great Bay, on the Maumee and Wabash, at Presqu' isle, at the junction of French Creek with the Alleghany, at the forks of the Ohio, and at less important localities in the West and South-West, were held by small English garrisons, while the French still occupied Vincennes on the Wabash and Chartres on the Mississippi, in the vicinity of the French settlements at Kaskaskia, Cahokia, and the present site of St. Louis.

Soon after the fall of Montreal, French traders from New Orleans and the French settlements on the Mississippi commenced to foment disaffection among the western Indians, who had strong sympathy with France, and were quite ready to believe the story that she would ere long regain Canada. The consequence was the rising of all the western tribes under the leadership of Pontiac, the principal chief of the Ottawas, whose warriors surrounded and besieged Detroit when he failed to capture it by a trick. Niagara was never attacked, and Detroit itself was successfully defended by Major Gladwin, a fearless soldier; but all the other forts and posts very soon fell into the hands of the Indians, who massacred the garrisons in several places. They also ravaged the border settlements of Pennsylvania and Virginia, and carried off a number of women and children to their wigwams. Fort Pitt at the confluence of the Alleghany and the Monongahela rivers—the site of the present city of Pittsburg—was in serious peril for a time, until Colonel Bouquet, a brave and skilful officer, won a signal victory over the Indians, who fled in dismay to their forest fastnesses. Pontiac failed to capture Detroit, and Bouquet followed up his first success by a direct march into the country of the Shawnees, Mingoes and Delawares, and forced them to agree to stern conditions of peace on the banks of the Muskingum. The power of the western Indians was broken for the time, and the British in 1765 took possession of the French forts of Chartres and Vincennes, when the *fleur-de-lys* disappeared for ever from the valley of the Mississippi. The French settlers on the Illinois and the Mississippi preferred to remain under British rule rather than cross the great river and become subjects of Spain, to whom Western Louisiana had been ceded by France. From this time forward France ceased to be an influential factor in the affairs of Canada or New France, and the Indian tribes recognized the fact that they could no longer expect any favour or aid from their old ally. They therefore transferred their friendship to England, whose power they had felt in the Ohio valley, and whose policy was now framed with a special regard to their just treatment.

This Indian war was still in progress when King George III issued his proclamation for the temporary government of his new dependencies in North America. As a matter of fact, though the proclamation was issued in England on the 7th October, 1763, it did not reach Canada and come into effect until the 10th August, 1764. The four governments of Quebec, Grenada, East Florida, and West Florida were established in the territories ceded by France and Spain. The eastern limit of the province of Quebec did not extend beyond St. John's River at the mouth of the St. Lawrence, nearly opposite to Anticosti, while that island itself and the Labrador country, east of the St. John's as far as the Straits of Hudson, were placed under the jurisdiction of Newfoundland. The islands of Cape Breton and St. John, now Prince Edward, became subject to the Government of Nova Scotia, which then included the present province of New Brunswick. The northern limit of the province did not extend beyond the territory known as Rupert's Land under the charter given to the

Hudson's Bay Company in 1670, while the western boundary was drawn obliquely from Lake Nipissing as far as Lake St. Francis on the St. Lawrence; the southern boundary then followed line 45° across the upper part of Lake Champlain, whence it passed along the highlands which divide the rivers that empty themselves into the St. Lawrence from those that flow into the sea—an absurdly defined boundary since it gave to Canada as far as Cape Rosier on the Gaspé peninsula a territory only a few miles wide. No provision whatever was made in the proclamation for the government of the country west of the Appalachian range, which was claimed by Pennsylvania, Virginia, and other colonies under the indefinite terms of their original charters, which practically gave them no western limits. Consequently the proclamation was regarded with much disfavour by the English colonists on the Atlantic coast. No provision was even made for the great territory which extended beyond Nipissing as far as the Mississippi and included the basin of the great lakes. It is easy to form the conclusion that the intention of the British government was to restrain the ambition of the old English colonies east of the Appalachian range, and to divide the immense territory to their north-west at some future and convenient time into several distinct and independent governments. No doubt the British government also found it expedient for the time being to keep the control of the fur-trade so far as possible in its own hands, and in order to achieve this object it was necessary in the first place to conciliate the Indian tribes, and not allow them to come in any way under the jurisdiction of the chartered colonies. The proclamation itself, in fact, laid down entirely new, and certainly equitable, methods of dealing with the Indians within the limits of British sovereignty. The governors of the old colonies were expressly forbidden to grant authority to survey lands beyond the settled territorial limits of their respective governments. No person was allowed to purchase land directly from the Indians. The government itself thenceforth could alone give a legal title to Indian lands, which must, in the first place, be secured by treaty with the tribes that claimed to own them. This was the beginning of that honest policy which has distinguished the relations of England and Canada with the Indian nations for over a hundred years, and which has obtained for the present Dominion the confidence and friendship of the many thousand Indians, who roamed for many centuries in Rupert's Land and in the Indian Territories where the Hudson's Bay Company long enjoyed exclusive privileges of trade.

The language of the proclamation with respect to the government of the province of Quebec was extremely unsatisfactory. It was ordered that so soon as the state and circumstances of the colony admitted, the governor-general could with the advice and consent of the members of the council summon a general assembly, "in such manner and form as is used and directed in those colonies and provinces in America which are under our immediate government." Laws could be made by the governor, council, and representatives of the people for the good government of the colony, "as near as may be agreeable to the laws of England, and under such regulations and restrictions as are used in other colonies." Until such an assembly could be called, the governor could with the advice of his council constitute courts for the trial and determination of all civil and criminal cases, "according to law and equity, and as near as may be agreeable to the laws of England," with liberty to appeal, in all civil cases, to the privy council of England. General Murray, who had been in the province since the battle on the Plains of Abraham, was appointed to administer the government. Any persons elected to serve in an assembly were required, by his commission and instructions, before they could sit and vote, to take the oaths of allegiance and supremacy, and subscribe a declaration against transubstantiation, the adoration of the Virgin, and the Sacrifice of the Mass.

This proclamation—in reality a mere temporary expedient to give time for considering the whole state of the colony—was calculated to do infinite harm, since its principal importance lay in the fact that it attempted to establish English civil as well as criminal law, and at the same time required oaths which effectively prevented the French Canadians from serving in the very assembly which it professed a desire on the part of the king to establish. The English-speaking or Protestant people in the colony did not number in 1764 more than three hundred persons, of little or no standing, and it was impossible to place all power in their hands and to ignore nearly seventy thousand French Canadian Roman Catholics. Happily the governor,

General Murray, was not only an able soldier, as his defence of Quebec against Lévis had proved, but also a man of statesmanlike ideas, animated by a high sense of duty and a sincere desire to do justice to the foreign people committed to his care. He refused to lend himself to the designs of the insignificant British minority, chiefly from the New England colonies, or to be guided by their advice in carrying on his government. His difficulties were lessened by the fact that the French had no conception of representative institutions in the English sense, and were quite content with any system of government that left them their language, religion, and civil law without interference. The stipulations of the capitulations of 1759-1760, and of the treaty of Paris, with respect to the free exercise of the Roman Catholic religion, were always observed in a spirit of great fairness: and in 1766 Monseigneur Briand was chosen, with the governor's approval, Roman Catholic bishop of Quebec. He was consecrated at Paris after his election by the chapter of Quebec, and it does not appear that his recognition ever became the subject of parliamentary discussion. This policy did much to reconcile the French Canadians to their new rulers, and to make them believe that eventually they would receive full consideration in other essential respects.

For ten years the government of Canada was in a very unsatisfactory condition, while the British ministry was all the while worried with the condition of things in the old colonies, then in a revolutionary ferment. The Protestant minority continued to clamour for an assembly, and a mixed system of French and English law, in case it was not possible to establish the latter in its entirety. Attorney-General Masères, an able lawyer and constitutional writer, was in favour of a mixed system, but his views were notably influenced by his strong prejudices against Roman Catholics. The administration of the law was extremely confused until 1774, not only on account of the ignorance and incapacity of the men first sent out from England to preside over the courts, but also as a consequence of the steady determination of the majority of French Canadians to ignore laws to which they had naturally an insuperable objection. In fact, the condition of things became practically chaotic. It might have been much worse had not General Murray, at first, and Sir Guy Carleton, at a later time, endeavoured, so far as lay in their power, to mitigate the hardships to which the people were subject by being forced to observe laws of which they were entirely ignorant.

At this time the governor-general was advised by an executive council, composed of officials and some other persons chosen from the small Protestant minority of the province. Only one French Canadian appears to have been ever admitted to this executive body. The English residents ignored the French as far as possible, and made the most unwarrantable claims to rule the whole province.

A close study of official documents from 1764 until 1774 goes to show that all this while the British government was influenced by an anxious desire to show every justice to French Canada, and to adopt a system of government most conducive to its best interests In 1767 Lord Shelburne wrote to Sir Guy Carleton that "the improvement of the civil constitution of the province was under their most serious consideration." They were desirous of obtaining all information "which can tend to elucidate how far it is practicable and expedient to blend the English with the French laws, in order to form such a system as shall be at once equitable and convenient for His Majesty's old and new subjects." From time to time the points at issue were referred to the law officers of the crown for their opinion, so anxious was the government to come to a just conclusion. Attorney-General Yorke and Solicitor-General De Grey in 1766 severely condemned any system that would permanently "impose new, unnecessary and arbitrary rules (especially as to the titles of land, and the mode of descent, alienation and settlement), which would tend to confound and subvert rights instead of supporting them." In 1772 and 1773 Attorney-General Thurlow and Solicitor-General Wedderburne dwelt on the necessity of dealing on principles of justice with the province of Quebec. The French Canadians, said the former, "seem to have been strictly entitled by the *jus gentium* to their property, as they possessed it upon the capitulation and treaty of peace, together with all its qualities and incidents by tenure or otherwise." It seemed a necessary consequence that all those laws by which that property was created, defined, and secured, must be continued to them. The Advocate-General Marriott, in 1773, also made a number of valuable suggestions in the same spirit, and at the same time expressed the opinion that under the existent conditions of the country it was not possible or expedient to call an assembly. Before the imperial government came to a positive conclusion on the vexed questions before it, they had the advantage of the wise experience of Sir Guy Carleton, who visited England and remained there for some time. The result of the deliberation of years was the passage through the British parliament of the measure known as "The Quebec Act," which has always been considered the charter of the special privileges which the French Canadians have enjoyed ever since, and which, in the course of a century, made their province one of the most influential sections of British North America.

The preamble of the Quebec Act fixed new territorial limits for the province. It comprised not only the country affected by the proclamation of 1763, but also all the eastern territory which had been previously annexed to Newfoundland. In the west and southwest the province was extended to the Ohio and the Mississippi, and in fact embraced all the lands beyond the Alleghanies coveted and claimed by the old English colonies, now hemmed in between the Atlantic and the Appalachian range. It was now expressly enacted that the Roman Catholic inhabitants of Canada should thenceforth "enjoy the free exercise" of their religion, "subject to the king's supremacy declared and established" by law, and on condition of taking an oath of allegiance, set forth in the act. The Roman Catholic clergy were allowed "to hold, receive, and enjoy their accustomed dues and rights, with respect to such persons only as shall confess the said religion"—that is, one twenty-sixth part of the produce of the land, Protestants being specially exempted. The French Canadians were allowed to enjoy all their property, together with all customs and usages incident thereto, "in as large, ample and beneficial manner," as if the proclamation or other acts of the crown "had not been made", but the religious orders and communities were excepted in accordance with the terms of the capitulation of Montreal—the effect of which exception I have already briefly stated. In "all matters of controversy relative to property and civil rights," resort was to be had to the old civil law of French Canada "as the rule for the decision of the same", but the criminal law of England was extended to the province on the indisputable ground that its "certainty and lenity" were already "sensibly felt by the inhabitants from an experience of more than nine years." The government of the province was entrusted to a governor and a legislative council appointed by the crown, "inasmuch as it was inexpedient to call an assembly." The council was to be composed of not more than twenty-three residents of the province. At the same time the British parliament made special enactments for the imposition of certain customs duties "towards defraying the charges of the administration of justice and the support of the civil government of the province." All deficiencies in the revenues derived from these and other sources had to be supplied by the imperial treasury. During the passage of the act through parliament, it evoked the bitter hostility of Lord Chatham, who was then the self-constituted champion of the old colonies, who found the act most objectionable, not only because it established the Roman Catholic religion, but placed under the government of Quebec the rich territory west of the Alleghanies. Similar views were expressed by the Mayor and Council of London, but they had no effect. The king, in giving his assent, declared that the measure "was founded on the clearest principles of justice and humanity, and would have the best effect in quieting the minds and promoting the happiness of our Canadian subjects." In French Canada the act was received without any popular demonstration by the French Canadians, but the men to whom the great body of that people always looked for advice and guidance—the priests, curés, and seigniors—naturally regarded these concessions to their nationality as giving most unquestionable evidence of the considerate and liberal spirit in which the British government was determined to rule the province. They had had ever since the conquest satisfactory proof that their religion was secure from all interference, and now the British parliament itself came forward with legal guarantees, not only for the free exercise of that religion, with all its incidents and tithes, but also for the permanent establishment of the civil law to which they attached so much importance. The fact that no provision was made for a popular assembly could not possibly offend a people to whom local self-government in any form was entirely unknown. It was impossible to constitute an assembly from the few hundred Protestants who were living in Montreal and Quebec, and it was equally impossible, in view of the religious prejudices dominant in England and the English colonies, to give eighty thousand French Canadian Roman

Catholics privileges which their co-religionists did not enjoy in Great Britain and to allow them to sit in an elected assembly. Lord North seemed to voice the general opinion of the British parliament on this difficult subject, when he closed the debate with an expression of "the earnest hope that the Canadians will, in the course of time, enjoy as much of our laws and as much of our constitution as may be beneficial to that country and safe for this", but "that time," he concluded, "had not yet come." It does not appear from the evidence before us that the British had any other motive in passing the Quebec Act than to do justice to the French Canadian people, now subjects of the crown of England. It was not a measure primarily intended to check the growth of popular institutions, but solely framed to meet the actual conditions of a people entirely unaccustomed to the working of representative or popular institutions. It was a preliminary step in the development of self-government.

On the other hand the act was received with loud expressions of dissatisfaction by the small English minority who had hoped to see themselves paramount in the government of the province. In Montreal, the headquarters of the disaffected, an attempt was made to set fire to the town, and the king's bust was set up in one of the public squares, daubed with black, and decorated with a necklace made of potatoes, and bearing the inscription *Voilà le pape du Canada & le sot Anglais*. The author of this outrage was never discovered, and all the influential French Canadian inhabitants of the community were deeply incensed that their language should have been used to insult a king whose only offence was his assent to a measure of justice to themselves.

Sir Guy Carleton, who had been absent in England for four years, returned to Canada on the 18th September, 1774, and was well received in Quebec. The first legislative council under the Quebec Act was not appointed until the beginning of August, 1775. Of the twenty-two members who composed it, eight were influential French Canadians bearing historic names. The council met on the 17th August, but was forced to adjourn on the 7th September, on account of the invasion of Canada by the troops of the Continental Congress, composed of representatives of the rebellious element of the Thirteen Colonies. In a later chapter I shall very shortly review the effects of the American revolution upon the people of Canada; but before I proceed to do so it is necessary to take my readers first to Nova Scotia on the eastern seaboard of British North America and give a brief summary of its political development from the beginning of British rule.

SECTION 2.—The foundation of Nova Scotia (1749—1783).

The foundation of Halifax practically put an end to the Acadian period of Nova Scotian settlement. Until that time the English occupation of the country was merely nominal. Owing largely to the representations of Governor Shirley, of Massachusetts—a statesman of considerable ability, who distinguished himself in American affairs during a most critical period of colonial history—the British government decided at last on a vigorous policy in the province, which seemed more than once on the point of passing out of their hands. Halifax was founded by the Honourable Edward Cornwallis on the slope of a hill, whose woods then dipped their branches into the very waters of the noble harbour long known as Chebuctou, and renamed in honour of a distinguished member of the Montague family, who had in those days full control of the administration of colonial affairs.

Colonel Cornwallis, a son of the Baron of that name—a man of firmness and discretion—entered the harbour, on the 21st of June, old style, or 2nd July present style, and soon afterwards assumed his duties as governor of the province. The members of his first council were sworn in on board one of the transports in the harbour. Between 2000 and 3000 persons were brought at this time to settle the town and country. These people were chiefly made up of retired military and naval officers, soldiers and sailors, gentlemen, mechanics, farmers—far too few—and some Swiss, who were extremely industrious and useful. On the whole, they were not the best colonists to build up a prosperous industrial community. The government gave the settlers large inducements in the shape of free grants of land, and practically supported them for the first two or three years. It was not until the Acadian population were removed, and their lands were available, that the foundation of the agricultural prosperity of the peninsula was really laid. In the summer of 1753 a considerable number of Germans were placed in the present county of Lunenburg, where their descendants still prosper, and take a most active part in all the occupations of life.

With the disappearance of the French Acadian settlers Nova Scotia became a British colony in the full sense of the phrase. The settlement of 1749 was supplemented in 1760, and subsequent years, by a valuable and large addition of people who were induced to leave Massachusetts and other colonies of New England and settle in townships of the present counties of Annapolis, King's, Hants, Queen's, Yarmouth, Cumberland, and Colchester, especially in the beautiful townships of Cornwallis and Horton, where the Acadian meadows were the richest. A small number also settled at Maugerville and other places on the St. John River.

During the few years that had elapsed since the Acadians were driven from their lands, the sea had once more found its way through the ruined dykes, which had no longer the skilful attention of their old builders. The new owners of the Acadian lands had none of the special knowledge that the French had acquired, and were unable for years to keep back the ever-encroaching tides. Still there were some rich uplands and low-lying meadows, raised above the sea, which richly rewarded the industrious cultivator. The historian, Haliburton, describes the melancholy scene that met the eyes of the new settlers when they reached, in 1760, the old homes of the Acadians at Mines. They came across a few straggling families of Acadians who "had eaten no bread for years, and had subsisted on vegetables, fish, and the more hardy part of the cattle that had survived the severity of the first winter of their abandonment." They saw everywhere "ruins of the houses that had been burned by the Provincials, small gardens encircled by cherry-trees and currant-bushes, and clumps of apple-trees." In all parts of the country, where the new colonists established themselves, the Indians were unfriendly for years, and it was necessary to erect stockaded houses for the protection of the settlements.

No better class probably could have been selected to settle Nova Scotia than these American immigrants. The majority were descendants of the Puritans who settled in New England, and some were actually sprung from men and women who had landed from "The Mayflower" in 1620. Governor Lawrence recognized the province was entrusted to a governor and a legislative council appointed by the crown, "inasmuch as it was inexpedient to call an assembly." The council was to be composed of not more than twenty-three residents of the province. At the same time the British parliament made special enactments for the imposition of certain customs duties "towards defraying the charges of the administration of justice and the support of the civil government of the province." All deficiencies in the revenues derived from these and other sources had to be supplied by the imperial treasury. During the passage of the act through parliament, it evoked the bitter hostility of Lord Chatham, who was then the self-constituted champion of the old colonies, who found the act most objectionable, not only because it established the Roman Catholic religion, but placed under the government of Quebec the rich territory west of the Alleghanies. Similar views were expressed by the Mayor and Council of London, but they had no effect. The king, in giving his assent, declared that the measure "was founded on the clearest principles of justice and humanity, and would have the best effect in quieting the minds and promoting the happiness of our Canadian subjects." In French Canada the act was received without any popular demonstration by the French Canadians, but the men to whom the great body of that people always looked for advice and guidance—the priests, curés, and seigniors—naturally regarded these concessions to their nationality as giving most unquestionable evidence of the considerate and liberal spirit in which the British government was determined to rule the province. They had had ever since the conquest satisfactory proof that their religion was secure from all interference, and now the British parliament itself came forward with legal guarantees, not only for the free exercise of that religion, with all its incidents and tithes, but also for the permanent establishment of the civil law to which they attached so much importance. The fact that no provision was made for a popular assembly could not possibly offend a people to whom local self-government in any form was entirely unknown. It was impossible to constitute an assembly from the few hundred Protestants who were living in Montreal and Quebec, and it was equally impossible, in view of the religious prejudices dominant in England and the English colonies, to give eighty thousand French Canadian Roman

Catholics privileges which their co-religionists did not enjoy in Great Britain and to allow them to sit in an elected assembly. Lord North seemed to voice the general opinion of the British parliament on this difficult subject, when he closed the debate with an expression of "the earnest hope that the Canadians will, in the course of time, enjoy as much of our laws and as much of our constitution as may be beneficial to that country and safe for this", but "that time," he concluded, "had not yet come." It does not appear from the evidence before us that the British had any other motive in passing the Quebec Act than to do justice to the French Canadian people, now subjects of the crown of England. It was not a measure primarily intended to check the growth of popular institutions, but solely framed to meet the actual conditions of a people entirely unaccustomed to the working of representative or popular institutions. It was a preliminary step in the development of self-government.

On the other hand the act was received with loud expressions of dissatisfaction by the small English minority who had hoped to see themselves paramount in the government of the province. In Montreal, the headquarters of the disaffected, an attempt was made to set fire to the town, and the king's bust was set up in one of the public squares, daubed with black, and decorated with a necklace made of potatoes, and bearing the inscription *Voilà le pape du Canada & le sot Anglais*. The author of this outrage was never discovered, and all the influential French Canadian inhabitants of the community were deeply incensed that their language should have been used to insult a king whose only offence was his assent to a measure of justice to themselves.

Sir Guy Carleton, who had been absent in England for four years, returned to Canada on the 18th September, 1774, and was well received in Quebec. The first legislative council under the Quebec Act was not appointed until the beginning of August, 1775. Of the twenty-two members who composed it, eight were influential French Canadians bearing historic names. The council met on the 17th August, but was forced to adjourn on the 7th September, on account of the invasion of Canada by the troops of the Continental Congress, composed of representatives of the rebellious element of the Thirteen Colonies. In a later chapter I shall very shortly review necessity of having a sturdy class of settlers, accustomed to the climatic conditions and to agricultural labour in America, and it was through his strenuous efforts that these immigrants were brought into the province. They had, indeed, the choice of the best land of the province, and everything was made as pleasant as possible for them by a paternal government, only anxious to establish British authority on a sound basis of industrial development.

In 1767, according to an official return in the archives of Nova Scotia, the total population of what are now the provinces of Nova Scotia, New Brunswick, and Prince Edward Island, reached 13,374 souls; of whom 6913 are given as Americans, 912 as English, 2165 as Irish, 1946 as Germans, and 1265 as Acadian French, the latter being probably a low estimate. Some of these Irish emigrated directly from the north of Ireland, and were Presbyterians. They were brought out by one Alexander McNutt, who did much for the work of early colonization; others came from New Hampshire, where they had been settled for some years. The name of Londonderry in New Hampshire is a memorial of this important class, just as the same name recalls them in the present county of Colchester, in Nova Scotia.

The Scottish immigration, which has exercised such an important influence on the eastern counties of Nova Scotia—and I include Cape Breton—commenced in 1772, when about thirty families arrived from Scotland and settled in the present county of Pictou, where a very few American colonists from Philadelphia had preceded them. In later years a steady tide of Scotch population flowed into eastern Nova Scotia and did not cease until 1820. Gaelic is still the dominant tongue in the eastern counties, where we find numerous names recalling the glens, lochs, and mountains of old Scotland. Sir William Alexander's dream of a new Scotland has been realised in a measure in the province where his ambition would have made him "lord paramount."

Until the foundation of Halifax the government of Nova Scotia was vested solely in a governor who had command of the garrison stationed at Annapolis. In 1719 a commission was issued to Governor Phillips, who was authorised to appoint a council of not less than twelve persons. This council had advisory and judicial functions, but its legislative authority was of a very limited scope. This provisional system of government lasted until 1749, when Halifax became the seat of the new administration of public affairs. The governor had a right to appoint a council of twelve persons—as we have already seen, he did so immediately—and to summon a general assembly "according to the usage of the rest of our colonies and plantations in America." He was, "with the advice and consent" of the council and assembly, "to make, constitute and ordain laws" for the good government of the province. During nine years the governor-in-council carried on the government without an assembly, and passed a number of ordinances, some of which imposed duties on trade for the purpose of raising revenue. The legality of their acts was questioned by Chief Justice Belcher, and he was sustained by the opinion of the English law officers, who called attention to the governor's commission, which limited the council's powers. The result of this decision was the establishment of a representative assembly, which met for the first time at Halifax on the 2nd October, 1758.

Governor Lawrence, whose name will be always unhappily associated with the merciless expatriation of the French Acadians, had the honour of opening the first legislative assembly of Nova Scotia in 1758. One Robert Sanderson, of whom we know nothing else, was chosen as the first speaker, but he held his office for only one session, and was succeeded by William Nesbitt, who presided over the house for many years. The first sittings of the legislature were held in the court house, and subsequently in the old grammar school at the corner of Barrington and Sackville Streets, for very many years one of the historic memorials of the Halifax of the eighteenth century.

At this time the present province of New Brunswick was for the most part comprised in a county known as Sunbury, with one representative in the assembly of Nova Scotia. The island of Cape Breton also formed a part of the province, and had the right to send two members to the assembly, but the only election held for that purpose was declared void on account of there not being any freeholders entitled by law to vote. The island of St. John, named Prince Edward in 1798, in honour of the Duke of Kent, who was commander-in-chief of the British forces for some years in North America, was also annexed to Nova Scotia in 1763, but it never sent representatives to its legislature. In the following year a survey was commenced of all the imperial dominions on the Atlantic. Various schemes for the cultivation and settlement of the island were proposed as soon as the surveys were in progress. The most notable suggestion was made by the Earl of Egmont, first lord of the admiralty; he proposed the division of the island into baronies, each with a castle or stronghold under a feudal lord, subject to himself as lord paramount, under the customs of the feudal system of Europe. The imperial authorities rejected this scheme, but at the same time they adopted one which was as unwise as that of the noble earl. The whole island, with the exception of certain small reservations and royalties, was given away by lottery in a single day to officers of the army and navy who had served in the preceding war, and to other persons who were ambitious to be great landowners, on the easy condition of paying certain quit-rents—a condition constantly broken. This ill-advised measure led to many troublesome complications for a hundred years, until at last they were removed by the terms of the arrangement which brought the island into the federal union of British North America in 1873. In 1769 the island was separated from Nova Scotia and granted a distinct government, although its total population at the time did not exceed one hundred and fifty families. An assembly of eighteen representatives was called so early as 1773, when the first governor, Captain Walter Paterson, still administered public affairs. The assembly was not allowed to meet with regularity during many years of the early history of the island. During one administration it was practically without parliamentary government for ten years. The land question always dominated public affairs in the island for a hundred years.

From the very beginning of a regular system of government in Nova Scotia the legislature appears to have practically controlled the administration of local affairs except so far as it gave, from time to time, powers to the courts of quarter sessions to regulate taxation and carry out certain small public works and improvements. In the first session of the legislature a joint committee of the council and assembly chose the town officers for Halifax. We have abundant evidence that at this time the authorities viewed with disfavour any attempt to establish a system of town government similar to that so long in operation in New England. The town meeting was considered the nursery of sedition in New England, and it is no wonder that the British authorities in Halifax frowned upon all attempts to reproduce it in their province.

Soon after his arrival in Nova Scotia, Governor Cornwallis established courts of law to try and determine civil and criminal cases in accordance with the laws of England. In 1774 there were in the province courts of general session, similar to the courts of the same name in England; courts of common pleas, formed on the practice of New England and the mother country, and a supreme court, court of assize and general gaol delivery, composed of a chief justice and two assistant judges. The governor-in-council constituted a court of error in certain cases, and from its decisions an appeal could be made to the king-in-council. Justices of peace were also appointed in the counties and townships, with jurisdiction over the collection of small debts.

We must now leave the province of Nova Scotia and follow the revolutionary movement, which commenced, soon after the signing of the Treaty of Paris, in the old British colonies on the Atlantic seaboard, and ended in the acknowledgement of their independence in 1783, and in the forced migration of a large body of loyal people who found their way to the British provinces.

CHAPTER III.

THE AMERICAN REVOLUTION AND THE UNITED EMPIRE LOYALISTS (1763—1784).

SECTION I.—The successful Revolution of the Thirteen Colonies in America.

When Canada was formally ceded to Great Britain the Thirteen Colonies were relieved from the menace of the presence of France in the valleys of the St. Lawrence, the Ohio, and the Mississippi. Nowhere were there more rejoicings on account of this auspicious event than in the homes of the democratic Puritans. The names of Pitt and Wolfe were honoured above all others of their countrymen, and no one in England, certainly not among its statesmen, imagined that in the colonies, which stretched from the river Penobscot to the peninsula of Florida, there was latent a spirit of independence which might at any moment threaten the rule of Great Britain on the American continent. The great expenses of the Seven Years' War were now pressing heavily on the British taxpayer. British statesmen were forced to consider how best they could make the colonies themselves contribute towards their own protection in the future, and relieve Great Britain in some measure from the serious burden which their defence had heretofore imposed on her. In those days colonies were considered as so many possessions to be used for the commercial advantage of the parent state. Their commerce and industries had been fettered for many years by acts of parliament which were intended to give Great Britain a monopoly of their trade and at the same time prevent them from manufacturing any article that they could buy from the British factories. As a matter of fact, however, these restrictive measures of imperial protection had been for a long time practically dead-letters. The merchants and seamen of New England carried on smuggling with the French and Spanish Indies with impunity, and practically traded where they pleased.

The stamp act was only evidence of a vigorous colonial policy, which was to make the people of the colonies contribute directly to their own defence and security, and at the same time enforce the navigation laws and acts of trade and put an end to the general system of smuggling by which men, some of the best known merchants of Boston, had acquired a fortune. George Grenville, who was responsible for the rigid enforcement of the navigation laws and the stamp act, had none of that worldly wisdom which Sir Robert Walpole showed when, years before, it was proposed to him to tax the colonies. "No," said that astute politician, "I have old England set against me already, and do you think I will have New England likewise?" But Grenville and his successors, in attempting to carry out a new colonial policy, entirely misunderstood the conditions and feelings of the colonial communities affected and raised a storm of indignation which eventually led to independence. The stamp act was in itself an equitable measure, the proceeds of which were to be exclusively used for the benefit of the colonies themselves; but its enactment was most unfortunate at a time when the influential classes in New England were deeply irritated at the enforcement of a policy which was to stop the illicit trade from which they had so largely profited in the past. The popular indignation, however, vented itself against the stamp act, which imposed internal taxation, was declared to be in direct violation of the principles of political liberty and self-government long enjoyed by the colonists as British subjects, and was repealed as a result of the violent opposition it met in the colonies. Parliament contented itself with a statutory declaration of its supremacy in all matters over every part of the empire; but not long afterwards the determination of some English statesmen to bring the colonies as far as practicable directly under the dominion of British law in all matters of commerce and taxation, and to control their government as far as possible, found full expression in the Townshend acts of 1767 which imposed port duties on a few commodities, including tea, imported into those countries. At the same time provision was made for the due execution of existing laws relating to trade. The province of New York was punished for openly refusing to obey an act of parliament which required the authorities to furnish the British troops with the necessaries of life. Writs of assistance, which allowed officials to search everywhere for smuggled goods, were duly legalised. These writs were the logical sequence of a rigid enforcement of the laws of trade and navigation, and had been vehemently denounced by James Otis, so far back as 1761, as not only irreconcilable with the colonial charters, but as inconsistent with those natural rights which a people "derived from nature and the Author of nature"—an assertion which obtained great prominence for the speaker. This bold expression of opinion in Massachusetts should be studied by the historian of those times in connection with the equally emphatic revolutionary argument advanced by Patrick Henry of Virginia, two years later, against the ecclesiastical supremacy of the Anglican clergy and the right of the king to veto legislation of the colony. Though the prerogative of the crown was thus directly called into question in a Virginia court, the British government did not take a determined stand on the undoubted rights of the crown in the case. English statesmen and lawyers probably regarded such arguments, if they paid any attention to them at all in days when they neglected colonial opinion, as only temporary ebullitions of local feeling, though in reality they were so many evidences of the opposition that was sure to show itself whenever there was a direct interference with the privileges and rights of self-governing communities. Both Henry and Otis touched a key-note of the revolution, which was stimulated by the revenue and stamp acts and later measures affecting the colonies.

It is somewhat remarkable that it was in aristocratic Virginia, founded by Cavaliers, as well as in democratic Massachusetts, founded by Puritans, that the revolutionary element gained its principal strength during the controversy with the parent state. The makers of Massachusetts were independents in church government and democrats in political principle. The whole history of New England, in fact, from the first charters until the argument on the writs of assistance, is full of incidents which show the growth of republican ideas. The Anglican church had no strength in the northern colonies, and the great majority of their people were bitterly opposed to the pretensions of the English hierarchy to establish an episcopate in America. It is not therefore surprising that Massachusetts should have been the leader in the revolutionary agitation; on the other hand in Virginia the Anglican clergy belonged to what was essentially an established church, and the whole social fabric of the colony rested on an aristocratic basis. No doubt before the outbreak of the revolution there was a decided feeling against England on account of the restrictions on the sale of tobacco; and the quarrel, which I have just referred to, with respect to the stipends of the clergy, which were to be paid in this staple commodity according to its market value at the time of payment, had spread discontent among a large body of the people. But above all such causes of dissatisfaction was the growing belief that the political freedom of the people, and the very existence of the colony as a self-governing community, were jeopardised by the indiscreet acts of the imperial authorities after 1763. It is easy then to understand that the action of the British government in 1767 renewed the agitation, which had been allayed for the moment by the repeal of the stamp act and the general belief that there would be no rigid enforcement of old regulations which meant the ruin of the most profitable trade of New England. The measures of the ministry were violently assailed in parliament by Burke and other eminent men who availed themselves of so excellent an opportunity of exciting the public mind against a government which was doing so much to irritate the colonies and injure British trade. All the political conditions were unfavourable to a satisfactory adjustment of the colonial difficulty. Chatham had been one of the earnest opponents of the stamp act, but he was now buried in retirement—labouring under some mental trouble—and Charles Townshend, the chancellor of the exchequer in the cabinet of which Chatham was the real head, was responsible for measures which his chief would have repudiated as most impolitic and inexpedient in the existing temper of the colonies.

The action of the ministry was for years at once weak and irritating. One day they asserted the supremacy of the British parliament, and on the next yielded to the violent opposition of the colonies and the appeals of British merchants whose interests were at stake. Nothing remained eventually but the tea duty, and even that was so arranged that the colonists could buy their tea at a much cheaper rate than the British consumer. But by this time a strong anti-British party was in course of formation throughout the colonies. Samuel Adams of Massachusetts, Patrick Henry of Virginia, and a few other political managers of consummate ability, had learned their own power, and the weakness of English ministers. Samuel Adams, who had no love in his heart for England, was undoubtedly by this time insidiously working towards the independence of the colonies. Violence and outrage formed part of his secret policy. The tea in Boston harbour was destroyed by a mob disguised as Mohawk Indians, and was nowhere allowed to enter into domestic consumption. The patience of English ministers was now exhausted, and they determined to enter on a vigorous system of repression, which might have had some effect at an earlier stage of the revolutionary movement, when the large and influential loyal body of people in the colonies ought to have been vigorously supported, and not left exposed to the threats, insults, and even violence of a resolute minority, comprising many persons influenced by purely selfish reasons—the stoppage of illicit trade from which they had profited—as well as men who objected on principle to a policy which seemed to them irreconcilable with the rights of the people to the fullest possible measure of local self-government. As it was, however, the insults and injuries to British officials bound to obey the law, the shameless and continuous rioting, the destruction of private property, the defiant attitude of the opposition to England, had at last awakened the home authorities to the dangers latent in the rebellious spirit that reckless agitators had aroused in colonies for which England had sacrificed so much of her blood and treasure when their integrity and dearest interests were threatened by France. The port of Boston, where the agitators were most influential and the most discreditable acts of violence had taken place, was closed to trade; and important modifications were made in the charter granted to Massachusetts by William III in 1692. Another obnoxious act provided that persons "questioned for any acts in execution of the laws" should be tried in England—a measure intended to protect officials and soldiers in the discharge of their duty against the rancour of the colonial community where they might be at that time. These measures, undoubtedly unwise at this juncture, were calculated to evoke the hostility of the other colonies and to show them what was probably in store for themselves. But while the issue certainly proved this to be the case, the course pursued by the government under existing conditions had an appearance of justification. Even Professor Goldwin Smith, who will not be accused of any sympathy with the British cabinet of that day, or of antagonism to liberal principles, admits that "a government thus bearded and insulted had its choice between abdication and repression," and "that repression was the most natural" course to pursue under the circumstances. Lord North gave expression to what was then a largely prevailing sentiment in England when he said "to repeal the tea duty would stamp us with timidity," and that the destruction of the property of private individuals, such as took place at Boston, "was a fitting culmination of years of riot and lawlessness." Lord North, we all know now, was really desirous of bringing about a reconciliation between the colonies and the parent state, but he servilely yielded his convictions to the king, who was determined to govern all parts of his empire, and was in favour of coercive measures. It is quite evident that the British ministry and their supporters entirely underrated the strength of the colonial party that was opposing England. Even those persons who, when the war broke out, remained faithful to their allegiance to the crown, were of opinion that the British government was pursuing a policy unwise in the extreme, although they had no doubt of the abstract legal right of that government to pass the Grenville and Townshend acts for taxing the colonies. Chatham, Burke, Conway, and Barré were the most prominent public men who, in powerful language, showed the dangers of the unwise course pursued by the "king's friends" in parliament.

As we review the events of those miserable years we can see that every step taken by the British government, from the stamp act until the closing of the port of Boston and other coercive measures, had the effect of strengthening the hands of Samuel Adams and the other revolutionary agitators. Their measures to create a feeling against England exhibited great cunning and skill. The revolutionary movement was aided by the formation of "Sons of Liberty"—a phrase taken from one of Barré's speeches,—by circular letters and committees of correspondence between the colonies, by petitions to the king winch were framed in a tone of independence not calculated to conciliate that uncompromising sovereign, by clever ingenious appeals to public patriotism, by the assembling of a "continental congress," by acts of "association" which meant the stoppage of all commercial intercourse with Great Britain. New England was the head and front of the whole revolution, and Samuel Adams was its animating spirit. Even those famous committees of correspondence between the towns of Massachusetts, which gave expression to public opinion and stimulated united action when the legislative authority was prevented by the royal governor from working, were the inspiration of this astute political manager. Prominent Virginians saw the importance of carrying out this idea on a wider field of action, and Virginia accordingly inaugurated a system of intercolonial correspondence which led to the meeting of a continental congress, and was the first practical step towards political independence of the parent state. Adams's decision to work for independence was made, or confirmed, as early as 1767, when Charles Townshend succeeded in passing the measures which were so obnoxious to the colonists, and finally led to civil war.

At a most critical moment, when the feelings of a large body of people were aroused to a violent pitch, when ideas of independence were ripening in the minds of others besides Samuel Adams, General Gage, then in command of the British regular troops in Boston, sent a military force to make prisoners of Adams and Hancock at Lexington, and seize some stores at Concord. Then the "embattled farmers" fired the shot "which was heard around the world." Then followed the capture of Ticonderoga and Crown Point, and the battle of Bunker's Hill, on the same day that Washington was appointed by congress to command the continental army. At this critical juncture, John Adams and other prominent colonists—not excepting Washington—were actually disavowing all desire to sever their relations with the parent state in the face of the warlike attitude of congress—an attitude justified by the declaration that it was intended to force a redress of grievances. Tom Paine, a mere adventurer, who had not been long in the country, now issued his pamphlet, "Common Sense," which was conceived in a spirit and written in a style admirably calculated to give strength and cohesion to the arguments of the people, who had been for some time coming to the conclusion that to aim at independence was the only consistent and logical course in the actual state of controversy between England and the colonies. On March 14th, 1776, the town of Boston, then the most important in America, was given up to the rebels; and British ships carried the first large body of unhappy and disappointed Loyalists to Halifax. On July the fourth of the same year the Declaration of Independence was passed, after much hesitation and discussion, and published to the world by the continental congress assembled at Philadelphia. The signal victory won by the continental army over Burgoyne at Saratoga in the autumn of the following year led to an alliance with France, without whose effective aid the eventual success of the revolutionists would have been very doubtful The revolutionists won their final triumph at Yorktown in the autumn of 1781, when a small army of regulars and Loyalists, led by Cornwallis, was obliged to surrender to the superior American and French forces, commanded by Washington and Rochambeau, and supported by a French fleet which effectively controlled the approaches to Chesapeake Bay.

The conduct of the war on the part of England was noted for the singular incapacity of her generals. Had there been one of any energy or ability at the head of her troops, when hostilities commenced, the undisciplined American army might easily have been beaten and annihilated Boston need never have been evacuated had Howe taken the most ordinary precautions to occupy the heights of Dorchester that commanded the town. Washington could never have organised an army had not Howe given him every possible opportunity for months to do so. The British probably had another grand opportunity of ending the war on their occupation of New York, when Washington and his relatively insignificant army were virtually in their power while in retreat. The history of the war is full of similar instances of lost opportunities to overwhelm the continental troops. All the efforts of the British generals appear to have been devoted to the occupation of the important towns in a country stretching for a thousand miles from north to south, instead of following and crushing the constantly retreating, diminishing, and discouraged forces of the revolutionists. The evacuation of Philadelphia at a critical moment of the war was another signal illustration of the absence of all military foresight and judgment, since it disheartened the Loyalists and gave up an important base of operation against the South. Even Cornwallis, who fought so bravely and successfully in the southern provinces, made a most serious mistake when he chose so weak a position as Yorktown, which was only defensible whilst the army of occupation had free access to the sea. Admiral Rodney, then at St. Eustatius, is open to censure for not having sent such naval reinforcements as would have enabled the British to command Chesapeake Bay, and his failure in this respect explains the inability of Clinton, an able general, to support Cornwallis in his hour of need. The moment the French fleet appeared in the Chesapeake, Cornwallis's position became perfectly untenable, and he was obliged to surrender to the allied armies, who were vastly superior in number and equipment to his small force, which had not even the advantage of fighting behind well-constructed and perfect defences. No doubt, from the beginning to the end of the war—notably in the case of Burgoyne—the British were seriously hampered by the dilatory and unsafe counsels of Lord George Germaine, who was allowed by the favour of the king to direct military operations, and who, we remember, had disgraced himself on the famous battlefield of Minden.

All the conditions in the country at large were favourable to the imperial troops had they been commanded by generals of ability. The Loyalists formed a large available force, rendered valueless time after time by the incapacity of the men who directed operations. At no time did the great body of the American people warmly respond to the demands made upon them by congress to support Washington. Had it not been for New England and Virginia the war must have more than once collapsed for want of men and supplies. It is impossible to exaggerate the absence of public spirit in the States during this critical period of their history. The English historian, Lecky, who has reviewed the annals of those times with great fairness, has truly said: "The nobility and beauty of the character of Washington can hardly be surpassed; several of the other leaders of the revolution were men of ability and public spirit, and few armies have ever shown a nobler self-devotion than that which remained with Washington through the dreary winter at Valley Forge. But the army that bore those sufferings was a very small one, and the general aspect of the American people during the contest was far from heroic or sublime." This opinion is fully borne out by those American historians who have reviewed the records of their national struggle in a spirit of dispassionate criticism. We know that in the spring of 1780 Washington himself wrote that his troops were "constantly on the point of starving for want of provisions and forage." He saw "in every line of the army the most serious features of mutiny and sedition." Indeed he had "almost ceased to hope," for he found the country in general "in such a state of insensibility and indifference to its interests" that he dare not flatter himself "with any change for the better." The war under such circumstances would have come to a sudden end had not France liberally responded to Washington's appeals and supported him with her money, her sailors and her soldiers. In the closing years of the war Great Britain had not only to fight France, Spain, Holland and her own colonies, but she was without a single ally in Europe. Her dominion was threatened in India, and the king prevented the intervention of the only statesman in the kingdom to whom the colonists at any time were likely to listen with respect. When Chatham died with a protest on his lips "against the dismemberment of this ancient monarchy," the last hope of bringing about a reconciliation between the revolutionists and the parent state disappeared for ever, and the Thirteen Colonies became independent at Yorktown.

SECTION 2.—Canada and Nova Scotia during the Revolution.

If Canada was saved to England during the American Revolution it was not on account of the energy and foresight shown by the king and his ministers in providing adequately for its defence, but mainly through the coolness and excellent judgment displayed by Governor Carleton. The Quebec act, for which he was largely responsible, was extremely unpopular in the Thirteen Colonies, on account of its having extended the boundaries of the province and the civil law to that western country beyond the Alleghanies, which the frontiersmen of Pennsylvania and Virginia regarded as specially their own domain. The fact that the Quebec act was passed by parliament simultaneously with the Boston port bill and other measures especially levelled against Massachusetts, gave additional fuel to the indignation of the people, who regarded this group of acts as part of a settled policy to crush the British-speaking colonies.

Under these circumstances, the invasion of Canada by Arnold in 1775, with the full approval of the continental congress, soon after the taking of Crown Point and Ticonderoga by the "Green Mountain boys" of Vermont, was a most popular movement which, it was hoped generally, would end in the easy conquest of a province, occupied by an alien people, and likely to be a menace in the future to the country south of the St. Lawrence. The capture of Chambly and St. John's—the keys of Canada, by way of Lake Champlain—was immediately followed by the surrender of Montreal, which was quite indefensible, and the flight of Carleton to Quebec, where he wisely decided to make a stand against the invaders. At this time there were not one thousand regular troops in the country, and Carleton's endeavour to obtain reinforcements from Boston had failed in consequence of the timidity of Admiral Graves, who expressed his opinion that it was not safe to send vessels up the St. Lawrence towards the end of the month of October. No dependence apparently could be placed at this critical juncture on a number of the French *habitants*, as soon as the districts of Richelieu, Montreal and Three Rivers were occupied by the continental troops. Many of them were quite ready to sell provisions to the invaders, provided they were paid in coin, and a few of them even joined Montgomery on his march to Quebec. Happily, however, the influence of the clergy and the *seigneurs* was sufficiently powerful to make the great mass of the people neutral during this struggle for supremacy in the province.

The bishop and the priests, from the outset, were quite alive to the gravity of the situation. They could not forget that the delegates to the continental congress, who were now appealing to French Canada to join the rebellious colonists, had only a few weeks before issued an address to the people of England in which they expressed their astonishment that the British parliament should have established in Canada "a religion that had deluged their land in blood and dispersed impiety, bigotry, persecution, murder, and rebellion through every part of the world." Almost simultaneously with the capture of the forts on Lake Champlain, Bishop Briand issued a *mandement* in which he dwelt with emphasis on the great benefits which the people of French Canada had already derived from the British connection and called upon them all to unite in the defence of their province. No doubt can exist that these opinions had much effect at a time when Carleton had reason to doubt even the loyalty of the English population, some of whom were notoriously in league with the rebels across the frontier, and gave material aid to the invaders as soon as they occupied Montreal. It was assuredly the influence of the French clergy that rendered entirely ineffectual the mission of Chase, Franklin, and the Carrolls of Maryland—one of whom became the first Roman Catholic archbishop of the United States—who were instructed by congress to offer every possible inducement to the Roman Catholic subjects of England in Canada to join the revolutionary movement.

Richard Montgomery, who had commanded the troops invading Canada, had served at Louisbourg and Quebec, and had subsequently become a resident of New York, where his political opinions on the outbreak of the revolution had been influenced by his connection, through marriage, with the Livingstones, bitter opponents of the British government. His merit as a soldier naturally brought him into prominence when the war began, and his own ambition gladly led him to obey the order to go to Canada, where he hoped to emulate the fame of Wolfe and become the captor of Quebec. He formed a junction, close to the ancient capital, with the force under Benedict Arnold, who was at a later time to sully a memorable career by an act of the most deliberate treachery to his compatriots. When Montgomery and Arnold united their forces before Quebec, the whole of Canada, from Lake Champlain to Montreal, and from that town to the walls of the old capital, was under the control of the continental troops. Despite the great disadvantages under which he laboured, Carleton was able to perfect his defences of the city, which he determined to hold until reinforcements should arrive in the spring from England. Montgomery had neither men nor artillery to storm the fortified city which he had hoped to surprise and easily occupy with the aid of secret friends within its walls. Carleton, however, rallied all loyal men to his support, and the traitors on whom the invaders had relied were powerless to carry out any treacherous design they may have formed. The American commanders at once recognised the folly of a regular investment of the fortress during a long and severe winter, and decided to attempt to surprise the garrison by a night assault. This plan was earned out in the early morning of the thirty-first of December, 1775, when the darkness was intensified by flurries of light blinding snow, but it failed before the assailants could force the barricades which barred the way to the upper town, where all the principal offices and buildings were grouped, just below the château and fort of St. Louis, which towers above the historic heights. Montgomery was killed, Arnold was wounded at the very outset, and a considerable number of their officers and men were killed or wounded.

Carleton saved Quebec at this critical hour and was able in the course of the same year, when General Burgoyne arrived with reinforcements largely composed of subsidised German regiments, to drive the continental troops in confusion from the province and destroy the fleet which congress had formed on Lake Champlain. Carleton took possession of Crown Point but found the season too late—it was now towards the end of autumn—to attempt an attack on Ticonderoga, which was occupied by a strong and well-equipped garrison. After a careful view of the situation he concluded to abandon Crown Point until the spring, when he could easily occupy it again, and attack Ticonderoga with every prospect of success. But Carleton, soon afterwards, was ordered to give up the command of the royal troops to Burgoyne, who was instructed by Germaine to proceed to the Hudson River, where Howe was to join him. Carleton naturally resented the insult that he received and resigned the governor-generalship, to which General Haldimand was appointed. Carleton certainly brought Canada securely through one of the most critical epochs of her history, and there is every reason to believe that he would have saved the honour of England and the reputation of her generals, had he rather than Burgoyne and Howe been entrusted with the direction of her armies in North America.

Carleton's administration of the civil government of the province was distinguished by a spirit of discretion and energy which deservedly places him among the ablest governors who ever presided over the public affairs of a colony. During the progress of the American war the legislative council was not able to meet until nearly two years after its abrupt adjournment in September, 1775. At this session, in 1777, ordinances were passed for the establishment of courts of King's bench, common pleas, and probate.

A critical perusal of the valuable documents, placed of late years in the archives of the Dominion, clearly proves that it was a fortunate day for Canada when so resolute a soldier and far-sighted administrator as General Haldimand was in charge of the civil and military government of the country after the departure of Carleton. His conduct appears to have been dictated by a desire to do justice to all classes, and it is most unfair to his memory to declare that he was antagonistic to French Canadians. During the critical time when he was entrusted with the public defence it is impossible to accuse him of an arrogant or unwarrantable exercise of authority, even when he was sorely beset by open and secret enemies of the British connection. The French Canadian *habitant* found himself treated with a generous consideration that he never obtained during the French régime, and wherever his services were required by the state, he was paid, not in worthless card money, but in British coin. During Haldimand's administration the country was in a perilous condition on account of the restlessness and uncertainty that prevailed while the French naval and military expeditions were in America, using every means of exciting a public sentiment hostile to England and favourable to France among the French Canadians. Admiral D'Estaing's proclamation in 1778 was a passionate appeal to the old national sentiment of the people, and was distributed in every part of the province. Dr. Kingsford believes that it had large influence in creating a powerful feeling which might have seriously threatened British dominion had the French been able to obtain permission from congress to send an army into the country. Whatever may have been the temper of the great majority of the French Canadians, it does not appear that many of them openly expressed their sympathy with France, for whom they would naturally still feel a deep love as their motherland. The assertion that many priests secretly hoped for the appearance of the French army is not justified by any substantial evidence except the fact that one La Valinière was arrested for his disloyalty, and sent a prisoner to England. It appears, however, that this course was taken with the approval of the bishop himself, who was a sincere friend of the English connection throughout the war. Haldimand arrested a number of persons who were believed to be engaged in treasonable practices against England, and effectively prevented any successful movement being made by the supporters of the revolutionists, or sympathisers with France, whose emissaries were secretly working in the parishes.

Haldimand's principal opponent during these troublous times was one Pierre du Calvet, an unscrupulous and able intriguer, whom he imprisoned on the strong suspicion of treasonable practices; but the evidence against Calvet at that time appears to have been inadequate, as he succeeded in obtaining damages against the governor-general in an English court. The imperial government, however, in view of all the circumstances brought to their notice, paid the cost of the defence of the suit. History now fully justifies the action of Haldimand, for the publication of Franklin's correspondence in these later times shows that Calvet—who was drowned at sea and never again appeared in Canada—was in direct correspondence with congress, and the recognised emissary of the revolutionists at the very time he was declaring himself devoted to the continuance of British rule in Canada.

Leaving the valley of the St. Lawrence, and reviewing the conditions of affairs in the maritime provinces, during the American revolution, we see that some of the settlers from New England sympathised with their rebellious countrymen. The people of Truro, Onslow, and Londonderry, with the exception of five persons, refused to take the oath of allegiance, and were not allowed for some time to be represented in the legislature. The assembly was always loyal to the crown, and refused to consider the appeals that were made to it by circular letters, and otherwise, to give active aid and sympathy to the rebellious colonies During the war armed cruisers pillaged the small settlements at Charlottetown, Annapolis, Lunenburg, and the entrance of the St. John River. One expedition fitted out at Machias, in the present state of Maine, under the command of a Colonel Eddy, who had been a resident of Cumberland, attempted to seize Fort Cumberland—known as Beauséjour in French Acadian days—at the mouth of the Missiquash. In this section of the country there were many sympathisers with the rebels, and Eddy expected to have an easy triumph. The military authorities were happily on the alert, and the only result was the arrest of a number of persons on the suspicion of treasonable designs. The inhabitants of the county of Yarmouth—a district especially exposed to attack—only escaped the frequent visits of privateers by secret negotiations with influential persons in Massachusetts. The settlers on the St. John River, at Maugerville, took measures to assist their fellow-countrymen in New England, but the defeat of the Cumberland expedition and the activity of the British authorities prevented the disaffected in Sunbury county—in which the original settlements of New Brunswick were then comprised—from rendering any practical aid to the revolutionists. The authorities at Halifax authorised the fitting out of privateers in retaliation for the damages inflicted on western ports by the same class of cruisers sailing from New England. The province was generally impoverished by the impossibility of carrying on the coasting trade and fisheries with security in these circumstances. The constant demand for men to fill the army and the fleet drained the country when labour was imperatively needed for necessary industrial pursuits, including the cultivation of the land. Some Halifax merchants and traders alone found profit in the constant arrival of troops and ships. Apart, however, from the signs of disaffection shown in the few localities I have mentioned, the people generally appear to have been loyal to England, and rallied, notably in the townships of Annapolis, Horton and Windsor, to the defence of the country, at the call of the authorities.

In 1783 the humiliated king of England consented to a peace with his old colonies, who owed their success not so much to the unselfishness and determination of the great body of the rebels as to the incapacity of British generals and to the patience, calmness, and resolution of the one great man of the revolution, George Washington. I shall in a later chapter refer to this treaty in which the boundaries between Canada and the new republic were so ignorantly and clumsily defined that it took half a century and longer to settle the vexed questions that arose in connection with territorial rights, and then the settlement was to the injury of Canada. So far as the treaty affected the Provinces its most important result was the forced migration of that large body of people who had remained faithful to the crown and empire during the revolution.

SECTION 3.—The United Empire Loyalists

John Adams and other authorities in the United States have admitted that when the first shot of the revolution was fired by "the embattled farmers" of Concord and Lexington, the Loyalists numbered one-third of the whole population of the colonies, or seven hundred thousand whites. Others believe that the number was larger, and that the revolutionary party was in a minority even after the declaration of independence. The greater number of the Loyalists were to be found in the present state of New York, where the capital was in possession of the British from September, 1776, until the evacuation in 1783. They were also the majority in Pennsylvania and the southern colonies of South Carolina and Georgia. In all the other states they represented a large minority of the best class of their respective communities. It is estimated that there were actually from thirty to thirty-five thousand, at one time or other, enrolled in regularly organised corps, without including the bodies which waged guerilla warfare in South Carolina and elsewhere.

It is only within a decade of years that some historical writers in the United States have had the courage and honesty to point out the false impressions long entertained by the majority of Americans with respect to the Loyalists, who were in their way as worthy of historical eulogy as the people whose efforts to win independence were crowned with success. Professor Tyler, of Cornell University, points out that these people comprised "in general a clear majority of those who, of whatever grade of culture or of wealth, would now be described as conservative people." A clear majority of the official class, of men representing large commercial interests and capital, of professional training and occupation, clergymen, physicians, lawyers and teachers, "seem to have been set against the ultimate measures of the revolution". He assumes with justice that, within this conservative class, one may "usually find at least a fair portion of the cultivation, of the moral thoughtfulness, of the personal purity and honour, existing in the community to which they happen to belong." He agrees with Dr. John Fiske, and other historical writers of eminence in the United States, in comparing the Loyalists of 1776 to the Unionists of the southern war of secession from 1861 until 1865. They were "the champions of national unity, as resting on the paramount authority of the general government." In other words they were the champions of a United British Empire in the eighteenth century.

"The old colonial system," says that thoughtful writer Sir J.R. Seeley, "was not at all tyrannous; and when the breach came the grievances of which the Americans complained, though perfectly real, were smaller than ever before or since led to such mighty consequences." The leaders among the Loyalists, excepting a few rash and angry officials probably, recognised that there were grievances which ought to be remedied. They looked on the policy of the party in power in Great Britain as injudicious in the extreme, but they believed that the relations between the colonies and the mother-state could be placed on a more satisfactory basis by a spirit of mutual compromise, and not by such methods as were insidiously followed by the agitators against England. The Loyalists generally contended for the legality of the action of parliament, and were supported by the opinion of all high legal authorities; but the causes of difficulty were not to be adjusted by mere lawyers, who adhered to the strict letter of the law, but by statesmen who recognised that the time had come for reconsidering the relations between the colonies and the parent state, and meeting the new conditions of their rapid development and political freedom. These relations were not to be placed on an equitable and satisfactory basis by mob-violence and revolution. All the questions at issue were of a constitutional character, to be settled by constitutional methods.

Unhappily, English statesmen of that day paid no attention to, and had no conception of, the aspirations, sentiments and conditions of the colonial peoples when the revolutionary war broke out. The king wished to govern in the colonies as well as in the British Isles, and unfortunately the unwise assertion of his arrogant will gave dangerous men like Samuel Adams, more than once, the opportunity they wanted to stimulate public irritation and indignation against England.

It is an interesting fact, that the relations between Great Britain and the Canadian Dominion are now regulated by just such principles as were urged in the interests of England and her colonies a hundred and twenty years ago by Governor Thomas Hutchinson, a great Loyalist, to whom justice is at last being done by impartial historians in the country where his motives and acts were so long misunderstood and misrepresented. "Whatever measures," he wrote to a correspondent in England, "you may take to maintain the authority of parliament, give me leave to pray they may be accompanied with a declaration that it is not the intention of parliament to deprive the colonies of their subordinate power of legislation, nor to exercise the supreme power except in such cases and upon such occasions as an equitable regard to the interests of the whole empire shall make necessary." But it took three-quarters of a century after the coming of the Loyalists to realise these statesmanlike conceptions of Hutchinson in the colonial dominions of England to the north of the dependencies which she lost in the latter part of the eighteenth century.

Similar opinions were entertained by Joseph Galloway, Jonathan Boucher, Jonathan Odell, Samuel Seabury, Chief Justice Smith, Judge Thomas Jones, Beverley Robinson and other men of weight and ability among the Loyalists, who recognised the short-sightedness and ignorance of the British authorities, and the existence of real grievances. Galloway, one of the ablest men on the constitutional side, and a member of the first continental congress, suggested a practical scheme of imperial federation, well worthy of earnest consideration at that crisis in imperial affairs. Eminent men in the congress of 1774 supported this statesmanlike mode of placing the relations of England and the colonies on a basis which would enable them to work harmoniously, and at the same time give full scope to the ambition and the liberties of the colonial communities thus closely united; but unhappily for the empire the revolutionary element carried the day. The people at large were never given an opportunity of considering this wise proposition, and the motion was erased from the records of congress. In its place, the people were asked to sign "articles of association" which bound them to cease all commercial relations with England. Had Galloway's idea been carried out to a successful issue, we might have now presented to the world the noble spectacle of an empire greater by half a continent and seventy-five millions of people.

But while Galloway and other Loyalists failed in their measures of adjusting existing difficulties and remedying grievances, history can still do full justice to their wise counsel and resolute loyalty, which refused to assist in tearing the empire to fragments. These men, who remained faithful to this ideal to the very bitter end, suffered many indignities at the hands of the professed lovers of liberty, even in those days when the questions at issue had not got beyond the stage of legitimate argument and agitation. The courts of law were closed and the judges prevented from fulfilling their judicial functions. No class of persons, not even women, were safe from the insults of intoxicated ruffians. The clergy of the Church of England were especially the object of contumely.

During the war the passions of both parties to the controversy were aroused to the highest pitch, and some allowance must be made for conditions which were different from those which existed when the questions at issue were still matters of argument. It is impossible in times of civil strife to cool the passions of men and prevent them from perpetrating cruelties and outrages which would be repugnant to their sense of humanity in moments of calmness and reflection. Both sides, more than once, displayed a hatred of each other that was worthy of the American Iroquois themselves. The legislative bodies were fully as vindictive as individuals in the persecution of the Loyalists. Confiscation of estate, imprisonment, disqualification for office, banishment, and even death in case of return from exile, were among the penalties to which these people were subject by the legislative acts of the revolutionary party.

If allowance can be made for the feelings of revenge and passion which animate persons under the abnormal conditions of civil war, no extenuating circumstances appear at that later period when peace was proclaimed and congress was called upon to fulfil the terms of the treaty and recommend to the several independent states the restoration of the confiscated property of Loyalists. Even persons who had taken up arms were to have an opportunity of receiving their estates back on condition of refunding the money which had been paid for them, and protection was to be afforded to those persons during twelve months while they were engaged in obtaining the restoration of their property. It was also solemnly agreed by the sixth article of the treaty that there should be no future confiscations or prosecutions, and that no person should "suffer any future loss or damage, either in his person, liberty or property," for the part he might have taken in the war. Now was the time for generous terms, such terms as were even shown by the triumphant North to the rebellious South at the close of the war of secession. The recommendations of congress were treated with contempt by the legislatures in all the states except in South Carolina, and even there the popular feeling was entirely opposed to any favour or justice being shown to the beaten party. The sixth article of the treaty, a solemn obligation, was violated with malice and premeditation. The Loyalists, many of whom had returned from Great Britain with the hope of receiving back their estates, or of being allowed to remain in the country, soon found they could expect no generous treatment from the successful republicans. The favourite Whig occupation of tarring and feathering was renewed. Loyalists were warned to leave the country as soon as possible, and in the south some were shot and hanged because they did not obey the warning. The Loyalists, for the most part, had no other course open to them than to leave the country they still loved and where they had hoped to die.

The British government endeavoured, so far as it was in its power, to compensate the Loyalists for the loss of their property by liberal grants of money and land, but despite all that was done for them the majority felt a deep bitterness in their hearts as they landed on new shores of which they had heard most depressing accounts. More than thirty-five thousand men, women and children, made their homes within the limits of the present Dominion. In addition to these actual American Loyalists, there were several thousands of negroes, fugitives from their owners, or servants of the exiles, who have been generally counted in the loose estimates made of the migration of 1783, and the greater number of whom were at a later time deported from Nova Scotia to Sierra Leone. Of the exiles at least twenty-five thousand went to the maritime colonies, and built up the province of New Brunswick, where representative institutions were established in 1784. Of the ten thousand people who sought the valley of the St Lawrence, some settled in Montreal, at Chambly, and in parts of the present Eastern Townships, but the great majority accepted grants of land on the banks of the St. Lawrence—from River Beaudette, on Lake St. Francis, as far as the beautiful Bay of Quinté—in the Niagara District, and on the shores of Lake Erie. The coming of these people, subsequently known by the name of "U.E. Loyalists"—a name appropriately given to them in recognition of their fidelity to a United Empire—was a most auspicious event for the British-American provinces, the greater part of which was still a wilderness. As we have seen in the previous chapters, there was in the Acadian provinces, afterwards divided into New Brunswick and Nova Scotia, a British population of only some 14,000 souls, mostly confined to the peninsula. In the valley of the St. Lawrence there was a French population of probably 100,000 persons, dwelling chiefly on the banks of the St. Lawrence between Quebec and Montreal. The total British population of the province of Quebec did not exceed 2000, residing for the most part in the towns of Quebec and Montreal. No English people were found west of Lake St. Louis; and what is now the populous province of Ontario was a mere wilderness, except where loyal refugees had gathered about the English fort at Niagara, or a few French settlers had made homes for themselves on the banks of the Detroit River and Lake St. Clair. The migration of between 30,000 and 40,000 Loyalists to the maritime provinces and the valley of the St. Lawrence was the saving of British interests in the great region which England still happily retained in North America.

The refugees who arrived in Halifax in 1783 were so numerous that hundreds had to be placed in the churches or in cabooses taken from the transports and ranged along the streets. At Guysborough, in Nova Scotia—so named after Sir Guy Carleton—the first village, which was hastily built by the settlers, was destroyed by a bush fire, and many persons only saved their lives by rushing into the sea. At Shelburne, on the first arrival of the exiles, there were seen "lines of women sitting on the rocky shore and weeping at their altered condition." Towns and villages, however, were soon built for the accommodation of the people. At Shelburne, or Port Roseway—anglicised from the French *Razoir*—a town of fourteen thousand people, with wide streets, fine houses, some of them containing furniture and mantel-pieces brought from New York, arose in two or three years. The name of New Jerusalem had been given to the same locality some years before, but it seemed a mockery to the Loyalists when they found that the place they had chosen for their new home was quite unsuited for settlement. A beautiful harbour lay in front, and a rocky country unfit for farmers in the rear of their ambitious town, which at one time was the most populous in British North America. In the course of a few years the place was almost deserted, and sank for a time into insignificance. A pretty town now nestles by the side of the beautiful and spacious harbour which attracted the first too hopeful settlers; and its residents point out to the tourist the sites of the buildings of last century, one or two of which still stand, and can show many documents and relics of those early days.

Over twelve thousand Loyalists, largely drawn from the disbanded loyal regiments of the old colonies, settled in New Brunswick. The name of Parrtown was first given, in honour of the governor of Nova Scotia, to the infant settlement which became the city of St. John, in 1785, when it was incorporated. The first landing of the loyal pioneers took place on the 18th of May, 1783, at what is now the Market Slip of this interesting city. Previous to 1783, the total population of the province did not exceed seven hundred souls, chiefly at Maugerville and other places on the great river. The number of Loyalists who settled on the St. John River was at least ten thousand, of whom the greater proportion were established at the mouth of the river, which was the base of operations for the peopling of the new province. Some adventurous spirits took possession of the abandoned French settlements at Grimross and St. Anne's, where they repaired some ruined huts of the original Acadian occupants, or built temporary cabins. This was the beginning of the settlement of Fredericton, which four years later became the political capital on account of its central position, its greater security in time of war, and its location on the land route to Quebec. Many of the people spent their first winter in log-huts, bark camps, and tents covered with spruce, or rendered habitable only by the heavy banks of snow which were piled against them. A number of persons died through exposure, and "strong, proud men"—to quote the words of one who lived in those sorrowful days—"wept like children and lay down in their snow-bound tents to die."

A small number of loyal refugees had found their way to the valley of the St. Lawrence as early as 1778, and obtained employment in the regiments organised under Sir John Johnson and others. It was not until 1783 and 1784 that the large proportion of the exiles came to Western Canada. They settled chiefly on the northern banks of the St. Lawrence, in what are now the counties of Glengarry, Stormont, Dundas, Grenville, Leeds, Frontenac, Addington, Lennox, Hastings and Prince Edward, where their descendants have acquired wealth and positions of honour and trust. The first township laid out in Upper Canada, now Ontario, was Kingston. The beautiful Bay of Quinté is surrounded by a country full of the memories of this people, and the same is true of the picturesque district of Niagara.

Among the Loyalists of Canada must also be honourably mentioned Joseph Brant (Thayendanega), the astute and courageous chief of the

Mohawks, the bravest nation of the Iroquois confederacy, who fought on the side of England during the war. At its close he and his people settled in Canada, where they received large grants from the government, some in a township by the Bay of Quinté, which still bears the Indian title of the great warrior, and the majority on the Grand River, where a beautiful city and county perpetuate the memory of this loyal subject of the British crown. The first Anglican church built in Upper Canada was that of the Mohawks, near Brantford, and here the church bell first broke the silence of the illimitable forest.

The difficulties which the Upper Canadian immigrants had to undergo before reaching their destination were much greater than was the case with the people who went direct in ships from American ports to Halifax and other places on the Atlantic coast. The former had to make toilsome journeys by land, or by *bateaux* and canoes up the St. Lawrence, the Richelieu, the Genesee, and other streams which gave access from the interior of the United States to the new Canadian land. The British government did its best to supply the wants of the population suddenly thrown upon its charitable care, but, despite all that could be done for them in the way of food and means of fighting the wilderness, they suffered naturally a great deal of hardship. The most influential immigration found its way to the maritime provinces, where many received congenial employment and adequate salaries in the new government of New Brunswick. Many others, with the wrecks of their fortunes or the pecuniary aid granted them by the British government, were able to make comfortable homes and cultivate estates in the valleys of the St. John and Annapolis, and in other fertile parts of the lower provinces. Of the large population that founded Shelburne a few returned to the United States, but the greater number scattered all over the provinces. The settlers in Upper Canada had to suffer many trials for years after their arrival, and especially in a year of famine, when large numbers had to depend on wild fruits and roots. Indeed, had it not been for the fish and game which were found in some, but not in all, places, starvation and death would have been the lot of many hundreds of helpless people.

Many of the refugees could trace their descent to the early immigration that founded the colonies of Plymouth and Massachusetts Bay. Some were connected with the Cavalier and Church families of Virginia. Others were of the blood of persecuted Huguenots and German Protestants from the Rhenish or Lower Palatinate. Not a few were Highland Scotchmen, who had been followers of the Stuarts, and yet fought for King George and the British connection during the American revolution. Among the number were notable Anglican clergymen, eminent judges and lawyers, and probably one hundred graduates of Harvard, Yale, King's, Pennsylvania, and William and Mary Colleges. In the records of industrial enterprise, of social and intellectual progress, of political development for a hundred years, we find the names of many eminent men, sprung from these people, to whom Canada owes a deep debt of gratitude for the services they rendered her in the most critical period of her chequered history.

CHAPTER IV.

DEVELOPMENT OF REPRESENTATIVE INSTITUTIONS (1784—1812).

SECTION I—Beginnings of the provinces of New Brunswick, Lower Canada and Upper Canada.

On the 16th August, 1784, as a consequence of the coming of over ten thousand Loyalists to the valley of the St. John River, a new province was formed out of that portion of the ancient limits of Acadia, which extended northward from the isthmus of Chignecto to the province of Quebec, and eastward from the uncertain boundary of the St. Croix to the Gulf of St. Lawrence. It received its present name in honour of the Brunswick-Luneburg or Hanoverian line which had given a royal dynasty to England, and its first governor was Colonel Thomas Carleton, a brother of the distinguished governor-general, whose name is so intimately associated with the fortunes of Canada during a most critical period of its history. The first executive council, which was also the legislative council, comprised some of the most eminent men of the Loyalist migration. For instance, George Duncan Ludlow; who had been a judge of the supreme court of New York; Jonathan Odell, the famous satirist and divine; William Hazen, a merchant of high reputation, who had large interests on the St. John River from 1763, and had proved his fidelity to the crown at a time when his countrymen at Maugerville were disposed to join the revolutionary party; Gabriel G. Ludlow, previously a colonel in a royal regiment; Edward Winslow, Daniel Bliss and Isaac Allen, all of whom had borne arms in the royal service and had suffered the loss of valuable property, confiscated by the successful rebels.

The constitution of 1784 provided for an assembly of twenty-six members who were elected in 1785, and met for the first time on the 3rd of January, 1786, at the Mallard House, a plain two-storey building on the north side of King Street. The city of St. John ceased to be the seat of government in 1787, when the present capital, Fredericton, first known as St. Anne's, was chosen. Of the twenty-six members elected to this assembly, twenty-three were Loyalists, and the same class necessarily continued for many years to predominate in the legislature. The first speaker was Amos Botsford, the pioneer of the Loyalist migration to New Brunswick, whose grandson occupied the same position for a short time in the senate of the Dominion of Canada.

Coming to the province of Lower Canada we find it contained at this time a population of about a hundred thousand souls, of whom six thousand lived in Quebec and Montreal respectively. Only two thousand English-speaking persons resided in the province, almost entirely in the towns. Small as was the British minority, it continued that agitation for an assembly which had been commenced long before the passage of the Quebec act. A nominated council did not satisfy the political ambition of this class, who obtained little support from the French Canadian people. The objections of the latter arose from the working of the act itself. Difficulties had grown up in the administration of the law, chiefly in consequence of its being entrusted exclusively to men acquainted only with English jurisprudence, and not disposed to comply with the letter and intention of the imperial statute. As a matter of practice, French law was only followed as equity suggested; and the consequence was great legal confusion in the province. A question had also arisen as to the legality of the issue of writs of *habeas corpus*, and it was eventually necessary to pass an ordinance to remove all doubts on this important point.

The Loyalist settlers on the St. Lawrence and Niagara Rivers sent a petition in 1785 to the home government, praying for the establishment of a new district west of the River Beaudette "with the blessings of British laws and British government, and of exemption from French tenure of property." While such matters were under the consideration of the imperial authorities, Sir Guy Carleton, once more governor-general of Canada, and lately raised to the peerage as Lord Dorchester, established, in 1788, five new districts for the express object of providing for the temporary government of the territory where the Loyalists had settled. These districts were known as Luneburg, Mecklenburg, Nassau and Hesse, in the western country, and Gaspé in the extreme east of the province of Quebec, where a small number of the same class of people had also found new homes. Townships, ranging from eighty to forty thousand acres each, were also surveyed within these districts and parcelled out with great liberality among the Loyalists. Magistrates wore appointed to administer justice with the simplest possible machinery at a time when men trained in the law were not available.

The grants of land made to the Loyalists and their children were large, and in later years a considerable portion passed into the hands of speculators who bought them up at nominal sums. It was in connection with these grants that the name of "United Empire Loyalists" originated. An order-in-council was passed on the 9th of November, 1780, in accordance with the wish of Lord Dorchester "to put a mark of honour upon the families who had adhered to the *unity of the empire* and joined the royal standard in America before the treaty of separation in 1783." Accordingly the names of all persons falling under this designation were to be recorded as far as possible, in order that "their posterity may be discriminated from future settlers in the parish lists and rolls of militia of their respective districts, and other public remembrances of the province."

The British cabinet, of which Mr. Pitt, the famous son of the Earl of Chatham, was first minister, now decided to divide the province of Quebec into two districts, with separate legislatures and governments. Lord Grenville, while in charge of the department of colonial affairs, wrote in 1789 to Lord Dorchester that the "general object of the plan is to assimilate the constitution of the province to that of Great Britain as nearly as the differences arising from the names of the people and from the present situation of the province will admit." He also emphatically expressed the opinion that "a considerable degree of attention is due to the prejudices and habits of the French inhabitants, and every degree of caution should be used to continue to them the enjoyment of those civil and religious rights which were secured to them by the capitulation of the province, or have since been granted by the liberal and enlightened spirit of the British government." When the bill for the formation of the two provinces of Upper Canada and Lower Canada came before the house of commons, Mr. Adam Lymburner, an influential merchant of Quebec, appeared at the Bar and ably opposed the separation "as dangerous in every point of view to British interests in America, and to the safety, tranquillity and prosperity of the inhabitants of the province of Quebec" He pressed the repeal of the Quebec act in its entirety and the enactment of a perfectly new constitution "unclogged and unembarrassed with any laws prior to this period" He professed to represent the views "of the most intelligent and respectable of the French Canadians"; but their antagonism was not directed against the Quebec act in itself, but against the administration of the law, influenced as this was by the opposition of the British people to the French civil code. Nor does it appear, as Mr. Lymburner asserted, that the western Loyalists were hostile to the formation of two distinct provinces. He represented simply the views of the English-speaking inhabitants of Lower Canada, who believed that the proposed division would place them in a very small minority in the legislature and, as the issue finally proved, at the mercy of the great majority of the French Canadian representatives, while on the other hand the formation of one large province extending from Gaspé to the head of the great lakes would ensure an English representation sufficiently formidable to lessen the danger of French Canadian domination. However, the British government seems to have been actuated by a sincere desire to do justice to the French Canadians and the Loyalists of the upper province at one and the same time. When introducing the bill in the house of commons on the 7th March, 1791, Mr. Pitt expressed the hope that "the division would remove the differences of opinion which had arisen between the old and new inhabitants, since each province would have the right of enacting laws desired in its own house of assembly." He believed a division to be essential, as "otherwise he could not reconcile the clashing interests known to exist." Mr. Burke was of opinion that "to attempt to amalgamate two populations composed of races of men diverse in language, laws and customs, was a complete absurdity", and he consequently approved of the division. Mr. Fox, from whom Burke became alienated during this debate, looked at the question in an entirely different light and was strongly of opinion that "it was most desirable to see the French and English inhabitants coalesce into one body, and the different distinctions of people extinguished for ever."

The Constitutional act of 1791 established in each province a legislative council and assembly, with powers to make laws. The legislative council was to be appointed by the king for life, in Upper

Canada it was to consist of not less than seven, and in Lower Canada of not less than fifteen members. The sovereign might, if he thought proper, annex hereditary titles of honour to the right of being summoned to the legislative council in either province—a provision which was never brought into operation. The whole number of members in the assembly of Upper Canada was not to be less than sixteen; in Lower Canada not less than fifty—to be chosen by a majority of votes in either case. The British parliament reserved to itself the right of levying and collecting customs-duties, for the regulation of navigation and commerce to be carried on between the two provinces, or between either of them and any other part of the British dominions or any foreign country. Parliament also reserved the power of directing the payment of these duties, but at the same time left the exclusive apportionment of all moneys levied in this way to the legislature, which could apply them to such public uses as it might deem expedient. The free exercise of the Roman Catholic religion was guaranteed permanently. The king was to have the right to set apart, for the use of the Protestant clergy in the colony, a seventh part of all uncleared crown lands. The governor might also be empowered to erect parsonages and endow them, and to present incumbents or ministers of the Church of England. The English criminal law was to obtain in both provinces.

In the absence of Lord Dorchester in England, the duty devolved on Major-General Alured Clarke, as lieutenant-governor, to bring the Lower Canadian constitution into force by a proclamation on the 18th February, 1791. On the 7th May, in the following year, the new province of Lower Canada was divided into fifty electoral districts, composed of twenty-one counties, the towns of Montreal and Quebec, and the boroughs of Three Rivers and William Henry (now Sorel). The elections to the assembly took place in June, and a legislative council of fifteen influential Canadians was appointed. The new legislature was convoked "for the despatch of business" on the 17th December, in the same year, in an old stone building known as the Bishop's Palace, which stood on a rocky eminence in the upper town of the old capital.

Chief Justice Smith took the chair of the legislative council under appointment by the crown, and the assembly elected as its speaker

Mr. Joseph Antome Panet, an eminent advocate, who was able to speak the two languages. In the house there were only sixteen members of British origin—and in later parliaments there was even a still smaller representation—while the council was nearly divided between the two nationalities. When the house proceeded to business, one of its first acts was to order that all motions, bills and other proceedings should be put in the two languages. We find in the list of French Canadian members of the two houses representatives of the most ancient and distinguished families of the province. A descendant of Pierre Boucher, governor of Three Rivers in 1653, and the author of a rare history of Canada, sat in the council of 1792 just as a Boucherville sits now-a-days in the senate of the Dominion. A Lotbinière had been king's councillor in 1680. A Chaussegros de Lery had been an engineer in the royal colonial corps; a Lanaudière had been an officer in the Carignan regiment in 1652; a Salaberry was a captain in the royal navy, and his family won further honours on the field of Chateauguay in the war of 1812-15, when the soil of Lower Canada was invaded. A Taschereau had been a royal councillor in 1732. The names of Belestre, Valtric, Bonne, Rouville, St. Ours, and Duchesnay, are often met in the annals of the French régime, and show the high character of the representation in the first parliament of Lower Canada.

The village of Newark was chosen as the capital of Upper Canada by Colonel (afterwards Major-General) Simcoe, the first lieutenant-governor of the province. He had served with much distinction during the revolution as the commander of the Queen's Rangers, some of whom had settled in the Niagara district. He was remarkable for his decision of character and for his ardent desire to establish the principles of British government in the new province. He was a sincere friend of the Loyalists, whose attachment to the crown he had had many opportunities of appreciating during his career in the rebellious colonies, and, consequently, was an uncompromising opponent of the new republic and of the people who were labouring to make it a success on the other side of the border. The new parliament met in a wooden building nearly completed on the sloping bank of the river, at a spot subsequently covered by a rampart of Fort George, which was constructed by Governor Simcoe on the surrender of Fort Niagara. A large boulder has been placed on the top of the rampart to mark the site of the humble parliament house of Upper Canada, which had to be eventually demolished to make place for new fortifications. The sittings of the first legislature were not unfrequently held under a large tent set up in front of the house, and having an interesting history of its own, since it had been carried around the world by the famous navigator, Captain Cook.

As soon as Lieutenant-Governor Simcoe assumed the direction of the government, he issued a proclamation dividing the province of Upper Canada into nineteen counties, some of winch were again divided into ridings for the purpose of electing the sixteen representatives to which the province was entitled under the act of 1791. One of the first acts of the legislature was to change the names of the divisions, proclaimed in 1788, to Eastern, Midland, Home, and Western Districts, which received additions in the course of years until they were entirely superseded by the county organisations. These districts were originally intended for judicial and legal purposes.

The legislature met under these humble circumstances at Newark on the 17th September, 1792. Chief Justice Osgoode was the speaker of the council, and Colonel John Macdonell, of Aberchalder, who had gallantly served in the royal forces during the revolution, was chosen presiding officer of the assembly. Besides him, there were eleven Loyalists among the sixteen members of the lower house. In the council of nine members there were also several Loyalists, the most prominent being the Honourable Richard Cartwright, the grandfather of the minister of trade and commerce in the Dominion ministry of 1896-1900.

SECTION 2.—Twenty years of political development (1792-1812).

The political conditions of the two decades from 1792 until 1812, when war broke out between England and the United States, were for the greater part of the time quite free from political agitation, and the representatives of the people in both the provinces of Canada were mostly occupied with the consideration of measures of purely provincial and local import. Nevertheless a year or two before the close of this period we can see in the province of Lower Canada premonitions of that irrepressible conflict between the two houses—

one elected by the people and the other nominated by and under the influence of the crown—which eventually clogged the machinery of legislation. We can also see the beginnings of that strife of races which ultimately led to bloodshed and the suspension of the constitution given to Lower Canada in 1791.

In 1806 *Le Canadien*, published in the special interest of "Nos institutions, notre langue, et nos lois," commenced that career of bitter hostility to the government which steadily inflamed the antagonism between the races. The arrogance of the principal officials, who had the ear of the governor, and practically engrossed all the influence in the management of public affairs, alienated the French Canadians, who came to believe that they were regarded by the British as an inferior race. As a matter of fact, many of the British inhabitants themselves had no very cordial feelings towards the officials, whose social exclusiveness offended all who did not belong to their special "set." In those days the principal officials were appointed by the colonial office and the governor-general, and had little or no respect for the assembly, on which they depended in no wise for their continuance in office or their salaries. The French Canadians eventually made few distinctions among the British but looked on them as, generally speaking, enemies to their institutions.

It was unfortunate, at a time when great discretion and good temper were so essential, that Sir James Craig should have been entrusted with the administration of the government of Lower Canada. The critical state of relations with the United States no doubt influenced his appointment, which, from a purely military point of view, was excellent. As it was, however, his qualities as a soldier were not called into requisition, while his want of political experience, his utter incapacity to understand the political conditions of the country, his supreme indifference to the wishes of the assembly, made his administration an egregious failure. Indeed it may he said that it was during his time that the seed was sown for the growth of that political and racial antagonism which led to the rebellion of 1837. It is not possible to exaggerate the importance of the consequences of his unjustifiable dismissal of Mr. Speaker Panet, and other prominent French Canadians, from the militia on the ground that they had an interest in the *Canadien*, or of his having followed up this very indiscreet act by the unwarrantable arrest of Mr. Bedard and some other persons, on the charge that they were the authors or publishers of what he declared to be treasonable writings. It is believed that the governor's action was largely influenced by the statements and advice of Chief Justice Sewell, the head of the legislative council and the official class. Several persons were released when they expressed regret for the expression of any opinions considered extreme by the governor and his advisers, but Mr. Bedard remained in prison for a year rather than directly or indirectly admit that the governor had any justification for his arbitrary act Sir James attempted to obtain the approval of the home government; but his agent, a Mr. Ryland, a man of ability and suavity, prominent always in the official life of the country, signally failed to obtain the endorsement of his master's action. He was unable to secure a promise that the constitution of 1791 should be repealed, and the legislative council of the Quebec act again given the supremacy in the province. Mr. Bedard was released just before the governor left the country, with the declaration that "his detention had been a matter of precaution and not of punishment"—by no means a manly or graceful withdrawal from what was assuredly a most untenable position from the very first moment Mr. Bedard was thrown into prison. Sir James Craig left the province a disappointed man, and died in England a few months after his return, from the effects of an incurable disease to which he had been a victim for many years. He was hospitable, generous and charitable, but the qualities of a soldier dominated all his acts of civil government.

In the other provinces, happily, there were no racial differences to divide the community and aggravate those political disputes that are sure to arise in the working of representative institutions in a British country. In Upper Canada for years the questions under discussion were chiefly connected with the disposal of the public lands, which in early times were too lavishly granted by Simcoe; and this led to the bringing in for a while of some undesirable immigrants from the United States —undesirable because they were imbued with republican and levelling ideas by no means favourable to the development and stability of English institutions of government. One of the first acts of the legislature was the establishment of courts of law and equity, in accordance with the practice and principles of

English jurisprudence. Another very important measure was one for the legalisation of marriages which had been irregularly performed during early times in the absence of the clergy of the Anglican Church by justices of the peace, and even the officers in charge of military posts. Magistrates were still allowed to perform the marriage ceremony according to the ritual of the Church of England, when the services of a clergyman of that denomination were not available. Not until 1830 were more liberal provisions passed and the clergy of any recognised creed permitted to unite persons legally in wedlock.

It was in the second session of the first parliament of Upper Canada, where the Loyalists were in so huge a majority, that an act was passed "to prevent the further introduction of slaves and to limit the term of contract for servitude within this province." A considerable number of slave servants accompanied their Loyalist masters to the provinces at the end of the war, and we find for many years after in the newspapers advertisements relating to runaway servants of this class. The Loyalists in the maritime provinces, like the same class in Upper Canada, never gave their approval to the continuance of slavery. So early as 1800 some prominent persons brought before the supreme court of New Brunswick the case of one Nancy Morton, a slave, on a writ of *habeas corpus*; and her right to freedom was argued by Ward Chipmim, one of the Loyalist makers of New Brunswick. Although the argument in this case was not followed by a judicial conclusion—the four judges being divided in opinion—slavery thereafter practically ceased to exist, not only in New Brunswick, but in the other maritime provinces, leaving behind it a memory so faint, that the mere suggestion that there ever was a slave in either of these provinces is very generally received with surprise, if not with incredulity.

The early history of representative government in Prince Edward Island is chiefly a dull narrative of political conflict between the governors and the assemblies, and of difficulties and controversies arising out of the extraordinary concessions of lands to a few proprietors, who generally infringed the conditions of their grants and retarded the settlement of the island. In New Brunswick the legislature was entirely occupied with the consideration of measures for the administration of justice and local affairs in an entirely new country. Party government had not yet declared itself, and the Loyalists who had founded the province controlled the legislature for many years until a spirit of liberalism and reform found full expression and led to the enlargement of the public liberty.

In Nova Scotia the Loyalists gradually acquired considerable influence in the government of the province, as the imperial authorities felt it incumbent on them to provide official positions for those men who had sacrificed so much for the empire. Their power was increased after the arrival of Governor John Wentworth—afterwards made a baronet—who had been the royal governor of New Hampshire, and had naturally a strong antipathy to democratic principles in any form. In his time there grew up an official oligarchy, chiefly composed of members of the legislative council, then embodying within itself executive, legislative and judicial powers. A Liberal party soon arose in Nova Scotia, not only among the early New England settlers of the time of Governor Lawrence, but among the Loyalists themselves, for it is inevitable that wherever we find an English people, the spirit of popular liberty and the determination to enjoy self-government in a complete sense will sooner or later assert itself among all classes of men. The first prominent leader of the opposition to the Tory methods of the government was one William Cottnam Tonge, who was for some years in the employ of the naval department. Sir John Wentworth carried his hostility to the extent of dismissing him from his naval office and also of refusing to accept him as speaker of the assembly—the first example in colonial history of an extreme exercise of the royal prerogative by a governor. Mr. Tonge's only crime appears to have been his bold assertion from time to time of the privileges of the house of assembly, as the guardian of the revenues and expenditures, against the interference of the governor and council. We find in Nova Scotia, as in the other provinces, during the period in question, the elements of perpetual discord, which found more serious expression after the war of 1812-15, and led to important constitutional changes.

The governors of those times became, from the very nature of their position, so many provincial autocrats, brought constantly into conflict with the popular body, and unable to conceive any system of government possible that did not place the province directly under the control of the imperial authorities, to whom appeals must be made in the most trivial cases of doubt or difficulty. The representative of the crown brooked no interference on the part of the assembly with what he considered his prerogatives and rights, and as a rule threw himself into the arms of the council, composed of the official oligarchy. In the course of time, the whole effort of the Liberal or Reform party, which gathered strength after 1815, was directed against the power of the legislative council. We hear nothing in the assemblies or the literature of the period under review in advocacy of the system of parliamentary or responsible government which was then in existence in the parent state and which we now enjoy in British North America. In fact, it was not until the beginning of the fourth decade of the nineteenth century that the Liberal politicians of Nova Scotia, like those of Upper Canada, recognised that the real remedy for existing political grievances was to be found in the harmonious operation of the three branches of the legislature. Even then we look in vain for an enunciation of this essential principle of representative government in the speeches or writings of a single French Canadian from 1791 until 1838, when the constitution of Lower Canada was suspended as a result of rebellion.

During the twenty years of which I am writing the government of Canada had much reason for anxiety on account of the unsatisfactory state of the relations between Great Britain and the United States, and of the attempts of French emissaries after the outbreak of the revolution in France to stir up sedition in Lower Canada. One of the causes of the war of 1812-15 was undoubtedly the irritation that was caused by the retention of the western posts by Great Britain despite the stipulation in the definitive treaty of peace to give them up "with all convenient speed." This policy of delay was largely influenced by the fact that the new republic had failed to take effective measures for the restitution of the estates of the Loyalists or for the payment of debts due to British creditors; but in addition there was probably still, as in 1763 and 1774, a desire to control the fur-trade and the Indians of the west, who claimed that the lands between the Canadian frontier and the Ohio were exclusively their hunting-grounds, not properly included within the territory ceded to the United States. Jay's treaty, arranged in 1794, with the entire approval of Washington, who thereby incurred the hostility of the anti-British party, was a mere temporary expedient for tiding over the difficulties between England and the United States. Its most important result so far as it affected Canada was the giving up in 1797 of the western posts including Old Fort Niagara. It became then necessary to remove the seat of government from Niagara, as an insecure position, and York, which regained its original Indian name of Toronto in 1834, was chosen as the capital by Lord Dorchester in preference to a place suggested by Simcoe on the Tranche, now the Thames, near where London now stands. The second parliament of Upper Canada met in York on the first of June, 1797, when Mr. Russell, who had been secretary to Sir Henry Clinton during the American war, was administrator of the government after the departure of Lieutenant-Governor Simcoe from a province whose interests he had so deeply at heart.

After the declaration of war against England by the republican convention of France in 1793, French agents found their way into the French parishes of Lower Canada, and endeavoured to make the credulous and ignorant *habitants* believe that France would soon regain dominion in her old colony. During General Prescott's administration, one McLane, who was said to be not quite mentally responsible for his acts, was convicted at Quebec for complicity in the designs of French agents, and was executed near St. John's gate with all the revolting incidents of a traitor's death in those relentless times. His illiterate accomplice, Frechétte, was sentenced to imprisonment for life, but was soon released on the grounds of his ignorance of the serious crime he was committing. No doubt in these days some restlessness existed in the French Canadian districts, and the English authorities found it difficult for a time to enforce the provisions of the militia act. Happily for the peace and security of Canada, the influence of the Bishop and Roman Catholic clergy, who looked with horror on the murderous acts of the revolutionists of France, was successfully exerted for the support of British rule, whose justice and benignity their church had felt ever since the conquest. The name of Bishop Plessis must always be mentioned in terms of sincere praise by every English writer who reviews the history of those trying times, when British interests would have been more than once in jeopardy had it not been for the loyal conduct of this distinguished prelate and the priests under his direction.

I shall now proceed to narrate the events of the unfortunate war which broke out in 1812 between England and the United States, as a result of the unsettled relations of years, and made Canada a battle ground on which were given many illustrations of the patriotism and devotion of the Canadian people, whose conquest, the invaders thought, would be a very easy task.

CHAPTER V.

THE WAR OF 1812—15.

SECTION I.—Origin of the war between England and the United States.

The causes of the war of 1812-15 must be sought in the history of Europe and the relations between England and the United States for several decades before it actually broke out. Great Britain was engaged in a supreme struggle not only for national existence but even for the liberties of Europe, from the moment when Napoleon, in pursuance of his overweening ambition, led his armies over the continent on those victorious marches which only ended amid the ice and snow of Russia. Britain's battles were mainly to be fought on the sea where her great fleet made her supreme. The restriction of all commerce that was not British was a necessary element in the assertion of her naval superiority. If neutral nations were to be allowed freely to carry the produce of the colonies of Powers with whom Great Britain was at war, then they were practically acting as allies of her enemies, and were liable to search and seizure. For some time, however, Great Britain thought it expedient to concur in the practice that when a cargo was trans-shipped in the United States, and paid a duty there, it became to all intents and purposes American property and might be carried to a foreign country and there sold, as if it were the actual produce of the republic itself. This became a very profitable business to the merchants of the United States, as a neutral nation, during the years when Great Britain was at war with France, since they controlled a large proportion of all foreign commerce. Frauds constantly occurred during the continuance of this traffic, and at last British statesmen felt the injury to their commerce was so great that the practice was changed to one which made American vessels liable to be seized and condemned in British prize courts whenever it was clear that their cargoes were not American produce, but were actually purchased at the port of an enemy. Even provisions purchased from an enemy or its colonies were considered "contraband of war" on the ground that they afforded actual aid and encouragement to an enemy. The United States urged at first that only military stores could fall under this category, and eventually went so far as to assert the principle that under all circumstances "free ships make free goods," and that neutral ships had a right to carry any property, even that of a nation at war with another power, and to trade when and where they liked without fear of capture. England, however, would not admit in those days of trial principles which would practically make a neutral nation an ally of her foe. She persisted in restricting the commerce of the United States by all the force she had upon the sea.

This restrictive policy, which touched the American pocket and consequently the American heart so deeply, was complicated by another question of equal, if not greater, import. The forcible impressment of men to man the British fleet had been for many years a necessary evil in view of the national emergency, and of the increase in the mercantile marine which attracted large numbers to its service. Great abuses were perpetrated in the operation of this harsh method of maintaining an efficient naval force, and there was no part of the British Isles where the presence of a press gang did not bring dismay into many a home. Great Britain, then and for many years later, upheld to an extreme degree the doctrine of perpetual allegiance; she refused to recognise the right of any of her citizens to divest themselves of their national fealty and become by naturalisation the subject of a foreign power or a citizen of the United States Such a doctrine was necessarily most obnoxious to the government and people of a new republic like the United States, whose future development rested on the basis of a steady and large immigration, which lost much of its strength and usefulness as long as the men who came into the country were not recognised as American citizens at home and abroad. Great Britain claimed the right, as a corollary of this doctrine of indefeasible allegiance, to search the neutral ships of the United States during the war with France, to enquire into the nationality of the seaman on board of those vessels, to impress all those whom her officers had reason to consider British subjects by birth, and to pay no respect to the fact that they may have been naturalised in the country of their adoption. The assertion of the right to search a neutral vessel and to impress seamen who were British subjects has in these modern times been condemned as a breach of the sound principle, that a right of search can only be properly exercised in the case of a neutral's violation of his neutrality—that is to say, the giving of aid to one of the parties to the war The forcible abduction of a seaman under the circumstances stated was simply an unwarrantable attempt to enforce municipal law on board a neutral vessel, which was in effect foreign territory, to be regarded as sacred and inviolate except in a case where it was brought under the operation of a recognised doctrine of international law. Great Britain at that critical period of her national existence would not look beyond the fact that the acts of the United States as a neutral were most antagonistic to the energetic efforts she was making to maintain her naval supremacy during the European crisis created by Napoleon's ambitious designs.

The desertion of British seamen from British ships, for the purpose of finding refuge in the United States and then taking service in American vessels, caused great irritation in Great Britain and justified, in the opinion of some statesmen and publicists who only regarded national necessities, the harsh and arbitrary manner in which English officials stopped and searched American shipping on the high seas, seized men whom they claimed to be deserters, and impressed any whom they asserted to be still British subjects. In 1807 the British frigate "Leopard," acting directly under the orders of the admiral at Halifax, even ventured to fire a broadside into the United States cruiser "Chesapeake" a few miles from Chesapeake Bay, killed and wounded a number of her crew, and then carried off several sailors who were said to be, and no doubt were, deserters from the English service and who were the primary cause of the detention of this American man-of-war. For this unjustifiable act England subsequently made some reparation, but nevertheless it rankled for years in the minds of the party hostile to Great Britain and helped to swell the list of grievances which the American government in the course of years accumulated against the parent state as a reason for war.

The difficulties between England and the United States, which culminated in war before the present century was far advanced, were also intensified by disputes which commenced soon after the treaty of 1783. I have already shown that for some years the north-west posts were still retained by the English on the ground, it is understood, that the claims of English creditors, and especially those of the Loyalists, should be first settled before all the conditions of the treaty could be carried out. The subsequent treaty of 1794, negotiated by Chief Justice Jay, adjusted these and other questions, and led for some years to a better understanding with Great Britain, but at the same time led to a rupture of friendly relations with the French Directory, who demanded the repeal of that treaty as in conflict with the one made with France in 1778, and looked for some tangible evidence of sympathetic interest with the French revolution. The war that followed with the French republic was insignificant in its operations, and was immediately terminated by Napoleon when he overthrew the Directory, and seized the government for his own ambitious objects. Subsequently, the administration of the United States refused to renew the Jay Treaty when it duly expired, and as a consequence the relatively amicable relations that had existed between the Republic and England again became critical, since American commerce and shipping were exposed to all the irritating measures that England felt compelled under existing conditions to carry out in pursuance of the policy of restricting the trade of neutral vessels. Several attempts were made by the British government, between the expiry of the Jay Treaty and the actual rupture of friendly relations with the United States, to come to a better understanding with respect to some of the questions in dispute, but the differences between the two Powers were so radical that all negotiations came to naught. Difficulties were also complicated by the condition of political parties in the American republic and the ambition of American statesmen. When the democratic republicans or "Strict constructionists," as they have been happily named, with Jefferson at their head, obtained office, French ideas came into favour; while the federalists or "Broad constitutionalists," of whom Washington, Hamilton and Adams had been the first exponents, were anxious to keep the nation free from European complications and to settle international difficulties by treaty and not by war. But this party was in a hopeless minority, during the critical times when international difficulties were resolving themselves into war, and was unable to influence public opinion sufficiently to make negotiations for the maintenance of peace successful, despite the fact that it had a considerable weight in the states of New England.

The international difficulties of the United States entered upon a critical condition when Great Britain, in her assertion of naval supremacy and restricted commerce as absolutely essential to her national security, issued an order-in-council which declared a strict blockade of the European coast from Brest to the Elbe. Napoleon retaliated with the Berlin decree, which merely promulgated a paper blockade of the British Isles. Then followed the later British orders-in-council, which prevented the shipping of the United States from trading with any country where British vessels could not enter, and allowed them only to trade with other European ports where they made entries and paid duties in English custom-houses. Napoleon increased the duties of neutral commerce by the Milan decree of 1807, which ordered the seizure of all neutral vessels which might have been searched by English cruisers. These orders meant the ruin of American commerce, which had become so profitable; and the Washington government attempted to retaliate, first by forbidding the importation of manufactures from England and her colonies, and, when this effort was ineffective, by declaring an embargo in its own ports, which had only the result of still further crippling American commerce at home and abroad. Eventually, in place of this unwise measure, which, despite its systematic evasion, brought serious losses to the whole nation and seemed likely to result in civil war in the east, where the discontent was greatest, a system of non-intercourse with both England and France was adopted, to last so long as either should press its restrictive measures against the republic, but this new policy of retaliation hardly impeded American commerce, of which the profits were far greater than the risks. The leaders of the Democratic party were now anxious to conciliate France, and endeavoured to persuade the nation that Napoleon had practically freed the United States from the restrictions to which it so strongly objected. It is a matter beyond dispute that the French decrees were never exactly annulled; and the Emperor was pursuing an insidious policy which confiscated American vessels in French ports at the very moment he was professing friendship with the United States. His object was to force the government of that country into war with England, and, unfortunately for its interests, its statesmen lent themselves to his designs.

The Democratic leaders, determined to continue in power, fanned the flame against England, whose maritime superiority enabled her to inflict the greatest injury on American shipping and commerce. The governing party looked to the south and west for their principal support. In these sections the interests were exclusively agricultural, while in New England, where the Federalists were generally in the majority, the commercial and maritime elements predominated. In Kentucky, Ohio, and other states there was a strong feeling against England on account of the current belief that the English authorities in Canada had tampered with the Indian tribes and induced them to harass the settlers until Harrison, on the eve of the war of 1812, effectually cowed them. It is, however, now well established by the Canadian archives that Sir James Craig, when governor-general in 1807, actually warned the Washington government of the restlessness of the western Indians, and of the anxiety of the Canadian authorities to avoid an Indian war in the north-west, which might prejudicially operate against the western province. This fact was not, however, generally known, and the feeling against Canada and England was kept alive by the dominant party in the United States by the disclosure that one John Henry had been sent by the Canadian government in 1808 to ascertain the sentiment of the people of New England with respect to the relations between the two countries and the maintenance of peace. Henry's correspondence was really quite harmless, but when it had been purchased from him by Madison, on the refusal of the imperial government to buy his silence, it served the temporary purpose of making the people of the west believe that England was all the while intriguing against the national interests, and endeavouring to create a discontent which might end in civil strife. Under these circumstances the southern leaders, Clay of Kentucky, and Calhoun of South Carolina, who always showed an inveterate animosity against England, forced Madison, then anxious to be re-elected president, to send a warlike message to congress, which culminated in a formal declaration of hostilities on the 18th of June, 1812, only one day later than the repeal of the obnoxious order-in-council by England. When the repeal became known some weeks later in Canada and the United States, the province of Upper Canada had been actually invaded by Hull, and the government of the United States had no desire whatever to desist from warlike operations, which, they confidently believed, would end in the successful occupation of Canada at a time when England was unable, on account of her European responsibilities, to extend to its defenders effective assistance.

SECTION 2.—Canada during the war.

In 1812 there were five hundred thousand people living in the provinces of British North America. Of this number, the French people of Lower Canada made up at least one half. These people had some grievances, and political agitators, notably the writers of the *Canadien*, were creating jealousies and rivalries between the French and English races chiefly on the ground of the dominant influence of the British minority in the administration of public affairs. On the whole, however, the country was prosperous and the people generally contented with British rule, the freedom of which presented such striking contrast to the absolutism of the old French régime. The great majority of the eighty thousand inhabitants of Upper or Western Canada were Loyalists or descendants of Loyalists, who had become deeply attached to their new homes, whilst recalling with feelings of deep bitterness the sufferings and trials of the American revolution. This class was naturally attached to British rule and hostile to every innovation which had the least semblance of American republicanism. In the western part of the province of Upper Canada there was, however, an American element composed of people who had been brought into the country by the liberal grants of land made to settlers, and who were not animated by the high sentiments of the Loyalists of 1783 and succeeding years. These people, for some years previous to 1812, were misled by political demagogues like Wilcox and Marcle, both of whom deserted to the enemy soon after the outbreak of the war. Emissaries from the republic were busily engaged for months, we now know, in fomenting a feeling against England among these later immigrants, and in persuading them that the time was close at hand when Canada would be annexed to the federal republic. Some attempts were even made to create discontent among the French Canadians, but no success appears to have followed these efforts in a country where the bishop, priests and leading men of the rural communities perfectly appreciated the value of British connection.

The statesmen of the United States, who were responsible for the war, looked on the provinces as so many weak communities which could be easily invaded and conquered by the republican armies. Upper Canada, with its long and exposed frontier and its small and scattered population, was considered utterly indefensible and almost certain to be successfully occupied by the invading forces. There was not a town of one thousand souls in the whole of that province, and the only forts of any pretension were those on the Niagara frontier. Kingston was a fortified town of some importance in the eastern part of the province, but Toronto had no adequate means of defence. At the commencement of the war there were only fourteen hundred and fifty regular troops in the whole country west of Montreal, and these men were scattered at Kingston, York, Niagara, Chippewa, Erie, Amherstburg, and St. Joseph. The total available militia did not exceed four thousand men, the majority of whom had little or no knowledge of military discipline, and were not even in the possession of suitable arms and accoutrements, though, happily, all were animated by the loftiest sentiments of courage and patriotism. In the lower provinces of Eastern Canada and Nova Scotia there was a considerable military force, varying in the aggregate from four to five thousand men. The fortifications of Quebec were in a tolerable state of repair, but the citadel which dominates Halifax was in a dilapidated condition. The latter port was, however, the rendezvous of the English fleet, which always afforded adequate protection to British interests on the Atlantic coasts of British North America, despite the depredations of privateers and the successes attained during the first months of the war by the superior tonnage and equipment of the frigates of the republic. But the hopes that were entertained by the war party in the United States could be gathered from the speeches of Henry Clay of Kentucky, who believed that the issue would be favourable to their invading forces, who would even "negotiate terms of peace at Quebec or Halifax."

The United States had now a population of at least six millions and a half of whites. It was estimated that during the war the government had a militia force of between four and five hundred thousand men available for service, while the regular army amounted to thirty-four thousand officers and privates. The forces that invaded Canada by the way of Lake Champlain, Sackett's Harbour, the Niagara and

Detroit Rivers, were vastly superior in numbers to the Canadian army of defence, except in the closing months of the war, when Prevost had under his command a large body of Peninsular veterans. One condition was always in favour of Canada, and that was the sullen apathy or antagonism felt by the people of New England with respect to the war. Had they been in a different spirit, Lower Canada would have been in far greater danger of successful invasion and occupation than was the case at any time during the progress of the conflict. The famous march of Arnold on Quebec by the Kennebec and Chaudière Rivers might have been repeated with more serious consequences while Prevost, and not Guy Carleton, was in supreme command in the French Canadian province.

I can attempt to limn only the events which stand out most plainly on the graphic pages of this momentous epoch in Canadian history, and to pay a humble tribute to the memory of men, whose achievements saved Canada for England in those days of trial. From the beginning to the end of the conflict, Upper Canada was the principal battle ground upon which the combatants fought for the supremacy in North America. Its frontiers were frequently crossed, its territory was invaded, and its towns and villages were destroyed by the ruthless hand of a foe who entered the province not only with the sword of the soldier but even with the torch of the incendiary. The plan of operations at the outset of the campaign was to invade the province across the Niagara and Detroit Rivers, neither of which offered any real obstacles to the passage of a determined and well-managed army in the absence of strong fortifications, or a superior defensive force, at every vulnerable point along the Canadian banks. Queenston was to be a base of operations for a large force, which would overrun the whole province and eventually co-operate with troops which could come up from Lake Champlain and march on Montreal. The forces of the United States in 1812 acted with considerable promptitude as soon as war was officially declared, and had they been led by able commanders the result might have been most unfortunate for Canada. The resources for defence were relatively insignificant, and indecision and weakness were shown by Sir George Prevost, then commander-in-chief and governor-general—a well meaning man but wanting in ability as a military leader, who was also hampered by the vacillating counsels of the

Liverpool administration, which did not believe in war until the province was actually invaded. It was fortunate for Canada that she had then at the head of the government in the upper province General Brock, who possessed decision of character and the ability to comprehend the serious situation of affairs at a critical juncture, when his superiors both in England and Canada did not appear to understand its full significance.

The assembly of Upper Canada passed an address giving full expression to the patriotic sentiments which animated all classes of people when the perilous state of affairs and the necessity for energetic action became apparent to the dullest minds. The Loyalists and their descendants, as well as other loyal people, rallied at the moment of danger to the support of Brock; and the immediate result of his decided orders was the capture of the post of Michillimackinac, which had been, ever since the days of the French régime, a position of great importance on the upper lakes. Then followed the ignominious surrender of General Hull and his army to Brock, and the consequent occupation of Detroit and the present state of Michigan by the British troops. Later, on the Niagara frontier, an army of invaders was driven from Queenston Heights, but this victory cost the life of the great English general, whose promptitude at the commencement of hostilities had saved the province. Among other brave men who fell with Brock was the attorney-general of the province, Lieutenant-Colonel John Macdonell, who was one of the general's aides. General Sheaffe, the son of a Loyalist, took command and drove the enemy across the river, in whose rapid waters many were drowned while struggling to save themselves from the pursuing British soldiery, determined to avenge the death of their honoured chief. A later attempt by General Smyth to invade Canadian territory opposite Black Rock on the Niagara River, was also attended with the same failure that attended the futile attempts to cross the Detroit and to occupy the heights of Queenston. At the close of 1812 Upper Canada was entirely free from the army of the republic, the Union Jack floated above the fort at Detroit, and the ambitious plan of invading the French province and seizing Montreal was given up as a result of the disasters to the enemy in the west. The party of peace in New England gathered strength, and the promoters of the war had no consolation except the triumphs obtained at sea by some heavily armed and well manned frigates of the United States to the surprise of the government and people of England, who never anticipated that their maritime superiority could be in any way endangered by a nation whose naval strength was considered so insignificant. But these victories of the republic on the ocean during the first year of the war were soon effaced by the records of the two subsequent years when "The Chesapeake" was captured by "The Shannon" and other successes of the British ships restored the prestige of England on the sea.

During the second year of the war the United States won some military and naval successes in the upper province, although the final results of the campaign were largely in favour of the defenders of Canada. The war opened with the defeat of General Winchester at Frenchtown on the River Raisins in the present state of Michigan; but this success, which was won by General Procter, was soon forgotten in the taking of York, the capital of the province, and the destruction of its public buildings. This event forced General Sheaffe to retire to Kingston, while General Vincent retreated to Burlington Heights as soon as the invading army occupied Fort George and dominated the Niagara frontier. Sir George Prevost showed his military incapacity at Sackett's Harbour, where he had it in his power to capture a post which was an important base of operations against the province. On the other hand Colonel George Macdonell made a successful attack on Ogdensburg and fittingly avenged the raid that an American force had made a short time previously on Elizabethtown, which was called Brockville not long afterwards in honour of the noted general. An advance of the invading army against General Vincent was checked by the memorable success won at Stoney Creek by Colonel Harvey and the surrender at Beaver Dams of Colonel Boerstler to Lieutenant Fitzgibbon, whose clever strategy enabled him to capture a large force of the enemy while in command of a few soldiers and Indians. When September arrived, the small, though all-important, British fleet on Lake Erie, under the command of Captain Barclay, sustained a fatal defeat at Put-in-Bay, and the United States vessels under Commodore Perry held full control of Lake Erie. A few weeks later, General Procter lost the reputation which he had won in January by his defeat of Winchester, and was beaten, under circumstances which disgraced him in the opinion of his superiors, on the River Thames not far from the Indian village of Moraviantown. The American forces were led by General Harrison, who had won some reputation in the Indian campaign in the northwest and who subsequently became, as his son in later times, a president of the United States.

It was in this engagement that the Shawenese chief, Tecumseh, was killed, in him England lost a faithful and brave ally. English prospects in the west were consequently gloomy for some time, until the autumn of 1813, when the auspicious tidings spread from the lakes to the Atlantic that the forces of the republic, while on their march to Montreal by the way of Lake Champlain and the St. Lawrence, had been successfully met and repulsed at Chateauguay and Chrysler's Farm, two of the most memorable engagements of the war, when we consider the insignificant forces that checked the invasion and saved Canada at a most critical time.

In the last month of the same year Fort George was evacuated by the American garrison, but not before General McLure had shamelessly burned the pretty town of Niagara, and driven helpless women and children into the ice and snow of a Canadian winter. General Drummond, who was in command of the western army, retaliated by the capture of Fort Niagara and the destruction of all the villages on the American side of the river as far as Buffalo, then a very insignificant place. When the new year dawned the only Canadian place in possession of the enemy was Amherstburg on the western frontier.

The third and last year of the war was distinguished by the capture of Oswego and Prairie-des-Chiens by British expeditions; the repulse of a large force of the invaders at Lacolle Mills in Lower Canada; the surrender of Fort Erie to the enemy, the defeat of General Riall at Street's or Usher's Creek in the Niagara district, the hotly contested battle won at Lundy's Lane by Drummond, and the ignominious retreat from Plattsburg of Sir George Prevost, in command of a splendid force of peninsular veterans, after the defeat of Commodore Downey's fleet on Lake Champlain. Before the year closed and peace was proclaimed, Fort Erie was evacuated, the stars and stripes were driven from Lake Ontario, and all Canadian territory except Amherstburg was free from the invader. The capital of the United

States had been captured by the British and its public buildings burned as a severe retaliation for the conduct of the invading forces at York, Niagara, Moraviantown, St. David's and Port Dover. Both combatants were by this time heartily tired of the war, and terms of peace were arranged by the treaty of Ghent at the close of 1814; but before the news reached the south, General Jackson repulsed General Packenham with heavy losses at New Orleans, and won a reputation which made him president a few years later.

The maritime provinces never suffered from invasion, but on the contrary obtained some advantages from the presence of large numbers of British men-of-war in their seaports, and the expenditure on military and naval supplies during the three years of war. Following the example of the Canadas, the assemblies of New Brunswick and Nova Scotia voted large sums of money and embodied the militia for active service or general purposes of defence. The assembly of New Brunswick, essentially the province of the Loyalists, declared in 1813 that the people were "ready and determined to repel every aggression which the infatuated policy of the American government may induce it to commit on the soil of New Brunswick." But the war was so unpopular in the state of Maine and other parts of New England that the provinces by the sea were comparatively safe from aggression and conflict. Soon after the commencement of hostilities the governors of Maine and New Brunswick issued proclamations which prevented hostilities for two years along their respective borders. In Nova Scotia there was much activity during the war, and letters of marque were issued to privateers which made many captures, and offered some compensation for the losses inflicted on the coasting and fishing interests by the same class of American vessels. In 1814 it was decided by the imperial authorities to break the truce which had practically left Maine free from invasion, and Sir John Sherbrooke, then governor of Nova Scotia, and Rear-Admiral Griffith took possession of Machias, Eastport, Moose, and other islands in Passamaquoddy Bay.

The people of the United States generally welcomed the end of a war which brought them neither honour nor profit and seemed likely to break the union into fragments in consequence of the hostility that had existed in New England through the conflict from the very beginning. The news of Prevost's retreat from Plattsburg no doubt hastened the decision of the British government to enter into negotiations for peace, which was settled on terms by no means favourable to Canadian interests. The question of the New Brunswick boundary might have been then adjusted on conditions which would have prevented at a later day the sacrifice of a large tract of territory in Maine which would be now of great value to the Dominion. The only advantage which accrued to the Canadians was a later convention which gave the people of the provinces full control of fisheries, ignorantly sacrificed by the treaty of 1783.

No class of the people of Canada contributed more to the effectiveness of the militia and the successful defence of the country than the descendants of the Loyalists, who formed so large and influential a portion of the English population of British North America. All the loyal settlements on the banks of the St. Lawrence, on the Niagara frontier, and on the shores of Lake Erie, sent many men to fight by the side of the regular British forces. Even aged men, who had borne arms in the revolutionary war, came forward with an enthusiasm which showed that age had not impaired their courage or patriotism, and although they were exempted from active service, they were found most useful in stationary duties at a time when Canada demanded the experience of such veterans. "Their lessons and example," wrote General Sheaffe, "will have a happy influence on the youth of the militia ranks." When Hull invaded the province and issued his boastful and threatening proclamation he used language which must have seemed a mockery to the children of the Loyalists. They remembered too well the sufferings of their fathers and brothers during "the stormy period of the revolution," and it seemed derisive to tell them now that they were to be "emancipated from tyranny and oppression and restored to the dignified station of free men." The proclamation issued by Governor Brock touched the loyal hearts of a people whose family histories were full of examples of "oppression and tyranny," and of the kind consideration and justice of England in their new homes. "Where," asked Brock, with the confidence of truth, "is the Canadian subject who can truly affirm to himself that he has been injured by the government in his person, his property, or his liberty? Where is to be found, in any part of the world, a growth so rapid in prosperity and wealth as this colony exhibits?" These people, to whom this special appeal was made at this national crisis, responded with a heartiness which showed that gratitude and affection lay deep in their hearts. Even the women worked in the field that their husbands, brothers and sons might drive the invaders from Canadian soil. The 104th Regiment, which accomplished a remarkable march of thirteen days in the depth of winter, from Fredericton to Quebec—a distance of three hundred and fifty miles—and lost only one man by illness, was composed of descendants of the loyal founders of New Brunswick. This march was accomplished practically without loss, while more than three hundred men were lost by Benedict Arnold in his expedition of 1777 against Quebec by the way of Kennebec—a journey not more dangerous or arduous than that so successfully accomplished by the New Brunswick Loyalists. In 1814 considerable numbers of seamen for service in the upper lakes passed through New Brunswick to Quebec, and were soon followed by several companies of the 8th or King's Regiment. The patriotism of the Loyalists of New Brunswick was shown by grants of public money and every other means in their power, while these expeditions were on their way to the seat of war in the upper provinces.

Historians and poets have often dwelt on the heroism of Laura Secord, daughter and wife of Loyalists, who made a perilous journey in 1814 through the Niagara district, and succeeded in warning Lieutenant Fitzgibbon of the approach of the enemy, thus enabling him with a few soldiers and Indians to surprise Colonel Boerstler near Beaver Dams and force him by clever strategy to surrender with nearly 600 men and several cannon. Even boys fled from home and were found fighting in the field. The Prince Regent, at the close of the war, expressly thanked the Canadian militia, who had "mainly contributed to the immediate preservation of the province and its future security." The Loyalists, who could not save the old colonies to England, did their full share in maintaining her supremacy in the country she still owned in the valley of the St. Lawrence and on the shores of the Atlantic.

As Bishop Plessis stimulated a patriotic sentiment among the French Canadians, so Vicar-General Macdonell of Glengarry, subsequently the first Roman Catholic bishop of Upper Canada, performed good service by assisting in the formation of a Glengarry regiment, and otherwise taking an active part in the defence of the province, where his will always be an honoured name. Equally indefatigable in patriotic endeavour was Bishop Strachan, then rector of York, who established "The Loyal and Patriotic Society," which did incalculable good by relieving the necessities of women and children, when the men were serving in the battlefield, by providing clothing and food for the soldiery, and otherwise contributing towards the comfort and succour of all those who were taking part in the public defences. Of the engagements of the war there are two which, above all others, possess features on which the historian must always like to dwell. The battle which was fought against such tremendous odds on the banks of the Chateauguay by less than a thousand French Canadians, led by Salaberry and Macdonell, recalls in some respects the defeat of Braddock in 1755. The disaster to the British forces near the Monongahela was mainly the result of the strategy of the Indians, who were dispersed in the woods which reechoed to their wild yells and their ever fatal shots fired under cover of trees, rocks and stumps. The British were paralysed as they saw their ranks steadily decimated by the fire of an enemy whom they could never see, and who seemed multitudinous as their shrieks and shouts were heard far and wide in that Bedlam of the forest. The leaves that lay thick and deep on the ground were reddened with the blood of many victims helpless against the concealed, relentless savages. The woods of the Chateauguay did not present such a scene of carnage as was witnessed at the battle of the Monongahela, but nevertheless they seemed to the panic-stricken invaders, who numbered many thousands, alive with an enemy whose strength was enormously exaggerated as bugle sounds and Indian yells made a fearful din on every side. Believing themselves surrounded by forces far superior in numbers, the invaders became paralysed with fear and fled in disorder from an enemy whom they could not see, and who might close upon them at any moment. In this way Canadian pluck and strategy won a famous victory which saved the province of Lower Canada at a most critical moment of the war.

If we leave the woods of Chateauguay, where a monument has been raised in recognition of this brilliant episode of the war, and come to the country above which rises the mist of the cataract of Niagara, we see a little acclivity over which passes that famous thoroughfare called "Lundy's Lane." Here too rises a stately shaft in commemoration of another famous victory—in many respects the most notable of the war—won by a gallant Englishman, whose name still clings to the pretty town close by.

This battle was fought on a midsummer night, when less than three thousand British and Canadian troops fought six hours against a much superior force, led by the ablest officers who had taken part in the war. For three hours, from six to nine o'clock at night, less than two thousand held the height, which was the main object of attack from the beginning to the end of the conflict, and kept at bay the forces that were led against them with a stern determination to win the position. Sunlight gave way to the twilight of a July evening, and dense darkness at last covered the combatants, but still the fight went on. Columns of the enemy charged in such close and rapid succession that the British artillerymen were constantly assailed in the very act of sponging and loading their guns. The assailants once won the height, but only to find themselves repulsed the next instant by the resolute daring of the British. Happily at the most critical moment, when the defenders of the hill were almost exhausted by the heroic struggle, reinforcements arrived, and the battle was renewed with a supreme effort on both sides. For three hours longer, from nine o'clock to midnight, the battle was fought in the darkness, only relieved by the unceasing flashes from the guns, whose sharp reports mingled with the deep and monotonous roar of the great falls. It was a scene worthy of a painter whose imagination could grasp all the incidents of a situation essentially dramatic in its nature. The assailants of the Canadian position gave way at last and withdrew their wearied and disheartened forces. It was in all respects a victory for England and Canada, since the United States army did not attempt to renew the battle on the next day, but retired to Fort Erie, then in their possession. As Canadians look down "the corridors of time," they will always see those flashes from the musketry and cannon of Lundy's Lane, and hear the bugles which drove the invaders of their country from the woods of Chateauguay.

The war did much to solidify the various racial elements of British North America during its formative stage. Frenchmen, Englishmen, Scotsmen from the Lowlands and Highlands, Irishmen and Americans, united to support the British connection. The character of the people, especially in Upper Canada, was strengthened from a national point of view by the severe strain to which it was subjected. Men and women alike were elevated above the conditions of a mere colonial life and the struggle for purely material necessities, and became animated by that spirit of self-sacrifice and patriotic endeavour which tend to make a people truly great.

CHAPTER VI.

THE EVOLUTION OF RESPONSIBLE GOVERNMENT (1815—1839)

SECTION I.—The rebellion in Lower Canada.

Responsible government in Canada is the logical sequence of the political struggles, which commenced soon after the close of the war of 1812-15. As we review the history of Canada since the conquest we can recognise "one ever increasing purpose" through all political changes, and the ardent desire of men, entrusted at the outset with a very moderate degree of political responsibility, to win for themselves a larger measure of political liberty in the management of their own local affairs. Grave mistakes were often made by the advocates of reform in the government of the several provinces — notably, as I shall show, in Lower Canada, where the French Canadian majority were carried often beyond reason at the dictation of Papineau—but, whatever may have been the indiscretions of politicians, there were always at the bottom of their demands the germs of political development.

The political troubles that continued from 1817 until 1836 in Lower Canada eventually made the working of legislative institutions impracticable. The contest gradually became one between the governor-general representing the crown and the assembly controlled almost entirely by a French Canadian majority, with respect to the disposition of the public revenues and expenditures. Imperial statutes, passed as far back as 1774-1775, provided for the levying of duties, to be applied solely by the crown, primarily "towards defraying the expenses of the administration of justice and the support of the civil government of the province", and any sums that remained in the hands of the government were "for the future disposition of parliament." Then there were "the casual or territorial revenues," such as money arising from the Jesuits' estates, royal seigniorial dues, timber and land, all of which were also exclusively under the control of the government. The assembly had been given jurisdiction only over the amount of duties payable into the treasury under the authority of laws passed by the legislature itself. In case the royal revenues were not sufficient to meet the annual expenditure of the government, the deficiency was met until the war of 1812-15 by drawing on the military exchequer. As the expenses of the provincial administration increased the royal revenues became inadequate, while the provincial revenues gradually showed a considerable surplus over the expenditure voted by the legislature. In 1813 the cost of the war made it impossible for the government to use the military funds, and it resorted to the provincial moneys for the expenses of justice and civil government. In this way, by 1817, the government had incurred a debt of a hundred and twenty thousand pounds to the province without the direct authority of the legislature. The assembly of Lower Canada was not disposed to raise troublesome issues during the war, or in any way to embarrass the action of Sir George Prevost, who, whatever may have been his incompetency as a military chief, succeeded by his conciliatory and persuasive methods in winning the good opinions of the French Canadian majority and making himself an exceptionally popular civil governor. After closing the accounts of the war, the government felt it expedient to stop such irregular proceedings, to obtain from the legislature a general appropriation act, covering the amount of expenditures in the past, and to prevent the necessity of such a questionable application of provincial funds in the future. This may be considered the beginning of the financial controversies that were so constant, as years passed by, between the governors and the assemblies, and never ended until the rebellion broke out. The assembly, desirous of obtaining power in the management of public affairs, learned that it could best embarrass the government and force them to consider and adjust public grievances, as set forth by the majority in the house, by means of the appropriation bills required for the public service. The assembly not only determined to exercise sole control over its own funds but eventually demanded the disposal of the duties imposed and regulated by imperial statutes. The conflict was remarkable for the hot and uncompromising temper constantly exhibited by the majority on the discussion of the generally moderate and fair propositions submitted by the government for settling vexed questions. The assembly found a powerful argument in favour of their persistent contention for a complete control of the public revenues and expenditures in the defalcation of Mr. Caldwell, the receiver-general, who had been allowed for years to use the public funds in his business speculations, and whose property was entirely inadequate to cover the deficiency in his accounts.

The legislative council was always ready to resist what it often asserted to be unconstitutional acts on the part of the house and direct infringements of "the rights of the crown" sometimes a mere convenient phrase used in an emergency to justify resistance to the assembly. It often happened, however, that the upper chamber had law on its side, when the house became perfectly unreasonable and uncompromising in its attitude of hostility to the government. The council, on several occasions, rejected a supply bill because it contained provisions asserting the assembly's right to control the crown revenues and to vote the estimates, item by item, from the governor's salary down to that of the humblest official. Every part of the official and legislative machinery became clogged by the obstinacy of governor, councils, and assembly. To such an extent, indeed, did the assembly's assumption of power carry it in 1836, that the majority actually asserted its own right to amend the constitution of the council as defined in the imperial statute of 1791. Its indiscreet acts eventually alienated the sympathy and support of such English members as Mr. Neilson, a journalist and politician of repute, Mr. Andrew Stuart, a lawyer of ability, and others who believed in the necessity of constitutional reforms, but could not follow Mr. Papineau and his party in their reckless career of attack on the government, which they thought would probably in the end imperil British connection.

The government was in the habit of regularly submitting its accounts and estimates to the legislature, and expressed its desire eventually to grant that body the disposal of all the crown revenues, provided it would consent to vote a civil list for the king's life, or even for a fixed number of years, but the assembly was not willing to agree to any proposal which prevented it from annually taking up the expenditures for the civil government item by item, and making them matters of yearly vote. In this way every person in the public service would be subject to the caprice, or ill-feeling, of any single member of the legislature, and the whole administration of the public departments would probably be made ineffective. Under the plan suggested by the government in accordance with English constitutional forms, the assembly would have every opportunity of criticising all the public expenditures, and even reducing the gross sum in cases of extravagance. But the same contumacious spirit, which several times expelled Mr. Christie, member for Gaspé, on purely vexatious and frivolous charges, and constantly impeached judges without the least legal justification, simply to satisfy personal spite or political malice, would probably have been exhibited towards all officials had the majority in the assembly been given the right of voting each salary separately. The assembly never once showed a disposition to meet the wishes of the government even half-way. Whatever may have been the vacillation or blundering of officials in Downing Street, it must be admitted that the imperial government showed a conciliatory spirit throughout the whole financial controversy. Step by step it yielded to all the demands of the assembly on this point. In 1831, when Lord Grey was premier, the British parliament passed an act, making it lawful for the legislatures of Upper and Lower Canada to appropriate the duties raised by imperial statutes for the purpose of defraying the charges of the administration of justice and the support of civil government. The government consequently retained only the relatively small sum arising from casual and territorial dues. When Lord Aylmer, the governor-general, communicated this important concession to the legislature, he also sent a message setting forth the fact that it was the settled policy of the crown on no future occasion to nominate a judge either to the executive or the legislative council, the sole exception being the chief justice of Quebec. He also gave the consent of the government to the passage of an act declaring that judges of the supreme court should thereafter hold office "during good behaviour," on the essential condition that their salaries were made permanent by the legislature. The position of the judiciary had long been a source of great and even just complaint, and, in the time of Sir James Craig, judges were disqualified from sitting in the assembly on the demand of that body. They continued, however, to hold office "during the pleasure" of the crown, and to be called at its will to the executive and legislative councils. Under these circumstances they were, with some reason, believed to be more or less under the influence of the governor-general; and particular judges consequently fell at times under the ban of the assembly, and were attacked on the most frivolous grounds. The assembly passed a bill providing for the independence of the judiciary, but it had to be reserved because it was not in accordance with the conditions considered necessary by the crown for the protection of the bench.

The governor-general also in his message promised reforms of the judicial and legal systems, the disposal of the funds arising from the Jesuits' estates by the legislature, and, in fact, nearly all the reforms which had been demanded by the house for years. Yet when the government asked at the same time for a permanent civil list, the message was simply referred to a committee of the whole house which never reported. Until this time the efforts of the assembly to obtain complete control of the public revenues and expenditures had a justification in the fact that it is a recognised English principle that the elected house should impose the taxes and vote the supplies; but their action on this occasion, when the imperial government made most important concessions, giving them full control over the public funds, simply on condition that they should follow the English system of voting the salaries of the judiciary and civil list, showed that the majority were earned away by a purely factious spirit. During the progress of these controversies, Mr. Louis Joseph Papineau, a brilliant but an unsafe leader, had become the recognised chief of the French Canadian majority, who for years elected him speaker of the assembly. In the absence of responsible government, there was witnessed in those times the extraordinary spectacle—only now-a-days seen in the American congress—of the speaker, who should be above all political antagonisms, acting as the leader of an arrogant majority, and urging them to continue in their hostility to the government. It was Mr. Papineau who first brought the governor-general directly into the arena of political conflict by violent personal attacks; and indeed he went so far in the case of Lord Dalhousie, a fair-minded man anxious to act moderately within the limits of the constitution, that the latter felt compelled by a sense of dignity to refuse the confirmation of the great agitator as speaker in 1827. The majority in the assembly vehemently asserted their right to elect their speaker independently of the governor, whose confirmation was a mere matter of form, and not of statutory right; and the only course at last open to Lord Dalhousie was to prorogue the legislature. Mr. Papineau was re-elected speaker at the next session, when Lord Dalhousie had gone to England and Sir James Kempt was administrator.

After 1831, Mr. Papineau steadily evoked the opposition of the more conservative and thoughtful British Liberals who were not disposed to be carried into a questionable position, inimical to British connection and the peace of the country, Dr. Wolfred Nelson, and Dr. O'Callaghan, a journalist, were soon the only supporters of ability left him among the British and Irish, the great majority of whom rallied to the support of the government when a perilous crisis arrived in the affairs of the province. The British party dwindled away in every appeal to the people, and no French Canadian representative who presumed to differ from Mr. Papineau was ever again returned to the assembly. Mr. Papineau became not only a political despot but an "irreconcilable," whose vanity led him to believe that he would soon become supreme in French Canada, and the founder of *La Nation Canadienne* in the valley of the St. Lawrence. The ninety-two resolutions passed in 1834 may be considered the climax of the demands of his party, which for years had resisted immigration as certain to strengthen the British population, had opposed the establishment of registry offices as inconsistent with the French institutions of the province, and had thrown every possible opposition in the way of the progress of the Eastern Townships, which were attracting year by year an industrious and energetic British population from the British Isles and New England.

In these resolutions of 1834 there is not a single paragraph or even phrase which can be tortured into showing that the French Canadian agitator and his friends were in favour of responsible government. The key-note of the whole document is an elective legislative council, which would inevitably increase the power of the French Canadians and place the British in a hopeless minority. Mr. Roebuck, the paid agent of the assembly in England, is said to have suggested the idea of this elective body, and assuredly his writings and speeches were always calculated to do infinite harm, by helping to inflame discontent in Canada, and misrepresenting in England the true condition of affairs in the province. The resolutions are noteworthy for their verbosity and entire absence of moderate and wise suggestion. They were obviously written under the inspiration of Mr. Papineau with the object of irritating the British government, and preventing the settlement of political difficulties. They even eulogised the institutions of the neighbouring states which "commanded the affection of the people in a larger measure than those of any other country," and should be regarded "as models of government for Canada." They even went so far as "to remind parliament of the consequences of its efforts to overrule the wishes of the American colonies," in case they should make any "modification" in the constitution of the province "independently of the wishes of its people." Colonel Gugy, Mr. Andrew Stuart, Mr. Neilson and other prominent Englishmen opposed the passage of these resolutions, as calculated to do infinite harm, but they were carried by a very large French Canadian majority at the dictation of Mr. Papineau. Whatever may have been its effect for the moment, this wordy effusion has long since been assigned to the limbo where are buried other examples of the demagogism of those trying times.

In 1835 the imperial government decided to send three commissioners to examine into the various questions which had been so long matters of agitation in Lower Canada. Lord Aberdeen, then Colonial Secretary of State, emphatically stated that it was the intention of the government "to review and enquire into every alleged grievance and examine every cause of complaint, and apply a remedy to every abuse that may still be found to prevail."

The choice of the government as chief commissioner and governor-general was Lord Gosford, an amiable, inexperienced and weak man, who failed either to conciliate the French Canadian majority to whom he was even humble for a while, or to obtain the confidence of the British party to whose counsels and warnings he did not pay sufficient heed at the outset of the crisis which culminated during his administration. The majority in the assembly were determined not to abate one iota of their pretensions, which now included the control of the casual and territorial revenues; and no provision whatever was made for four years for the payment of the public service. The commissioners reported strongly against the establishment of an elected council, and in favour of a modified system of responsible government, not dependent on the vote of the house. They recommended also the surrender of the casual and territorial revenues on condition of proper provision for the payment of the civil service, and the administration of justice.

The imperial government immediately recognised that they had to face a very serious crisis in the affairs of Lower Canada. On the 6th March, 1836, Lord John Russell, then home secretary in Lord Melbourne's administration, introduced a series of ten resolutions, providing for the immediate payment of the arrears of £142,160. 14s. 6d., due to the public service, out of the moneys in the hands of the receiver-general. While it was admitted that measures should be taken to secure for the legislative council a greater degree of public confidence, the government deemed it inexpedient to make that body elective. The necessity of improving the position of the executive council was also acknowledged, but the suggestion of a ministry responsible to the assembly was not approved. This disapproval was quite in accordance with the policy adopted by Englishmen since 1822, when a measure had been introduced in parliament for the reunion of the two Canadas—the precursor of the measure of 1840. This measure originally provided that two members of the executive council should sit and speak in the assembly but not vote. Those parts of the bill of 1822 which provided for a union were not pressed on account of the objections raised in both the provinces, but certain other provisions became law under the title of "The Canadian Trade Acts," relieving Upper Canada from the capricious action of Lower Canada with respect to the duties from which the former obtained the principal part of her fund for carrying on her government. This share had been originally fixed at one-fifth of the proceeds of the customs duties collected by the province of Lower Canada, but when the population of the western section increased considerably and consumed a far greater quantity of dutiable goods, its government justly demanded a larger proportion of the revenues collected in the ports of the lower St. Lawrence. The legislature of Lower Canada paid no attention to this equitable demand, and eventually even refused to renew the legislation providing for the payment of one-fifth of the duties. Under these circumstances the imperial government found it necessary to intervene, and pass the "Trade Acts," making the past legislation of Lower Canada on the subject permanent, and preventing its legislature from imposing new duties on imports without the consent of the upper province. As this was a question of grave import, the resolutions of 1836 gave authority to the legislatures of Upper and Lower Canada to provide joint legislation "for determining and adjusting all questions respecting the trade and commerce of the provinces."

As soon as the passage of these resolutions became known throughout Lower Canada, Papineau and his supporters commenced an active campaign of denunciation against England, from whom, they declared, there was no redress whatever to be expected. Wherever the revolutionists were in the majority, they shouted, "*Vive la liberté!*" "*Vive la Nation Canadienne!*" "*Vive Papineau!*" "*Point de despotisme!*": while flags and placards were displayed with similar illustrations of popular frenzy. *La Nation Canadienne* was now launched on the turbulent waves of a little rebellion in which the phrases of the French revolution were glibly shouted by the *habitants* with very little conception of their real significance. The British or Constitutional party took active steps in support of British connection, but Lord Gosford, unhappily still governor-general, did not for some time awaken to the reality of the public danger. Happily for British interests, Sir John Culhorne, afterwards Lord Seaforth, a courageous and vigilant soldier, was in the country, and was able, when orders were given him by the reluctant governor, to deal determinedly with the rebels who had taken up arms in the Richelieu district. Dr. Wolfred Nelson made a brave stand at St. Denis, and repulsed Colonel Gore's small detachment of regulars. Papineau was present for a while at the scene of conflict, but he took no part in it and lost no time in making a hurried flight to the United States—an ignominious close to a successful career of rhetorical flashes which had kindled a conflagration that he took very good care should not even scorch him. Colonel Wetherall defeated another band of rebels at St. Charles, and their commander, Mr. Thomas Storrow Brown, a well-meaning but gullible man, fled across the border. Dr. Wolfred Nelson was captured, and a number of other rebels of less importance were equally unfortunate. Some of the refugees made a public demonstration from Vermont, but precipitately fled before a small force which met them. At St. Eustache, one Girod, a plausible, mendacious Swiss or Alsatian, who had become a leader in the rebellious movement, and Dr. Chenier, a rash but courageous man, collected a considerable body of rebels, chiefly from St. Benoit, despite the remonstrances of Mr. Paquin, the curé of the village, and defended the stone church and adjacent buildings against a large force, led by Sir John Colborne himself. Dr. Chenier and many others—at least seventy, it is said on good authority—were killed, and the former has in the course of time been elevated to the dignity of a national hero and a monument raised in his honour on a public square of the French Canadian quarters of Montreal. Mad recklessness rather than true heroism signalised his action in this unhappy affair, when he led so many of his credulous compatriots to certain death, but at least he gave up his life manfully to a lost cause rather than fly like Papineau who had beguiled him to this melancholy conclusion. Even Girod showed courage and ended his own life when he found that he could not evade the law. The rebellious element at St. Benoit was cowed by the results at St. Eustache; and the Abbé Chartier, who had taken an active part in urging the people to resistance, fled to the United States whence he never returned. The greater part of the village was destroyed by fire, probably in retaliation for the losses and injuries suffered by the volunteers at the hands of the rebels in different parts of the district of Montreal.

One of the most unfortunate and discreditable incidents of the rising in the Richelieu district was the murder of Lieutenant Weir, who had been taken prisoner while carrying despatches to Sorel, and was literally hacked to pieces, when he tried to escape from a *calèche* in which he was being conveyed to St. Charles. An equally unhappy incident was the cold-blooded execution, after a mock trial, of one Chartrand, a harmless non-combatant who was accused, without a tittle of evidence, of being a spy. The temper of the country can be gauged by the fact that when it was attempted, some time later, to convict the murderers on clear evidence, it was impossible to obtain a verdict. Jolbert, the alleged murderer of Weir, was never punished, but François Nicholas and Amable Daumais, who had aided in the trial and execution of Chartrand, were subsequently hanged for having taken an active part in the second insurrection of 1838.

The rebellion of 1837 never reached any large proportions, and very few French Canadians of social or political standing openly participated in the movement. Monseigneur Lartigue, Roman Catholic bishop of Montreal, issued a *mandement* severely censuring the misguided men who had joined in the rebellious movement and caused so much misery throughout the province. In England, strange to say, there were men found, even in parliament, ready to misrepresent the facts and glory in a rebellion the causes of which they did not understand. The animating motive with these persons was then—and there were similar examples during the American revolution—to assail the government of the day and make political capital against them, but, it must be admitted, in all fairness to the reform ministry of that day and even to preceding cabinets for some years, that the policy of all was to be just and conciliatory in their relations with the provincial agitators, though it is also evident that a more thorough knowledge of political conditions and a more resolute effort to a reach the bottom of grievances might have long before removed causes of irritation and saved the loss of property and life in 1837 and 1838.

In the presence of a grave emergency, the British government felt compelled to suspend the constitution of Lower Canada, and send out Lord Durham, a Liberal statesman of great ability, to act as governor-general and high commissioner "for the determining of certain important questions depending in the provinces of Upper and Lower Canada respecting the form and future government of the said provinces" Despite a certain haughtiness of manner which was apt to wound his inferiors and irritate his equals in position, he was possessed of a great fund of accurate political knowledge and a happy faculty of grasping all the essential facts of a difficult situation, and suggesting the best remedy to apply under all the circumstances. He endeavoured, to the utmost of his ability, to redeem the pledge with which he entered on his mission to Canada, in the first instance "to assert the supremacy of her majesty's government," in the next "to vindicate the honour and dignity of the law," and above all "to know nothing of a British, a French, or a Canadian party," but "to look on them all alike as her majesty's subjects." After he had appointed a special council he set to work energetically to secure the peace of the country. Humanity was the distinguishing feature of his too short career in Canada. A comprehensive amnesty was proclaimed to all those engaged in the rebellion with the exception of Dr. Wolfred Nelson, R.S.M. Bouchette, Bonaventure Viger, Dr. Masson, and four others of less importance, who were ordered by an ordinance to be transported to Bermuda during the queen's pleasure. These persons, as well as sixteen others, including Papineau, who had fled from justice, were declared to be subject to death should they venture to enter the province. Not a single rebel suffered death on the scaffold during Lord Durham's administration. Unfortunately the ordinance, transporting a number of persons without trial to an island where the governor-general had no jurisdiction, gave an opportunity to Lord Brougham, who hated the high commissioner, to attack him in the house of lords. Lord Melbourne, then premier, was forced to repeal the ordinance and to consent to the passage of a bill indemnifying all those who had acted under its provisions Lord Glenelg, colonial secretary, endeavoured to diminish the force of this parliamentary censure by writing to the high commissioner that "her majesty's government repeat their approbation of the spirit in which these measures were conceived and state their conviction that they have been dictated by a judicious and enlightened humanity"; but a statesman of Lord Durham's haughty character was not ready to submit to such a rebuke as he had sustained in parliament He therefore immediately placed his resignation in the hands of the government which had commissioned him with powers to give peace and justice to distracted Canada, and yet failed to sustain him at the crucial moment. Before leaving the country he issued a proclamation in defence of his public acts. His course in this particular offended the ministry who, according to Lord Glenelg, considered it a dangerous innovation, as it was practically an appeal by a public officer to the public against the measures of parliament. Lord Durham may be pardoned under all the circumstances for resenting at the earliest possible moment his desertion by the government, who were bound in honour to defend him, at all hazards, in his absence, and should not have given him over for the moment to his enemies, led by a spiteful Scotch lawyer. Lord Durham left Canada with the assurance that he had won the confidence of all loyal British subjects and proved to all French

Canadians that there were English statesmen prepared to treat them with patience, humanity and justice.

Sir John Colborne became administrator on the departure of Lord Durham, and subsequently governor-general. Unhappily he was immediately called upon to crush another outbreak of the rebels, in November, 1838, in the counties watered by the Richelieu River, and in the district immediately south of Montreal. Dr. Robert Nelson and some other rebels, who had found refuge in the frontier towns and villages of Vermont and New York, organised this second insurrection, which had the support of a considerable number of *habitants*, though only a few actually took up arms. The rising, which began at Caughnawaga, was put down at Beauharnois, within a week from the day on which it commenced. The authorities now felt that the time had passed for such leniency as had been shown by Lord Durham; and Sir John Colborne accordingly established courts-martial for the trial of the prisoners taken during this second insurrection, as it was utterly impossible to obtain justice through the ordinary process of the courts. Only twelve persons, however, suffered the extreme penalty of the law; some were sent to New South Wales—where however they were detained only a short time; and the great majority were pardoned on giving security for good behaviour.

While these trials were in progress, and the government were anxious to give peace and security to the province, refugees in the border states were despatching hands of ruffians to attack and plunder the Loyalists in the Eastern Townships; but the government of the United States intervened and instructed its officers to take decisive measures for the repression of every movement in the territory of a friendly Power. Thus the mad insurrection incited by Papineau, but actually led by the Nelsons, Chenier and Brown, came at last to an end.

A new era of political development was now to dawn on the province, as a result of a more vigorous and remedial policy initiated by the imperial government, at last thoroughly awakened to an intelligent comprehension of the political conditions of the Canadas. But before I proceed to explain the details of measures fraught with such important consequences, I must give an historical summary of the events which led also to a rash uprising in Upper Canada, simultaneously with the one which ended so disastrously for its leaders in the French province.

SECTION 2.—The rebellion in Upper Canada.

The financial disputes between the executive and the assembly never attained such prominence in Upper Canada as in the lower province. In 1831 the assembly consented to make permanent provision for the civil list and the judiciary, on condition of the government's giving up to the legislature all the revenues previously at its own disposition. Three years later the legislature also passed an act to provide that the judges should hold their offices during good behaviour, and not at the pleasure of the crown—a measure rendered possible by the fact that the assembly had made the salaries of the bench permanent.

Nor did the differences between the assembly and the legislative council ever assume such serious proportions as they did in the French province. Still the leaders of the reform party of Upper Canada had strong objections to the constitution of the council; and a committee of grievances reported in 1835 in favour of an elected body as well as a responsible council, although it did not very clearly outline the methods of working out the system in a colony where the head of the executive was an imperial officer acting under royal instructions. The different lieutenant-governors, the executive and legislative councillors, and the whole body of officials, from the very moment responsible government was suggested in any form, threw every possible obstacle in the way of its concession by the imperial government.

It was largely the dominant influence of the official combination, long known in Canadian history as the "family compact," which prevented the concession of responsible government before the union of the Canadas. This phrase, as Lord Durham said in his report, was misleading inasmuch as there "was very little of family connection between the persons thus united." As a matter of fact the phrase represented a political and aristocratic combination, which grew up as a consequence of the social conditions of the province and eventually monopolised all offices and influence in government. This bureaucracy permeated all branches of government—the executive, the legislative council, and even the assembly where for years there sat several members holding offices of emolument under the crown. It practically controlled the banks and monetary circles. The Church of England was bound up in its interests. The judiciary was more or less under its influence while judges were appointed during pleasure and held seats in the councils. This governing class was largely composed of the descendants of the Loyalists of 1784, who had taken so important a part in the war with the United States and always asserted their claims to special consideration in the distribution of government favour. The old settlers—all those who had come into the country before the war—demanded and obtained greater consideration at the hands of the government than the later immigrants, who eventually found themselves shut out of office and influence. The result was the growth of a Liberal or Reform party, which, while generally composed of the later immigrants, comprised several persons of Loyalist extraction, who did not happen to belong to the favoured class or church, but recognised the necessity for a change in the methods of administration. Among these Loyalists must be specially mentioned Peter Perry, who was really the founder of the Reform party in 1834, and the Reverend Egerton Ryerson, a Methodist minister of great natural ability.

Unfortunately creed also became a powerful factor in the political controversies of Upper Canada. By the constitutional act of 1791 large tracts of land were set aside for the support of a "Protestant clergy", and the Church of England successfully claimed for years an exclusive right to these "clergy reserves" on the ground that it was the Protestant church recognised by the state. The clergy of the Church of Scotland in Canada, though very few in number for years, at a later time obtained a share of these grants as a national religious body; but all the dissentient denominations did not participate in the advantages of these reserves. The Methodists claimed in the course of years to be numerically equal to, if not more numerous than, the English Episcopalians, and were deeply irritated at the inferior position they long occupied in the province. So late as 1824 the legislative council, composed of members of the dominant church, rejected a bill allowing Methodist ministers to solemnise marriages, and it was not until 1831 that recognised ministers of all denominations were placed on an equality in this respect. Christian charity was not more a characteristic of those times than political liberality. Methodism was considered by the governing class as a sign of democracy and social inferiority. History repeated itself in Upper Canada. As the Puritans of New England feared the establishment of an Anglican episcopacy, and used it to stimulate a feeling against the parent state during the beginnings of the revolution, so in Upper Canada the dissenting religious bodies made political capital out of the favouritism shown to the Church of England in the distribution of the public lands and public patronage. The Roman Catholics and members of all Protestant sects eventually demanded the secularisation of the reserves for educational or other public purposes, or the application of the funds to the use of all religious creeds. The feeling against that church culminated in 1836, when Sir John Colborne, then lieutenant-governor, established forty-four rectories in accordance with a suggestion made by Lord Goderich some years previously. While the legality of Sir John Colborne's course was undoubted, it was calculated to create much indignant feeling among the dissenting bodies, who saw in the establishment of these rectories an evidence of the intention of the British government to create a state church so far as practicable by law within the province. This act, so impolitic at a critical time of political discussion, was an illustration of the potent influence exercised in the councils of the government by Archdeacon Strachan, who had come into the province from Scotland in 1799 as a schoolmaster. He had been brought up in the tenets of the Presbyterian Church, but some time after his arrival in Canada he became an ordained minister of the Church of England, in which he rose step by step to the episcopacy. He became a member of both the executive and legislative councils in 1816 and 1817, and exercised continuously until the union of 1841 a singular influence in the government of the province. He was endowed with that indomitable will, which distinguished his great countryman, John Knox. His unbending toryism was the natural outcome of his determination to sustain what he considered the just rights of his church against the liberalism of her opponents—chiefly dissenters—who wished to rob her of her clergy reserves and destroy her influence in education and public affairs generally. This very fidelity to his church became to some extent her weakness, since it evoked the bitter hostility of a large body of persons and created the impression that she was the church of the aristocratic and official class rather than that of the people—an impression which existed for many years after the fall of the "family compact."

The public grievances connected with the disposition of the public lands were clearly exposed by one Robert Gourlay, a somewhat meddlesome Scotchman, who had addressed a circular, soon after his arrival in Canada, to a number of townships with regard to the causes which retarded improvement and the best means of developing the resources of the province. An answer from Sandwich virtually set forth the feeling of the rural districts generally on these points. It stated that the reasons for the existing depression were the reserves of land for the crown and clergy, "which must for a long time keep the country a wilderness, a harbour for wolves, and a hindrance to compact and good neighbourhood; defects in the system of colonisation; too great a quantity of lands in the hands of individuals who do not reside in the province, and are not assessed for their property." Mr. Gourlay's questions were certainly asked in the public interest, but they excited the indignation of the official class who resented any interference with a state of things which favoured themselves and their friends, and were not desirous of an investigation into the management of public affairs. The subsequent treatment of Mr. Gourlay was shameful in the extreme. He was declared a most dangerous character when he followed up his circular by a pamphlet, attacking the methods by which public affairs generally were conducted, and contrasting them with the energetic and progressive system on the other side of the border. The indignation of the officials became a positive fever when he suggested the calling of public meetings to elect delegates to a provincial convention—a term which recalled the days of the American revolution, and was cleverly used by Gourlay's enemies to excite the ire and fear of the descendants of the Loyalists. Sir Peregrine Maitland succeeded in obtaining from the legislature an opinion against conventions as "repugnant to the constitution," and declaring the holding of such public meetings a misdemeanour, while admitting the constitutional right of the people to petition. These proceedings evoked a satirical reply from Gourlay, who was arrested for seditious libel, but the prosecutions failed. It was then decided to resort to the provisions of a practically obsolete statute passed in 1804, authorising the arrest of any person who had resided in the province for six months without taking the oath of allegiance, and was suspected to be a seditious character. Such a person could be ordered by the authorities to leave the province, or give security for good behaviour. This act had been originally passed to prevent the immigration of aliens unfavourable to England, especially of Irishmen who had taken part in the rebellion of 1798 and found refuge in the United States. Gourlay had been a resident of Upper Canada for nearly two years, and in no single instance had the law been construed to apply to an immigrant from the British Isles. Gourlay was imprisoned in the Niagara gaol, and when his friends attempted to bring him out on a writ of *habeas corpus* they failed simply because Chief Justice Powell, an able lawyer of a Loyalist family and head of the official party, refused to grant the writ on a mere technical plea, afterwards declared by the highest legal authorities in England to be entirely contrary to sound law. Gourlay consequently remained in prison for nearly eight months, and when he was brought again before the chief justice, his mental faculties were obviously impaired for the moment, but despite his wretched condition, which prevented him from conducting his defence, he was summarily convicted and ordered to leave the province within twenty-four hours, under penalty of death should he not obey the order or return to the country.

This unjust sentence created wide-spread indignation among all right-thinking people, especially as it followed a message of the lieutenant-governor to the legislature, that he did not feel justified in extending the grants of land, made to actors in the war of 1812-15, to "any of the inhabitants who composed the late convention of delegates, the proceedings of which were very properly subjected to your very severe animadversion" This undoubtedly illegal action of the lieutenant-governor only escaped the censure of the assembly by the casting vote of the speaker, but was naturally justified in the legislative council where Chief Justice Powell presided. Gourlay became a martyr in the opinion of a large body of people, and a Reform party began to grow up in the country. The man himself disappeared for years from Canadian history, and did not return to the province until 1856, after a chequered and unhappy career in

Great Britain and the United States. The assembly of the United Canadas in 1842 declared his arrest to be "unjust and illegal," and his sentence "null and void," and he was offered a pension as some compensation for the injuries he had received; but he refused it unless it was accompanied by an official declaration of the illegality of the conviction and its elision from the records of the courts. The Canadian government thought he should be satisfied with the action of the assembly and the offer of the pension. Gourlay died abroad, and his daughters on his death received the money which he rejected with the obstinacy so characteristic of his life.

During these days of struggle we find most prominent among the official class Attorney-General Robinson, afterwards chief justice of Upper Canada for many years. He was the son of a Virginian Loyalist, and a Tory of extreme views, calm, polished, and judicial in his demeanour. But whatever his opinions on the questions of the day he was too discreet a politician and too honest a judge ever to have descended to such a travesty of justice as had been shown by his predecessor in the case of Gourlay. His influence, however was never in the direction of liberal measures. He opposed responsible government and the union of the two provinces, both when proposed unsuccessfully in 1822, and when carried in Upper Canada eighteen years later.

The elections of 1825 had a very important influence on the political conditions of the upper province, since they brought into the assembly Peter Perry, Dr. Rolph, and Marshall Spring Bidwell, who became leading actors in the Reform movement which culminated in the concession of responsible government. But the most conspicuous man from 1826 until 1837 was William Lyon Mackenzie, a Scotchman of fair education, who came to Canada in 1820, and eventually embraced journalism as the profession most suited to his controversial temperament. Deeply imbued with a spirit of liberalism in politics, courageous and even defiant in the expression of his opinions, sadly wanting in sound judgment and common sense when his feelings were excited, able to write with vigour, but more inclined to emphatic vituperation than well-reasoned argument, he made himself a force in the politics of the province. In the *Colonial Advocate*, which he established in 1824, he commenced a series of attacks on the government which naturally evoked the resentment of the official class, and culminated in the destruction of his printing office in 1826 by a number of young men, relatives of the principal officials—one of them actually the private secretary of the lieutenant-governor, Sir Peregrine Maitland. Mr. Mackenzie obtained large damages in the courts, and was consequently able to continue the publication of his paper at a time when he was financially embarrassed. The sympathy felt for Mr. Mackenzie brought him into the assembly as member for York during the session of 1829. So obnoxious did he become to the governing class that he was expelled four times from the assembly between 1831 and 1834, and prevented from taking his seat by the orders of the speaker in 1835—practically the fifth expulsion. In 1832 he went to England and presented largely signed petitions asking for a redress of grievances. He appears to have made some impression on English statesmen, and the colonial minister recommended a few reforms to the lieutenant-governor, but they were entirely ignored by the official party. Lord Glenelg also disapproved of the part taken by Attorney-General Boulton—Mr. Robinson being then chief justice— and Solicitor-General Hagerman in the expulsion of Mr. Mackenzie; but they treated the rebuke with contempt and were removed from office for again assisting in the expulsion of Mr. Mackenzie.

In 1834 he was elected first mayor of Toronto, then incorporated under its present name, as a consequence of the public sympathy aroused in his favour by his several expulsions. Previous to the election of 1835, in which he was returned to the assembly, he made one of the most serious blunders of his life, in the publication of a letter from Mr. Joseph Hume, the famous Radical, whose acquaintance he had made while in England. Mr. Hume emphatically stated his opinion that "a crisis was fast approaching in the affairs of Canada which would terminate in independence and freedom from the baneful domination of the mother country, and the tyrannical conduct of a small and despicable faction in the colony." The official class availed themselves of this egregious blunder to excite the indignation of the Loyalist population against Mr. Mackenzie and other Reformers, many of whom, like the Baldwins and Perrys, disavowed all sympathy with such language. Mr. Mackenzie's motive was really to insult Mr. Ryerson, with whom he had quarrelled. Mr. Ryerson in the *Christian Guardian*, organ of the Methodists, had attacked Mr. Hume as a person unfit to present petitions from the Liberals of Canada, since he had opposed the measure for the emancipation of slaves in the West Indies, and had consequently alienated the confidence and sympathy of the best part of the nation. Mr. Hume then wrote the letter in question, in which he also stated that he "never knew a more worthless hypocrite or so base a man as Mr. Ryerson proved himself to be." Mr. Mackenzie in this way incurred the wrath of a wily clergyman and religious journalist who exercised much influence over the Methodists, and at the same time fell under the ban of all people who were deeply attached to the British connection. Moderate Reformers now looked doubtfully on Mackenzie, whose principal supporters were Dr. Duncombe, Samuel Lount, Peter Matthews, and other men who took an active part in the insurrection of 1837.

In the session of 1835 a committee of grievances, appointed on the motion of Mr. Mackenzie himself, reported in favour of a system of responsible government, an elective legislative council, the appointment of civil governors, a diminution of the patronage exercised by the crown, the independence of the legislature, and other reforms declared to be in the interest of good government. The report was temperately expressed, and created some effect for a time in England, but the colonial minister could not yet be induced to move in the direction of positive reform in the restrictive system of colonial government.

Unhappily, at this juncture, when good judgment and discretion were so necessary in political affairs, all the circumstances combined to hasten a perilous crisis, and to give full scope to the passionate impulses of Mackenzie's nature. Sir John Colborne was replaced in the government of the province by one of the most incapable governors ever chosen by the colonial office, Sir Francis Bond Head. He had been chiefly known in England as a sprightly writer of travels, and had had no political experience except such as could be gathered in the discharge of the duties of a poor-law commissioner in Wales. His first official act was an indiscretion. He communicated to the legislature the full text of the instructions which he had received from the king, although he had been advised to give only their substance, as least calculated to hamper Lord Gosford, who was then attempting to conciliate the French Canadian majority in Lower Canada. These instructions, in express terms, disapproved of a responsible executive and particularly of an elected legislative council, to obtain which was the great object of Papineau and his friends. Mr. Bidwell, then speaker of the assembly, recognised the importance of this despatch, and forwarded it immediately to Mr. Papineau, at that time speaker of the Lower Canadian house, with whom he and other Reformers had correspondence from time to time. Lord Gosford was consequently forced to lay his own instructions in full before the legislature and to show the majority that the British government was opposed to such vital changes in the provincial constitution as they persistently demanded. The action of the Lower Canadian house on this matter was communicated to the assembly of Upper Canada by a letter of Mr. Papineau to Mr. Bidwell, who laid it before his house just before the prorogation in 1835. In this communication the policy of the imperial government was described as "the naked deformity of the colonial system," and the royal commissioners were styled "deceitful agents," while the methods of government in the neighbouring states were again eulogised as in the ninety-two resolutions of 1834. Sir Francis Bond Head seized the opportunity to create a feeling against the Reformers, to whom he was now hostile. Shortly after he sent his indiscreet message to the legislature he persuaded Dr. Rolph, Mr. Bidwell and Receiver-General Dunn to enter the executive council on the pretence that he wished to bring that body more into harmony with public opinion. The new councillors soon found that they were not to be consulted in public affairs, and when the whole council actually resigned Sir Francis told them plainly that he alone was responsible for his acts, and that he would only consult them when he deemed it expedient in the public interest. This action of the lieutenant-governor showed the Reformers that he was determined to initiate no changes which would disturb the official party, or give self-government to the people. The assembly, in which the Liberals were dominant, passed an address to the king, declaring the lieutenant-governor's conduct "derogatory to the honour of the king," and also a memorial to the British house of commons charging him with "misrepresentation, and a deviation from candour and truth."

Under these circumstances Sir Francis eagerly availed himself of Papineau's letter to show the country the dangerous tendencies of the opinions and acts of the Reformers in the two provinces. In an answer he made to an address from some inhabitants of the Home District, he warned the people that there were individuals in Lower Canada, who were inculcating the idea that "this province is to be disturbed by the interference of foreigners, whose powers and influence will prove invincible"—an allusion to the sympathy shown by Papineau and his friends for the institutions of the United States. Then Sir Francis closed his reply with this rhodomontade: "In the name of every regiment of militia in Upper Canada, I publicly promulgate 'Let them come if they dare'" He dissolved the legislature and went directly to the country on the issue that the British connection was endangered by the Reformers. "He succeeded, in fact," said Lord Durham in his report of 1839, "in putting the issue in such a light before the province, that a great portion of the people really imagined that they were called upon to decide the question of separation by their votes." These strong appeals to the loyalty of a province founded by the Loyalists of 1784, combined with the influence exercised by the "family compact," who had all offices and lands at their disposal, defeated Mackenzie, Bidwell, Perry and other Reformers of less note, and brought into the legislature a solid phalanx of forty-two supporters of the government against eighteen elected by the opposition. It was a triumph dearly paid for in the end. The unfair tactics of the lieutenant-governor rankled in the minds of a large body of people, and hastened the outbreak of the insurrection of 1837. The British government seems for a time to have been deceived by this victory of the lieutenant-governor and actually lauded his "foresight, energy and moral courage"; but ere long, after more mature consideration of the political conditions of the province, it dawned upon the dense mind of Lord Glenelg that the situation was not very satisfactory, and that it would be well to conciliate the moderate element among the Reformers. Sir Francis was accordingly instructed to appoint Mr. Bidwell to the Bench, but he stated emphatically that such an appointment would be a recognition on disloyalty. He preferred to resign rather than obey the instructions of the colonial department, and greatly to his surprise and chagrin his proffer of resignation was accepted without the least demur. The colonial office by this time recognised the mistake they had made in appointing Sir Francis to a position, for which he was utterly unfit, but unhappily for the province they awoke too late to a sense of their own folly.

Mackenzie became so embittered by his defeat in 1836, and the unscrupulous methods by which it was accomplished, that he made up his mind that reform in government was not to be obtained except by a resort to extreme measures. At meetings of Reformers, held at Lloydtown and other places during the summer of 1837, resolutions were carried that it was their duty to arm in defence of their rights and those of their countrymen. Mackenzie visited many parts of the province, in order to stimulate a revolutionary movement among the disaffected people, a system of training volunteers was organised; pikes were manufactured and old arms were put in order. It was decided that Dr. Rolph should be the executive chief of the provisional government, and Mackenzie in the meantime had charge of all the details of the movement. Mr. Bidwell appears to have steadily kept aloof from the disloyal party, but Dr. Rolph was secretly in communication with Mackenzie, Lount, Matthews, Lloyd, Morrison, Duncombe, and other actors in the rebellion. The plan was to march on Toronto, where it was notorious that no precautions for defence were being taken, to seize the lieutenant-governor, to proclaim a provisional government, and to declare the independence of the province unless Sir Francis should give a solemn promise to constitute a responsible council. It is quite certain that Mackenzie entirely misunderstood the sentiment of the country, and exaggerated the support that would be given to a disloyal movement. Lord Durham truly said that the insurrectionary movements which did take place were "indicative of no deep rooted disaffection," and that "almost the entire body of the Reformers of the province sought only by constitutional means to obtain those objects for which they had so long peacefully struggled before the unhappy troubles occasioned by the violence of a few unprincipled adventurers and heated enthusiasts."

Despite the warnings that he was constantly receiving of the seditious doings of Mackenzie and his lieutenants, Sir Francis Bond Head could not be persuaded an uprising was imminent. So complete was his fatuity that he allowed all the regular troops to be withdrawn to Lower Canada at the request of Sir John Colborne. Had he taken adequate measures for the defence of Toronto, and showed he was prepared for any contingency, the rising of Mackenzie's immediate followers would never have occurred. His apathy and negligence at this crisis actually incited an insurrection. The repulse of Gore at St. Denis on the 23rd November (p. 134) no doubt hastened the rebellious movement in Upper Canada, and it was decided to collect all available men and assemble at Montgomery's tavern, only four miles from Toronto by way of Yonge Street, the road connecting Toronto with Lake Simcoe. The subsequent news of the dispersion of the rebels at St. Charles was very discouraging to Mackenzie and Lount, but they felt that matters had proceeded too far for them to stop at that juncture. They still hoped to surprise Toronto and occupy it without much difficulty. A Colonel Moodie, who had taken part in the war of 1812-15, had heard of the march of the insurgents from Lake Simcoe, and was riding rapidly to Toronto to warn the lieutenant-governor, when he was suddenly shot down and died immediately. Sir Francis was unconscious of danger when he was aroused late at night by Alderman Powell, who had been taken prisoner by the rebels but succeeded in making his escape and finding his way to Government House. Sir Francis at last awoke from his lethargy and listened to the counsels of Colonel Fitzgibbon—the hero of Beaver Dams in 1813— and other residents of Toronto, who had constantly endeavoured to force him to take measures for the public security. The loyal people of the province rallied with great alacrity to put down the revolt. The men of the western district of Gore came up in force, and the first man to arrive on the scene was Allan MacNab, the son of a Loyalist and afterwards prime minister of Canada. A large and well equipped force was at once organised under the command of Colonel Fitzgibbon.

The insurrection was effectually quelled on the 7th December at Montgomery's tavern by the militia and volunteer forces under Colonel Fitzgibbon. The insurgents had at no time mustered more than eight hundred men, and in the engagement on the 7th there were only four hundred, badly armed and already disheartened. In twenty minutes, or less time, the fight was over and the insurgents fled with the loss of one man killed and several seriously wounded. The Loyalists, who did not lose a single man, took a number of prisoners, who were immediately released by the lieutenant-governor on condition of returning quietly to their homes. Mackenzie succeeded in escaping across the Niagara frontier, but Matthews was taken prisoner as he was leading a detachment across the Don into Toronto. Lount was identified at Chippewa while attempting to find his way to the United States and brought back to Toronto. Rolph, Gibson and Duncombe found a refuge in the republic, but Van Egmond, who had served under Napoleon, and commanded the insurgents, was arrested and died in prison of inflammatory rheumatism. Mr. Bidwell was induced to fly from the province by the insidious representations of the lieutenant-governor, who used the fact of his flight as an argument that he had been perfectly justified in not appointing him to the Bench. In later years, the Canadian government, recognising the injustice Mr. Bidwell had received, offered him a judgeship, but he never could be induced to return to Canada Mackenzie had definite grievances against Sir Francis and his party; and a British people, always ready to sympathise with men who resent injustice and assert principles of popular government, might have soon condoned the serious mistake he had made in exciting a rash revolt against his sovereign. But his apologists can find no extenuating circumstances for his mad conduct in stirring up bands of ruffians at Buffalo and other places on the frontier to invade the province. The base of operations for these raids was Navy Island, just above the Niagara Falls in British territory. A small steamer, "The Caroline," was purchased from some Americans, and used to bring munitions of war to the island. Colonel MacNab was sent to the frontier, and successfully organised an expedition of boats under the charge of Captain Drew— afterwards an Admiral—to seize the steamer at Fort Schlosser, an insignificant place on the American side. The capture was successfully accomplished and the steamer set on fire and sent down the river, where she soon sank before reaching the cataract. Only one man was killed—one Durfee, a citizen of the United States. This audacious act of the Canadians was deeply resented in the republic as a violation of its territorial rights, and was a subject of international controversy until 1842 when it was settled with other questions at issue between Great Britain and the United States. Mackenzie now disappeared for some years from Canadian history, as the United States authorities felt compelled to imprison him for a time. It was not until the end of 1838 that the people of the Canada were free from filibustering expeditions organised in the neighboring states. "Hunters' Lodges" were formed under the pledge "never to rest until all tyrants of Britain cease to have any dominion or footing whatever in North America." These marauding expeditions on the exposed parts of the western frontier—especially on the St. Clair and Detroit Rivers—were successfully resisted. At Prescott, a considerable body of persons, chiefly youths under age, under the leadership of Von Schoultz, a Pole, were beaten at the Old Stone Windmill, which they attempted to hold against a Loyalist force. At Sandwich, Colonel Prince, a conspicuous figure in Canadian political history of later years, routed a band of filibusters, four of whom he ordered to instant death. This resolute deed created some excitement in England, where it was condemned by some and justified by others. Canadians, who were in constant fear of such raids, naturally approved of summary justice in the case of persons who were really brigands, not entitled to any consideration under the laws of war.

In 1838 President Buren issued a proclamation calling upon all citizens of the United States to observe the neutrality laws; but the difficulty in those days was the indisposition of the federal government to interfere with the states where such expeditions were organised. The vigilance of the Canadian authorities and the loyalty of the people alone saved the country in these trying times. A great many of the raiders were taken prisoners and punished with the severity due to their unjustifiable acts. Von Schoultz and eight others were hanged, a good many were pardoned, while others were transported to Van Diemen's Land, whence they were soon allowed to return. The names of these filibusters are forgotten, but those of Lount and Matthews, who perished on the scaffold, have been inscribed on some Canadian hearts as patriots. Sir George Arthur, who succeeded Sir Francis Head, was a soldier, who had had experience as a governor among the convicts of Van Diemen's Land, and the negro population of Honduras, where he had crushed a revolt of slaves. Powerful appeals were made to him on behalf of Lount and Matthews, but not even the tears and prayers of Lount's distracted wife could reach his heart. Such clemency as was shown by Lord Durham would have been a bright incident in Sir George Arthur's career in Canada, but he looked only to the approval of the Loyalists, deeply incensed against the rebels of 1837. His action in these two cases was regarded with disapprobation in England, and the colonial minister expressed the hope that no further executions would occur—advice followed in the case of other actors of the revolt of 1837. Sir George Arthur's place in colonial annals is not one of high distinction. Like his predecessors, he became the resolute opponent of responsible government, which he declared in a despatch to be "Mackenzie's scheme for getting rid of what Mr. Hume called 'the baneful domination' of the mother country"; "and never" he added, "was any scheme better devised to bring about such an end speedily".

SECTION 3.—Social and economic conditions of the Provinces in 1838.

We have now reached a turning-point in the political development of the provinces of British North America, and may well pause for a moment to review the social and economic condition of their people. Since the beginning of the century there had been a large immigration into the provinces, except during the war of 1812. In the nine years preceding 1837, 263,089 British and Irish immigrants arrived at Quebec, and in one year alone there were over 50,000. By 1838 the population of the five provinces of Upper Canada, Lower Canada, Nova Scotia, New Brunswick and Prince Edward Island had reached about 1,400,000 souls. In Upper Canada, with the exception of a very few people of German or Dutch descent, and some French Canadians opposite Detroit and on the Ottawa River, there was an entirely British population of at least 400,000 souls. The population of Lower Canada was estimated at 600,000, of whom hardly one-quarter were of British origin, living chiefly in Montreal, the Townships, and Quebec. Nova Scotia had nearly 200,000 inhabitants, of whom probably 16,000 were French Acadians, resident in Cape

Breton and in Western Nova Scotia. In New Brunswick there were at least 150,000 people, of whom some 15,000 were descendants of the original inhabitants of Acadie. The Island of Prince Edward had 30,000 people, of whom the French Acadians made up nearly one-sixth. The total trade of the country amounted, in round figures, to about £5,000,000 sterling in imports, and somewhat less in exports The imports were chiefly manufactures from Great Britain, and the exports were lumber, wheat and fish. Those were days when colonial trade was stimulated by differential duties in favour of colonial products, and the building of vessels was encouraged by the old navigation laws which shut out foreign commerce from the St. Lawrence and the Atlantic ports, and kept the carrying trade between Great Britain and the colonies in the hands of British and colonial merchants, by means of British registered ships. While colonists could not trade directly with foreign ports, they were given a monopoly for their timber, fish, and provisions in the profitable markets of the British West Indies.

The character of the immigration varied considerably, but on the whole the thrifty and industrious formed the larger proportion. In 1833 the immigrants deposited 300,000 sovereigns, or nearly a million and a half of dollars, in the Upper Canadian banks. An important influence in the settlement of Upper Canada was exercised by one Colonel Talbot, the founder of the county of Elgin. Mrs. Anna Jameson, the wife of a vice-chancellor of Upper Canada, describes in her *Winter Studies and Summer Rambles*, written in 1838, the home of this great proprietor, a Talbot of Malahide, one of the oldest families in the parent state. The château—as she calls it, perhaps sarcastically—was a "long wooden building, chiefly of rough logs, with a covered porch running along the south side." Such homes as Colonel Talbot's were common enough in the country. Some of the higher class of immigrants, however, made efforts to surround themselves with some of the luxuries of the old world. Mrs. Jameson tells us of an old Admiral, who had settled in the London district—now the most prosperous agricultural part of Ontario—and had the best of society in his neighbourhood; "several gentlemen of family, superior education, and large capital (among them the brother of an English and the son of an Irish peer, a colonel and a major in the army) whose estates were in a flourishing state."

The common characteristic of the Canadian settlements was the humble log hut of the poor immigrant, struggling with axe and hoe amid the stumps to make a home for his family. Year by year the sunlight was let into the dense forests, and fertile meadows soon stretched far and wide in the once untrodden wilderness. Despite all the difficulties of a pioneer's life, industry reaped its adequate rewards in the fruitful lands of the west, bread was easily raised in abundance, and animals of all kinds thrived.

Unhappily the great bane of the province was the inordinate use of liquor. "The erection of a church or chapel," says Mrs. Jameson, "generally preceded that of a school-house in Upper Canada, but the mill and the tavern invariably preceded both." The roads were of the most wretched character and at some seasons actually prohibitory of all social intercourse. The towns were small and ill-built. Toronto, long known as "muddy little York," had a population of about 10,000, but with the exception of the new parliament house, it had no public buildings of architectural pretensions. The houses were generally of wood, a few of staring ugly red brick; the streets had not a single side-walk until 1834, and in 1838 this comfort for the pedestrian was still exceptional. Kingston, the ancient Cataraqui, was even a better built town than Toronto, and had in 1838 a population of perhaps 4500 persons. Hamilton and London were beginning to be places of importance. Bytown, now Ottawa, had its beginnings in 1826, when Colonel By of the Royal Engineers, commenced the construction of the Rideau Canal on the chain of lakes and rivers between the Ottawa and the St. Lawrence at Kingston. The ambition of the people of Upper Canada was always to obtain a continuous and secure system of water navigation from the lakes to Montreal. The Welland Canal between Lakes Erie and Ontario was commenced as early as 1824 through the enterprise of Mr. William Hamilton Merritt, but it was very badly managed; and the legislature, which had from year to year aided the undertaking, was obliged eventually to acquire it as a provincial work. The Cornwall Canal was also undertaken, but work was stopped when it was certain that Lower Canada would not respond to the aspirations of the West and improve that portion of the St. Lawrence within its direct control. Flat-bottomed *bateaux* and Durham boats were generally in use for the carriage of goods on the inland waters, and it was not until the completion of a canal system between the lakes and Montreal, after the Union, that steamers came into vogue.

The province of Upper Canada had in 1838 reached a crisis in its affairs. In the course of the seven years preceding the rebellion, probably eighty thousand or one half of the immigrants, who had come to the province, had crossed the frontier into the United States, where greater inducements were held out to capital and population. As Mrs. Jameson floated in a canoe, in the middle of the Detroit River, she saw on the one side "all the bustle of prosperity and commerce," and on the other "all the symptoms of apathy, indolence, mistrust, hopelessness." At the time such comparisons were made, Upper Canada was on the very verge of bankruptcy.

Turning to Lower Canada, we find that the financial position of the province was very different from that of Upper Canada. The public accounts showed an annual surplus, and the financial difficulties of the province were caused entirely by the disputes between the executive and the assembly which would not vote the necessary supplies. The timber trade had grown to large proportions and constituted the principal export to Great Britain from Quebec, which presented a scene of much activity in the summer. Montreal was already showing its great advantages as a headquarters of commerce on account of its natural relations to the West and the United States. Quebec and Montreal had each about 35,000 inhabitants. Travellers admitted that Montreal, on account of the solidity of its buildings, generally of stone, compared most favourably with many of the finest and oldest towns in the United States. The Parish Church of Notre Dame was the largest ecclesiastical edifice in America, and notable for its simple grandeur. With its ancient walls girdling the heights first seen by Jacques Cartier, with its numerous churches and convents, illustrating the power and wealth of the Romish religion, with its rugged, erratic streets creeping through hewn rock, with its picturesque crowd of red-coated soldiers of England mingling with priests and sisters in sombre attire, or with the *habitants* in *étoffe du pays*,—the old city of Quebec, whose history went back to the beginning of the seventeenth century, was certainly a piece of mediaevalism transported from northern France. The plain stone buildings of 1837 still remain in all their evidences of sombre antiquity. None of the religious or government edifices were distinguished for architectural beauty—except perhaps the English cathedral—but represented solidity and convenience, while harmonising with the rocks amid which they had risen.

The parliament of Lower Canada still met in the Bishop's Palace, which was in want of repair. The old Château St. Louis had been destroyed by fire in 1834, and a terrace bearing the name of Durham was in course of construction over its ruins. It now gives one of the most picturesque views in the world on a summer evening as the descending sun lights up the dark green of the western hills, or brightens the tin spires and roofs of the churches and convents, or lingers amid the masts of the ships moored in the river or in the coves, filled with great rafts of timber.

As in the days of French rule, the environs of Quebec and Montreal, and the north side of the St. Lawrence between these two towns, presented French Canadian life in its most picturesque and favourable aspect. These settlements on the river formed one continuous village, with tinned spires rising every few miles amid poplars, maples and elms. While the homes of the seigniors and of a few professional men were more commodious and comfortable than in the days of French rule, while the churches and presbyteries illustrated the increasing prosperity of the dominant religion, the surroundings of the *habitants* gave evidences of their want of energy and enterprise. But crime was rare in the rural districts and intemperance was not so prevalent as in parts of the west.

Nearly 150,000 people of British origin resided in Lower Canada—a British people animated for the most part by that spirit of energy natural to their race. What prosperity Montreal and Quebec enjoyed as commercial communities was largely due to the enterprise of British merchants. The timber trade was chiefly in their hands, and the bank of Montreal was founded by this class in 1817—seven years before the bank of Upper Canada was established in Toronto. As political strife increased in bitterness, the differences between the races became accentuated. Papineau alienated all the British by his determination to found a "*Nation Canadienne*" in which the British would occupy a very inferior place. "French and British," said Lord Durham, "combined for no public objects or improvements, and could not harmonise even in associations of charity." The French Canadians looked with jealousy and dislike on the increase and prosperity of what they regarded as a foreign and hostile race. It is quite intelligible, then, why trade languished, internal development ceased, landed property decreased in value, the revenue showed a diminution, roads and all classes of local improvements were neglected, agricultural industry was stagnant, wheat had to be imported for the consumption of the people, and immigration fell off from 52,000 in 1832 to less than 5000 in 1838.

In the maritime provinces of Nova Scotia, New Brunswick, and Prince Edward Island, there were no racial antagonisms to affect internal development; and the political conflict never reached such proportions as to threaten the peace and security of the people. In New Brunswick the chief industry was the timber trade—deals especially—which received its first stimulus in 1809, when a heavy duty was placed on Baltic timber, while that from the colonies came free into the British Isles. Shipbuilding was also profitably followed in New Brunswick, and was beginning to be prosecuted in Nova Scotia, where, a few years later, it made that province one of the greatest ship-owning and ship-sailing communities of the world until iron steamers gradually drove wooden vessels from the carrying trade. The cod, mackerel, and herring fisheries—chiefly the first—were the staple industry of Nova Scotia, and kept up a large trade with the British West Indies, whence sugar, molasses and rum were imported. Prince Edward Island was chiefly an agricultural community, whose development was greatly retarded by the wholesale grant of lands in 1767 to absentee proprietors. Halifax and St. John had each a population of twenty thousand. The houses were mostly of wood, the only buildings of importance being the government house, finished in 1805, and the provincial or parliament house, considered in its day one of the handsomest structures in North America. In the beautiful valleys of Kings and Annapolis— now famous for their fruit—there was a prosperous farming population. Yarmouth illustrated the thrift and enterprise of the Puritan element that came into the province from New England at an early date in its development. The eastern counties, with the exception of Pictou, showed no sign of progress. The Scotch population of Cape Breton, drawn from a poor class of people in the north of Scotland, for years added nothing to the wealth of an island whose resources were long dormant from the absence of capital and enterprise.

Popular education in those days was at the lowest possible ebb. In 1837 there were in all the private and public schools of the provinces only one-fifteenth of the total population. In Lower Canada not one-tenth could write. The children of the *habitants* repeated the Catechism by rote, and yet could not read as a rule. In Upper Canada things were no better. Dr. Thomas Rolph tells us that, so late as 1833, Americans or other anti-British adventurers carried on the greater proportion of the common schools, where the youth were taught sentiments "hostile to the parent state" from books used in the United States—a practice stopped by statute in 1846.

Adequate provision, however, was made for the higher education of youth in all the provinces. "I know of no people," wrote Lord Durham of Lower Canada, "among whom a larger provision exists for the higher kinds of elementary education." The piety and benevolence of the early possessors of the country founded seminaries and colleges, which gave an education resembling the kind given in the English public schools, though more varied. In Upper Canada, so early as 1807, grammar schools were established by the government. By 1837 Upper Canada College—an institution still flourishing—offered special advantages to youths whose parents had some money. In Nova Scotia King's College—the oldest university in Canada—had its beginning as an academy as early as 1788, and educated many eminent men during its palmy days. Pictou Academy was established by the Reverend Dr. McCulloch as a remonstrance against the sectarianism of King's; and the political history of the province was long disturbed by the struggle of its promoters against the narrowness of the Anglicans, who dominated the legislative council, and frequently rejected the grant made by the assembly. Dalhousie College was founded in 1820 by Lord Dalhousie, then governor of Nova Scotia, to afford that higher education to all denominations which old King's denied. Acadia College was founded by the Baptists at Wolfville, on a gently rising ground overlooking the fertile meadows of Grand Pré. The foundations of the University of New Brunswick were laid in 1800.

McGill University, founded by one of those generous Montreal merchants who have always been its benefactors, received a charter in 1821, but it was not opened until 1829. The Methodists laid the foundation of Victoria College at Cobourg in 1834, but it did not commence its work until after the Union; and the same was the case with King's College, the beginning of the University of Toronto.

We need not linger on the literary output of those early times. Joseph Bouchette, surveyor-general, had made in the first part of the century a notable contribution to the geography and cartography of Lower Canada. Major Richardson, who had served in the war of 1812 and in the Spanish peninsula, wrote in 1833 "Wacousta or the Prophecy," a spirited romance of Indian life. In Nova Scotia the "Sayings and Doings of Sam Slick, of Slickville"—truly a remarkable original creation in humorous literature—first appeared in a Halifax paper. The author, Judge Haliburton, also published as early as 1829 an excellent work in two volumes on the history of his native province. Small libraries and book stores could only be seen in the cities.

In these early times of the provinces, when books and magazines were rarities, the newspaper press naturally exercised much influence on the social and intellectual conditions of the people at large. By 1838 there were no less than forty papers printed in the province of Upper Canada alone, some of them written with ability, though too often in a bitter, personal tone. In those days English papers did not circulate to any extent in a country where postage was exorbitant. People could hardly afford to pay postage rates on letters. The poor settler was often unable to pay the three or four shillings or even more, imposed on letters from their old homes across the sea; and it was not unusual to find in country post-offices a large accumulation of dead letters, refused or neglected on account of the expense. The management of the post-office by imperial officers was one of the grievances of the people of the provinces generally. It was carried on for the benefit of a few persons, and not for the convenience or solace of the many thousands who were anxious for news of their kin across the ocean.

Canada Under British Rule 1760-1900

CHAPTER VII.

A NEW ERA OF COLONIAL GOVERNMENT (1839—1867).

SECTION I.—The union of the Canadas and the establishment of responsible government.

Lord Durham's report on the affairs of British North America was presented to the British government on the 31st January, 1839, and attracted an extraordinary amount of interest in England, where the two rebellions had at last awakened statesmen to the absolute necessity of providing an effective remedy for difficulties which had been pressing upon their attention for years, but had never been thoroughly understood until the appearance of this famous state paper. A legislative union of the two Canadas and the concession of responsible government were the two radical changes which stood out prominently in the report among minor suggestions in the direction of stable government. On the question of responsible government Lord Durham expressed opinions of the deepest political wisdom. He found it impossible "to understand how any English statesman could have ever imagined that representative and irresponsible government could be successfully combined....To suppose that such a system would work well there, implied a belief that the French Canadians have enjoyed representative institutions for half a century, without acquiring any of the characteristics of a free people; that Englishmen renounce every political opinion and feeling when they enter a colony, or that the spirit of Anglo-Saxon freedom is utterly changed and weakened among those who are transplanted across the Atlantic[3]."

[3: For the full text of Lord Durham's report, which was laid before Parliament, 11 February, 1839, see *English Parliamentary Papers* for 1839.]

In June, 1839, Lord John Russell introduced a bill to reunite the two provinces, but it was allowed, after its second reading, to lie over for that session of parliament, in order that the matter might be fully considered in Canada. Mr. Poulett Thomson was appointed governor-general with the avowed object of carrying out the policy of the imperial government. Immediately after his arrival in Canada, in the autumn of 1839, the special council of Lower Canada and the legislature of Upper Canada passed addresses in favour of a union of the two provinces. These necessary preliminaries having been made, Lord John Russell, in the session of 1840, again brought forward "An act to reunite the provinces of Upper and Lower Canada, and for the government of Canada," which was assented to on the 23rd of July, but did not come into effect until the 10th of February in the following year.

The act provided for a legislative council of not less than twenty members, and for a legislative assembly in which each section of the united provinces would be represented by an equal number of members—that is to say, forty-two for each or eighty-four in all. The number of representatives allotted to each province could not be changed except with the concurrence of two-thirds of the members of each house. The members of the legislative council were appointed by the crown for life, and the members of the assembly were chosen by electors possessing a small property qualification. Members of both bodies were required to hold property to a certain amount. The assembly had a duration of four years, subject of course to be sooner dissolved by the governor-general.

Provision was made for a consolidated revenue fund, on which the first charges were expenses of collection, management and receipt of revenues, interest of public debt, payment of the clergy, and civil list. The English language alone was to be used in the legislative records. All votes, resolutions or bills involving the expenditure of public money were to be first recommended by the governor-general.

The first parliament of the United Canadas was opened on the 14th June, 1841, in the city of Kingston, by the governor-general, who had been created Baron Sydenham of Sydenham and of Toronto. This session was the commencement of a series of parliaments which lasted until the confederation of all the provinces in 1867, and forcibly illustrated the capacity of the people of Canada to manage their internal affairs. For the moment, I propose to refer exclusively to those political conditions which brought about responsible government, and the removal of grievances which had so long perplexed the imperial state and distracted the whole of British North America.

In Lord John Russell's despatches of 1839,—the sequence of Lord Durham's report—we can clearly see the doubt in the minds of the imperial authorities whether it was possible to work the system of responsible government on the basis of a governor directly responsible to the parent state, and at the same time acting under the advice of ministers who would be responsible to a colonial legislature. But the colonial secretary had obviously come to the opinion that it was necessary to make a radical change which would insure greater harmony between the executive and the popular bodies of the provinces. Her Majesty, he stated emphatically, "had no desire to maintain any system of policy among her North American subjects which opinion condemns", and there was "no surer way of gaining the approbation of the Queen than by maintaining the harmony of the executive with the legislative authorities." The new governor-general was expressly appointed to carry out this new policy. If he was extremely vain, at all events he was also astute, practical, and well able to gauge the public sentiment by which he should be guided at so critical a period of Canadian history. The evidence is clear that he was not individually in favour of responsible government, as it was understood by men like Mr. Baldwin and Mr. Howe, when he arrived in Canada. He believed that the council should be one "for the governor to consult and no more"; and voicing the doubts that existed in the minds of imperial statesmen, he added, the governor "cannot be responsible to the government at home" and also to the legislature of the province, if it were so, "then all colonial government becomes impossible." The governor, in his opinion, "must therefore be the minister [i.e. the colonial secretary], in which case he cannot be under control of men in the colony."

When the assembly met it was soon evident that the Reformers in that body were determined to have a definite understanding on the all-important question of responsible government; and the result was that the governor-general, a keen politician, immediately recognised the fact that, unless he yielded to the feeling of the majority, he would lose all his influence. There is every reason to believe that the resolutions which were eventually passed in favour of responsible government, in amendment to those moved by Mr. Baldwin, had his approval before their introduction. The two sets of resolutions practically differed little from each other, and the inference to be drawn from the political situation of these times is that the governor's friends in the council thought it advisable to gain all the credit possible with the public for the passage of resolutions on the all-absorbing question of the day, since it was obvious that it had to be settled in some satisfactory and definite form. These resolutions embodying the principles of the new constitution of Canada, were as follows: (1) "That the head of the executive government of the province, being within the limits of his government the representative of the sovereign, is responsible to the imperial authority alone, but that, nevertheless, the management of our local affairs can only be conducted by him with the assistance, counsel, and information of subordinate officers in the province. (2) That, in order to preserve between the different branches of the provincial parliament that harmony which is essential to the peace, welfare and good government of the province, the chief advisers of the representative of the sovereign, constituting a provincial administration under him, ought to be men possessed of the confidence of the representatives of the people; thus affording a guarantee that the well-understood wishes and interests of the people, which our gracious sovereign has declared shall be the rule of the provincial government, will on all occasions be faithfully represented and advocated. (3) That the people of this province have, moreover, the right to expect from such provincial administration, the exertion of their best endeavours that the imperial authority, within its constitutional limits, shall be exercised in the manner most consistent with their well-understood wishes and interests."

On the 4th September, 1841, Lord Sydenham met with a serious accident while riding, and as his constitution had been impaired for years he died a fortnight later, to the regret of all political parties. He was succeeded by Sir Charles Bagot, a Conservative and High Churchman, whose brief administration was notable for the display of infinite discretion on his part, and for his desire to do justice to the French Canadians even at the risk of offending the ultra-loyal party, who claimed special consideration in the management of public affairs. Responsible government was in a fair way of being permanently established when Sir Charles Bagot unhappily died in

1843 of dropsy, complicated by heart-disease; and Lord Metcalfe was brought from India to create—as it soon appeared—confusion and discord in the political affairs of the province. His ideas of responsible government were those which had been steadily inculcated by colonial secretaries since 1839, and were even entertained by Lord Sydenham himself, namely, that the governor should be as influential a factor as possible in the government, and should always remember that he was directly responsible to the crown, and should consider its prerogatives and interests as superior to all local considerations.

When Lord Metcalfe assumed the responsibilities of his post, he found in office a Liberal administration, led by Mr. Baldwin, the eminent Reform leader of Upper Canada, and Mr. Louis Hippolyte Lafontaine, afterwards chief justice of Lower Canada and a baronet, who had been at the outset, like all his countrymen, opposed to the union, as unjust to their province. What originally excited their antagonism were the conditions exacted by the legislature of Upper Canada: an equality of representation, though the French section had a population of two hundred thousand more than the western province, the exclusion of the French language from the legislature, and the imposition of the heavy debt of Upper Canada on the revenues of the united provinces. But unlike Mr. Papineau, with whom he had acted during the political struggles in Lower Canada, Mr. Lafontaine developed a high order of discreet statesmanship after the union, and recognised the possibility of making French Canada a force in government. He did not follow the example of Mr. John Neilson, who steadily opposed the union—but determined to work it out fairly and patiently on the principles of responsible government.

Lord Metcalfe, at the very outset, decided not to distribute the patronage of the crown under the advice of his responsible advisers, but to ignore them, as he declared, whenever he deemed it expedient. No responsible ministers could, with any regard to their own self-respect, or to the public interests, submit to a practice directly antagonistic to responsible government, then on its trial. Consequently, all the members of the Baldwin-Lafontaine government, with the exception of Mr. Daly, immediately resigned, when Lord Metcalfe followed so unconstitutional a course. Mr. Dominick Daly, afterwards knighted when governor of Prince Edward's Island—who had no party proclivities, and was always ready to support the crown in a crisis—became nominally head of a weak administration. The ministry was only completed after a most unconstitutional delay of several months, and was even then only composed of men whose chief merit was their friendliness to the governor, who dissolved the assembly and threw all the weight of the crown into the contest. The governor's party was returned with a very small majority, but it was a victory, like that of Sir Francis Bond Head in 1835, won at the sacrifice of the dignity of the crown, and at the risk of exciting once more public discontent to a dangerous degree. Lord Metcalfe's administration was strengthened when Mr. Draper resigned his legislative councillorship and took a seat in the assembly as leader. Lord Metcalfe's conduct received the approval of the imperial authorities, who elevated him to the peerage—so much evidence that they were not yet ready to concede responsible government in a complete sense. The result was a return to the days of old paternal government, when the parliamentary opposition was directed against the governor himself and the British government of which he was the organ. Lord Metcalfe had been a sufferer from cancer, and when it appeared again in its most aggravated form he returned to England, where he died a few months later (1846). The abuse that followed him almost to the grave was a discreditable exhibition of party rancour, but it indicated the condition to which the public mind had been brought by his unwise and unconstitutional conduct of public affairs—conduct for which his only apology must be the half-hearted, doubtful policy of the imperial authorities with regard to the province, and his own inability to understand the fundamental principles of responsible government.

Lord Metcalfe's successor was Lord Cathcart, who had served with distinction in the Peninsular War, and was appointed with a view to contingencies that might arise out of the dispute between England and the United States on the Oregon boundary question, to which I shall refer in another chapter. He pursued a judicious course at a time when politics were complicated by the fact that the industry and commerce of the country were seriously deranged by the adoption of free trade in England, and the consequent removal of duties which had given the preference in the British market to Canadian wheat, flour and other products. What aggravated the commercial situation was the fact that the navigation laws, being still in force, closed the St. Lawrence to foreign shipping and prevented the extension of trade to other markets so as to compensate Canadians for the loss of that with the parent state. Lord Cathcart was recalled within less than a year, when all prospect of war with the United States had disappeared, and was followed (1847) by a civil governor, the Earl of Elgin, who was chosen by the Whig ministry, in which Lord John Russell was prime minister, and Earl Grey the secretary of state for the colonies. It had dawned upon English statesmen that the time had come for giving the colonists of British North America a system of responsible government without such reserves as had so seriously shackled its beginnings. In all probability they thought that the free-trade policy of England had momentarily weakened the ties that had bound the colonies to the parent state, and that it was advisable to follow up the new commercial policy by removing causes of public discontent in the province.

Lord Elgin was happily chosen to inaugurate a new era of colonial self-government. Gifted with a judicial mind and no ordinary amount of political sagacity, able to originate as well as carry out a statesmanlike policy, animated, like Lord Durham—whose daughter he had married—by a sincere desire to give full scope to the aspirations of the people for self-government, so far as compatible with the supremacy of the crown, possessed of eloquence which at once charmed and convinced, Lord Elgin was able to establish on sure foundations the principles of responsible government, and eventually to leave Canada with the conviction that no subsequent representative of the crown could again impair its efficient operation, and convulse the public mind, as Lord Metcalfe had done. On his arrival he gave his confidence to the Draper ministry, who were still in office; but shortly afterwards its ablest member was elevated to the bench, and Mr. Sherwood became attorney-general and head of a government, chiefly interesting now for the fact that one of its members was Mr. John Alexander Macdonald, who, on becoming a member of the assembly in 1844, had commenced a public career which made him one of the most notable figures in the history of the colonial empire of England.

Parliament was dissolved, and the elections were held in January, 1848, when the government were defeated by a large majority and the second Lafontaine-Baldwin ministry was formed; a ministry conspicuous for the ability of its members, and the useful character of its legislation during the four years it remained in power. It is noteworthy here that Lord Elgin did not follow the example of his predecessors and select the ministers himself, but followed the strict constitutional usage of calling upon Mr. Lafontaine as a recognised leader of a party in parliament to form a government. It does not fall within the scope of this chapter to go into the merits of this great administration, whose coming into office may be considered the crowning of the principles adopted by Lord Elgin for the unreserved concession of responsible government, and never violated from that time forward by any governor of Canada.

We must now direct our attention to the maritime provinces, that we may complete this review of the progress of responsible government in British North America. In 1836 the revenues of New Brunswick had been placed at the disposal of the legislature, and administrative power entrusted to those who possessed the confidence of the assembly. The lieutenant-governor, Sir John Harvey, who had distinguished himself in the war of 1812-15, recognised in Lord John Russell's despatches "a new and improved constitution," and by an official memorandum informed the heads of departments that "thenceforward their offices would be held by the tenure of public confidence"; but after his departure (in 1841) an attempt was made by Sir William Colebrooke to imitate the example of Lord Metcalfe. He appointed to the provincial secretaryship a Mr. Reade, who had been only a few months in the province, and never represented a constituency or earned promotion in the public service. The members of the executive council were never consulted, and four of the most popular and influential councillors soon resigned. One of them, Mr. Lemuel A. Wilmot, the recognised leader of the Liberals, addressed a strong remonstrance to the lieutenant-governor, and vindicated those principles of colonial government "which require the administration to be conducted by heads of departments responsible to the legislature, and holding their offices contingently upon the approbation and confidence of the country, as expressed through the representatives of the people." The colonial secretary of state disapproved of the action of the lieutenant-governor, and constitutional government was strengthened in this province of the Loyalists. From that time there was a regularly organised administration and an opposition contending for office and popular favour.

In Nova Scotia a despatch from Lord Glenelg brought to a close in 1838 the agitation which had been going on for years for a separation of the executive from the legislative functions of the legislative council, and the formation of two distinct bodies in accordance with the existing English system. In this state paper—the first important step towards responsible government in the province—the secretary of state, Lord Glenelg, stated that it was her Majesty's pleasure that neither the chief justice nor any of his colleagues should sit in the council, that all the judges should entirely withdraw from all political discussions; that the assembly's claim to control and appropriate all the revenues arising in the province should be fully recognised by the government; that the two councils should be thereafter divided, and that the members of these bodies should be drawn from different parts of the province—Halifax previously having obtained all the appointments except one or two—and selected without reference to distinctions of religious opinions. Unfortunately for Nova Scotia there was at that time at the head of the executive a brave, obstinate old soldier, Sir Colin Campbell, who had petrified ideas on the subject of colonial administration, and showed no disposition to carry out the obvious desire of the imperial authorities to give a more popular form to the government of the province. One of his first official acts was to give to the Anglican Church a numerical superiority to which it had no valid claim. As in Upper Canada, at that time, there was a combination or compact, composed of descendants of English Tories or of the Loyalists of 1783, who belonged to the Anglican Church, and were opposed to popular government. Two men were now becoming most prominent in politics. One of these was Mr. James William Johnston, the son of a Georgia Loyalist, an able lawyer, gifted with a persuasive tongue which chimed most harmoniously with the views of Sir Colin. On the other side was Mr. Joseph Howe, the son of a Loyalist printer of Boston, who had no such aristocratic connections as Mr. Johnston, and soon became the dominant influence in the Reform party, which had within its ranks such able and eloquent men as S.G.W. Archibald, Herbert Huntington, Lawrence O'Connor Doyle, William and George R. Young, and, very soon, James Boyle Uniacke. Sir Colin Campbell completely ignored the despatches of Lord John Russell, which were recognised by Sir John Harvey as conferring "an improved constitution" upon the colonies. In February, 1840, Mr. Howe moved a series of resolutions, in which it was emphatically stated that "no satisfactory settlement of questions before the country could be obtained until the executive council was remodelled," and that, as then constituted, "it did not enjoy the confidence of the country." The motion was carried by a majority of eighteen votes, in a house of forty-two members, and indeed, so untenable was the position of the executive council that Mr. James Boyle Uniacke, a member of the government, retired, rather than vote, and subsequently placed his resignation in the hands of the lieutenant-governor, on the ground that it was his duty to yield to the opinions of the representative house, and facilitate the introduction of a better system of government, in accordance with the well-understood wishes of the people. From that time Mr. Uniacke became one of Mr. Howe's ablest allies in the struggle for self-government. Sir Colin, however, would not recede from the attitude he had assumed, but expressed the opinion, in his reply to the address of the legislature, that he could not recognise in the despatch of the colonial secretary of state "any instruction for a fundamental change in the colonial constitution." The assembly then prayed her Majesty, in a powerful and temperate address, to recall Sir Colin Campbell. Though Lord John Russell did not present the address to the Queen, the imperial government soon afterwards appointed Lord Falkland to succeed Sir Colin Campbell, whose honesty of purpose had won the respect of all parties.

Lord Falkland was a Whig, a lord of the bedchamber, and married to one of the Fitzclarences—a daughter of William IV and Mrs. Jordan. He arrived at Halifax in September, 1840, and his first political act was in the direction of conciliating the Liberals, who were in the majority in the assembly. He dismissed—to the disgust of the official party—four members of the executive who had no seats in either branch of the legislature, and induced Mr. Howe and Mr. James MacNab to enter the government, on the understanding that other Liberals would be brought in according as vacancies occurred, and that the members of the council should hold their seats only upon the tenure of public confidence. A dissolution took place, the coalition government was sustained, and the Liberals came into the assembly with a majority. Mr. Howe was elected speaker of the assembly, though an executive councillor—without salary; but he and others began to recognise the impropriety of one man occupying such positions, and in a later session a resolution was passed against the continuance of what was really an un-British and unconstitutional practice. It was also an illustration of the ignorance that prevailed as to the principles that should guide the words and acts of a cabinet, that members of the executive, who had seats in the legislative council, notably Mr. Stewart, stated openly, in contradiction of the assertions of Mr. Howe and his Liberal colleagues, that "no change had been made in the constitution of the country, and that responsible government in a colony was responsible nonsense, and meant independence." It was at last found necessary to give some sort of explanation of such extraordinary opinions, to avert a political crisis in the assembly. Then, to add to the political embarrassment, there was brought before the people the question of abandoning the practice of endowing denominational colleges, and of establishing in their place one large non-sectarian University. At this time the legislature voted annual grants to five sectarian educational institutions of a high class. The most important were King's College, belonging to the Anglican Church, and Acadia College, supported by the Baptists. The Anglican Church was still influential in the councils of the province, and the Baptists had now the support of Mr. Johnston, the able attorney-general, who had seceded from the Church of England. This able lawyer and politician had won the favour of the aristocratic governor, and persuaded him to dissolve the assembly, during the absence of Mr. Howe in the country, though it had continuously supported the government, and the people had given no signs of a want of confidence in the house as then constituted. The fact was, Mr. Johnston and his friends in the council thought it necessary to lose no time in arousing the feelings of the supporters of denominational colleges against Mr. Howe and other Liberals, who had commenced to hold meetings throughout the country in favour of a non-sectarian University. The two parties came back from the electors almost evenly divided, and Mr. Howe had an interview with Lord Falkland. He consented to remain in the cabinet until the assembly had an opportunity of expressing its opinion on the question at issue, when the governor himself precipitated a crisis by appointing to the executive and legislative councils Mr. M.B. Almon, a wealthy banker, and a brother-in-law of the attorney-general. Mr. Howe and Mr. MacNab at once resigned their seats in the government on the ground that Mr. Almon's appointment was a violation of the compact by which two Liberals had been induced to join the ministry, and was most unjust to the forty or fifty gentlemen who, in both branches, had sustained the administration for several years. Instead of authorising Mr. Johnston to fill the two vacancies and justify the course taken by the governor, the latter actually published a letter in a newspaper, in which he boldly stated that he was entirely opposed to the formation of a government composed of individuals of one political party, that he would steadily resist any invasion of the royal prerogatives with respect to appointments, and that he had chosen Mr. Almon, not simply on the ground that he had not been previously engaged in political life to any extent, but chiefly because he wished to show his own confidence in Mr. Johnston, Mr. Almon's brother-in-law. Lord Falkland had obviously thrown himself into the arms of the astute attorney-general and his political friends.

It was now a political war *à outrance* between Lord Falkland and Mr. Howe, from 1842 until the governor left the province in 1846. Lord Falkland made strenuous efforts to detach Mr. MacNab, Mr. Uniacke and other Liberals from Mr. Howe, and induce them to enter the government, but all to no purpose. He now gave up writing letters to the press, and attacked his opponents in official communications addressed to the colonial office, which supported him, as it did Lord Metcalfe, under analogous circumstances. These despatches were laid without delay on the tables of the houses, to be used far and wide against the recalcitrant Liberals. Mr. Howe had again renewed his connection with the press, which he had left on becoming speaker and councillor, and had become editor of the *Nova Scotian*, and the *Morning Chronicle*, of which Mr. Annand was the proprietor. In these influential organs of the Liberal party—papers still in existence—Mr. Howe attacked Lord Falkland, both in bitter prose and sarcastic verse. All this while the governor and his council contrived to control the assembly, sometimes by two or three votes, sometimes by a prorogation when it was necessary to dispose summarily of a troublesome question. Public opinion began to set in steadily against the government. The controversy between Lord Falkland and Mr. Howe reached its climax on the 21st February, 1846, when a despatch was brought down to the house, referring to the speaker, Mr. William Young, and his brother, George R. Young, as the associates of "reckless" and "insolvent" men—the reference being to Mr. Howe and his immediate political friends. When the despatch had been read, Mr. Howe became greatly excited, and declared amid much disorder that if "the infamous system" of libelling respectable colonists in despatches sent to the colonial office was continued, "without their having any means of redress ... some colonist would by-and-by, or he was much mistaken, hire a black fellow to horsewhip a lieutenant-governor."

It was time that this unhappy conflict should end. The imperial authorities wisely transferred Lord Falkland to Bombay, where he could do no harm, and appointed Sir John Harvey to the government of Nova Scotia. Like Lord Elgin in Canada, he was discreetly chosen by the Reform ministry, as the sequel showed. He was at first in favour of a coalition government like his predecessors, but he wisely dissolved the assembly when he found that the leading Liberals positively refused to go into an alliance with the members of the executive council, or any other set of men, until the people had decided between parties at the polls. The result was a victory for the Liberals, and as soon as the assembly met a direct motion of want of confidence was carried against the government, and for the first time in the history of the country the governor called to his council men exclusively belonging to the opposition in the popular branch. Mr. Howe was not called upon to form a cabinet—his quarrel with Lord Falkland had to be resented somehow—but the governor's choice was Mr. James Boyle Uniacke, who gave a prominent position in the new government to the great Liberal, to whom responsible government owed its final success in this maritime province.

Responsible government was not introduced into Prince Edward Island until 1851, when an address on the prosperous state of the island was presented to the imperial authorities, who at once consented to concede responsible government on the condition that adequate provision was made for certain public officers affected by the new order of things. The leader of the new government was the Honourable George Coles.

In the history of the past there is much to deplore, the blunders of English ministers, the want of judgment on the part of governors, the selfishness of "family compacts," the arrogance of office-holders, the recklessness of Canadian politicians. But the very trials of the crisis through which Canada passed brought out the fact, that if English statesmen had mistaken the spirit of the Canadian people, and had not always taken the best methods of removing grievances, it was not from any studied disposition to do these countries an injustice, but rather because they were unable to see until the very last moment that, even in a colony, a representative system must be worked in accordance with those principles that obtained in England, and that it was impossible to direct the internal affairs of dependencies many thousand miles distant through a colonial office, generally managed by a few clerks.

Of all the conspicuous figures of these memorable times, which already seem so far away from Canadians of the present day, who possess so many political rights, there are several who stand out more prominently than all others, and represent the distinct types of politicians, who influenced the public mind during the first half of the nineteenth century, when responsible government was in slow process of evolution from the political struggles which arose in the operation of representative institutions. Around the figure of Louis Joseph Papineau there has always been a sort of glamour which has helped to conceal his vanity, his rashness and his want of political sagacity, which would, under any circumstances, have prevented his success as a safe statesman, capable of guiding a people through a trying ordeal. His eloquence was fervid and had much influence over his impulsive countrymen, his sincerity was undoubted, and in all likelihood his very indiscretions made more palpable the defects of the political system against which he so persistently and so often justly declaimed. He lived to see his countrymen enjoy power and influence under the very union which they resented, and to find himself no longer a leader among men, but isolated from a great majority of his own people, and representing a past whose methods were antagonistic to the new régime that had grown up since 1838. It would have been well for his reputation had he remained in obscurity on his return from exile in 1847, when he and other rebels of 1837 were wisely pardoned, and had he never stood again on the floor of the parliament of Canada, as he did from 1848 until 1854, since he could only prove, in those later times, that he had never understood the true working of responsible government. While the Lafontaine-Baldwin ministry were in power, he revived an agitation for an elective legislative council and declared himself utterly hostile to responsible government; but his influence was at an end in the country, and he could make little impression on the assembly. The days of reckless agitation had passed, and the time for astute and calm statesmanship had come. Lafontaine and Morin were now safer political guides for his countrymen. He soon disappeared entirely from public view, and in the solitude of his picturesque château, amid the groves that overhang the Ottawa River, only visited from time to time by a few staunch friends, or by curious tourists who found their way to that quiet spot, he passed the remainder of his days with a tranquillity in wondrous contrast to the stormy and eventful drama of his life. The writer often saw his noble, dignified figure—erect even in age—passing unnoticed on the streets of Ottawa, when perhaps at the same time there were strangers, walking through the lobbies of the parliament house, asking for his portrait.

William Lyon Mackenzie is a far less picturesque figure in Canadian history than Papineau, who possessed an eloquence of tongue and a grace of demeanour which were not the attributes of the little peppery, undignified Scotchman who, for a few years, played so important a part in the English-speaking province. With his disinterestedness and unselfishness, with his hatred of political injustice and oppression, Canadians who remember the history of the constitutional struggles of England will always sympathise. Revolt against absolutism and tyranny is permissible in the opinion of men who love political freedom, but the conditions of Upper

Canada were hardly such as justified the rash insurrection into which he led his deluded followers, many to misery and some to death. Mackenzie lived long enough to regret these sad mistakes of a reckless period of his life, and to admit that "the success of the rebellion would have deeply injured the people of Canada," whom he believed he was then serving, and that it was the interest of the Canadian people to strengthen in every way the connection with England. Like Papineau, he returned to Canada in 1849 to find himself entirely unequal to the new conditions of political life, where a large constitutional knowledge, a spirit of moderation and a statesmanlike conduct could alone give a man influence in the councils of his country. One historian has attempted to elevate Dr. Rolph at his expense, but a careful study of the career of those two actors will lead fair-minded readers to the conclusion that even the reckless course followed at the last by Mackenzie was preferable to the double-dealing of his more astute colleague. Dr. Rolph came again into prominence as one of the founders of the Clear Grits, who formed in 1849 an extreme branch of the Reform party. Dr. Rolph's qualities ensured him success in political intrigue, and he soon became a member of the Hincks-Morin government, which was formed on the reconstruction of the Lafontaine-Baldwin ministry in 1851, when its two moderate leaders were practically pushed aside by men more in harmony with the aggressive elements of the Reform party. But Mr. Mackenzie could never win such triumphs as were won by his wily and more manageable associate of old times. He published a newspaper—*The Weekly Message*—replete with the eccentricities of the editor, but it was never a financial success, while his career in the assembly from 1851 until 1858 only proved him almost a nullity in public affairs. Until his death in 1861 his life was a constant fight with poverty, although his closing years were somewhat soothed by the gift of a homestead. He might have received some public position which would have given him comfort and rest, but he would not surrender what he called his political freedom to the men in office, who, he believed, wished to purchase his silence—the veriest delusion, as his influence had practically disappeared with his flight to the United States.

Joseph Howe, unlike the majority of his compeers who struggled for popular rights, was a prominent figure in public life until the very close of his career in 1873. All his days, even when his spirit was sorely tried by the obstinacy and indifference of some English ministers, he loved England, for he knew—like the Loyalists, from one of whom he sprung—it was in her institutions, after all, his country could best find prosperity and happiness. It is an interesting fact that, among the many able essays and addresses which the question of imperial federation has drawn forth, none can equal his great speech on the consolidation of the empire in eloquence, breadth, and fervour. Of all the able men Nova Scotia has produced no one has surpassed that great tribune of the people in his power to persuade and delight the masses by his oratory. Yet, strange to say, his native province has never raised a monument to his memory.

One of the most admirable figures in the political history of the Dominion was undoubtedly Robert Baldwin. Compared with other popular leaders of his generation, he was calm in council, unselfish in motive, and moderate in opinion. If there is any significance in the political phrase "Liberal-Conservative," it could be applied with justice to him. The "great ministry," of which he and Louis Hippolyte Lafontaine—afterwards a baronet and chief justice—were the leaders, left behind it many monuments of broad statesmanship, and made a deep impression on the institutions of the country. In 1851 he resigned from the Reform ministry, of which he had been the Upper Canadian leader, in consequence of a vote of the Reformers of that province adverse to the continuance of the court of chancery, the constitution of which had been improved chiefly by himself. When he presented himself as a candidate before his old constituency he was defeated by a nominee of the Clear Grits, who were then, as always, pressing their opinions with great vehemence and hostility to all moderate men. He illustrated the fickle character of popular favour, when a man will not surrender his principles and descend to the arts of the politician. He lived until 1858 in retirement, almost forgotten by the people for whom he had worked so fearlessly and sincerely.

In New Brunswick the triumph of responsible government must always be associated with the name of Lemuel A. Wilmot, the descendant of a famous United Empire Loyalist stock, afterwards a judge and a lieutenant-governor of his native province. He was in some respects the most notable figure, after Joseph Howe and J.W. Johnston, the leaders of the Liberal and Conservative parties in Nova Scotia, in that famous body of public men who so long brightened the political life of the maritime provinces. But neither those two leaders nor their distinguished compeers, James Boyle Uniacke, William Young, John Hamilton Gray and Charles Fisher, all names familiar to students of Nova Scotia and New Brunswick history, surpassed Mr. Wilmot in that magnetic eloquence which carries an audience off its feet, in versatility of knowledge, in humorous sarcasm, and in conversational gifts, which made him a most interesting personality in social life. He impressed his strong individuality upon his countrymen until the latest hour of his useful career.

In Prince Edward Island, the name most intimately connected with the struggle for responsible government is that of George Coles, who, despite the absence of educational and social advantages in his youth, eventually triumphed over all obstacles, and occupied a most prominent position by dint of unconquerable courage and ability to influence the opinions of the great mass of people.

SECTION 2.—Results of self-government from 1841 to 1864.

The new colonial policy, adopted by the imperial government immediately after the presentation of Lord Durham's report, had a remarkable effect upon the political and social development of the British North American provinces during the quarter of a century that elapsed between the union of the Canadas in 1841 and the federal union of 1867. In 1841 Mr. Harrison, provincial secretary of the upper province in the coalition government formed by Lord Sydenham, brought in a measure which laid the foundations of the elaborate system of municipal institutions which the Canadian provinces now enjoy. In 1843 Attorney-General Lafontaine presented a bill "for better serving the independence of the legislative assembly of this province," which became law in 1844 and formed the basis of all subsequent legislation in Canada.

The question of the clergy reserves continued for some years after the union to perplex politicians and harass governments. At last in 1854 the Hincks government was defeated by a combination of factions, and the Liberal-Conservative party was formed out of the union of the Conservatives and the moderate Reformers. Sir Allan MacNab was the leader of this coalition government, but the most influential member was Mr. John A. Macdonald, then attorney-general of Upper Canada, whose first important act was the settlement of the clergy reserves. Reform ministers had for years evaded the question, and it was now left to a government, largely composed of men who had been Tories in the early part of their political career, to yield to the force of public opinion and take it out of the arena of political agitation by means of legislation which handed over this property to the municipal corporations of the province for secular purposes, and at the same time made a small endowment for the protection of the clergy who had legal claims on the fund. The same government had also the honour of removing the old French seigniorial system, recognised to be incompatible with the modern condition of a country of free government, and injurious to the agricultural development of the province at large. The question was practically settled in 1854, when Mr. Drummond, then attorney-general for Lower Canada, brought in a bill providing for the appointment of a commission to ascertain the amount of compensation that could be fairly asked by the seigniors for the cession of their seigniorial rights. The seigniors, from first to last, received about a million of dollars, and it also became necessary to revise those old French laws which affected the land tenure of Lower Canada. Accordingly in 1856 Mr. George Cartier, attorney-general for Lower Canada in the Taché-Macdonald ministry, introduced the legislation necessary for the codification of the civil law. In 1857 Mr. Spence, post-master-general in the same ministry, brought in a measure to organise the civil service, on whose character and ability so much depends in the working of parliamentary institutions. From that day to this the Canadian government has practically recognised the British principle of retaining public officers without reference to a change of political administration.

Soon after the union the legislating obtained full control of the civil list and the post-office. The last tariff framed by the imperial parliament for British North America was mentioned in the speech at the opening of the Canadian legislature in 1842. In 1846 the British colonies in America were authorised by an imperial statute to reduce or repeal by their own legislation duties imposed by imperial acts upon foreign goods imported from foreign countries into the colonies in question. Canada soon availed herself of this privilege, which was granted to her as the logical sequence of the free-trade policy of Great Britain, and, from that time to the present, she has been enabled to legislate very freely with regard to her own commercial interests. In 1849 the imperial parliament repealed the navigation laws, and allowed the river St. Lawrence to be used by vessels of all nations. With the repeal of laws, the continuance of which had seriously crippled Canadian trade after the adoption of free trade by England, the provinces gradually entered on a new career of industrial enterprise.

No part of the constitution of 1840 gave greater offence to the French Canadian population than the clause restricting the use of the French language in the legislature. It was considered as a part of the policy, foreshadowed in Lord Durham's report, to denationalise, if possible, the French Canadian province. The repeal of the clause, in 1848, was one evidence of the harmonious operation of the union, and of a better feeling between the two sections of the population. Still later, provision was made for the gradual establishment of an elective legislative council, so long and earnestly demanded by the old legislature of Lower Canada.

The members of the Lafontaine-Baldwin government became the legislative executors of a troublesome legacy left to them by a Conservative ministry. In 1839 acts had been passed by the special council of Lower Canada and the legislature of Upper Canada to compensate the loyal inhabitants of those provinces for the loss they had sustained during the rebellions. In the first session of the union parliament the Upper Canadian act was amended, and money voted to reimburse all persons in Upper Canada whose property had been unnecessarily, or wantonly, destroyed by persons acting, or pretending to act, on behalf of the crown. An agitation then commenced for the application of the same principle to Lower Canada, and in 1845 commissioners were appointed by the Draper administration to inquire into the nature and value of the losses suffered by her Majesty's loyal subjects in Lower Canada. When their report was presented in favour of certain claims the Draper ministry brought in some legislation on the subject, but went out of office before any action could be taken thereon. The Lafontaine-Baldwin government then determined to set the question at rest, and introduced legislation for the issue of debentures to the amount of $400,000 for the payment of losses sustained by persons who had not been convicted of, or charged with, high treason or other offences of a treasonable nature, or had been committed to the custody of the sheriff in the gaol of Montreal and subsequently transported to the island of Bermuda. Although the principle of this measure was fully justified by the action of the Tory Draper government, extreme Loyalists and even some Reformers of Upper Canada declaimed against it in the most violent terms, and a few persons even declared that they would prefer annexation to the United States to the payment of the rebels. The bill, however, passed the legislature by a large majority, and received the crown's assent through Lord Elgin on the 25th April, 1849. A large crowd immediately assembled around the parliament house—formerly the St. Anne Market House—and insulted the governor-general by opprobrious epithets, and by throwing missiles at him as he drove away to Monklands, his residence in the country. The government and members of the legislature appear to have been unconscious of the danger to which they were exposed until a great crowd rushed into the building, which was immediately destroyed by fire with its fine collection of books and archives. A few days later, when the assembly, then temporarily housed in the hall of Bonsecours Market, attempted to present an address to Lord Elgin, he was in imminent danger of his life while on his way to the government house—then the old Château de Ramesay in Nôtre-Dame Street—and the consequences might have been most serious had he not evaded the mob on his return to Monklands. This disgraceful affair was a remarkable illustration not simply of the violence of faction, but largely of the discontent then so prevalent in Montreal and other industrial centres, on account of the commercial policy of Great Britain, which seriously crippled colonial trade and was the main cause of the creation of a small party which actually advocated for a short time annexation to the United States as preferable to the existing state of things. The result was the removal of the seat of government from Montreal, and the establishment of a nomadic system of government by which the legislature met alternately at Toronto and Quebec every five years until Ottawa was chosen by the Queen as a permanent political capital. Lord Elgin felt his position keenly, and offered his resignation to the imperial government, but they refused to entertain it, and his course as a constitutional governor under such trying circumstances was approved by parliament.

The material condition of the provinces—especially of Upper Canada, which now became the first in population and wealth—kept pace with the rapid progress of the people in self-government. The population of the five provinces had increased from about 1,500,000, in 1841, to about 3,200,000 when the census was taken in 1861 The greatest increase had been in the province of Upper Canada, chiefly in consequence of the large immigration which flowed into the country from Ireland, where the potato rot had caused wide-spread destitution and misery. The population of this province had now reached 1,396,091, or nearly 300,000 more than the population of Lower Canada—an increase which, as I shall show in the next chapter, had important effects on the political conditions of the two provinces. The eastern or maritime provinces received but a small part of the yearly immigration from Europe, and even that was balanced by an exodus to the United States. Montreal had a population of 100,000, or double that of Quebec, and was now recognised as the commercial capital of British North America. Toronto had reached 60,000, and was making more steady progress in population and wealth than any other city, except Montreal. Towns and villages were springing up with great rapidity in the midst of the enterprising farming population of the western province. In Lower Canada the townships showed the energy of a British people, but the *habitants* pursued the even tenor of ways which did not include enterprise and improved methods of agriculture.

The value of the total exports and imports of the provinces reached $150,000,000 by 1864, or an increase of $100,000,000 in a quarter of a century. The great bulk of the import trade was with Great Britain and the United States, but the value of the exports to the United States was largely in excess of the goods purchased by Great Britain—especially after 1854, when Lord Elgin arranged a reciprocity treaty with the United States. Lord Elgin represented

Great Britain in the negotiations at Washington, and the Congress of the United States and the several legislatures of the Canadian provinces passed the legislation necessary to give effect to the treaty. Its most important provisions established free trade between British North America and the United States in products of the forest, mine, and sea, conceded the navigation of the St. Lawrence to the Americans, and the use of the canals of Canada on the same terms as were imposed upon British subjects, gave Canadians the right to navigate Lake Michigan, and allowed the fishermen of the United States to fish on the sea-coasts of the British provinces without regard to distance from the shore, in return for a similar but relatively worthless privilege on the eastern shores of the republic, north of the 30th parallel of north latitude. During the thirteen years the treaty lasted the trade between the two countries rose from over thirty-three million dollars in 1854 to over eighty million dollars in 1866, when it was repealed by the action of the United States government itself, for reasons which I shall explain in a later chapter.

The navigation of the St. Lawrence was now made continuous and secure by the enlargement of the Welland and Lachine canals, and the construction of the Cornwall, Williamsburgh, and Beauharnois canals. Railways received their great stimulus during the government of Sir Francis Hincks, who largely increased the debt of Canada by guaranteeing in 1852 the bonds of the Grand Trunk Railway—a noble, national work, now extending from Quebec to Lake Michigan, with branches in every direction, but whose early history was marred by jobbery and mismanagement, which not only ruined or crippled many of the original shareholders, but cost Canada eventually twenty-three million dollars. In 1864 there were two thousand miles of railway working in British North America, of which the Grand Trunk Railway owned at least one-half. The railways in the maritime provinces were very insignificant, and all attempts to obtain the co-operation of the imperial and Canadian governments for the construction of an Intercolonial Railway through British American territory failed, despite the energetic efforts of Mr. Howe to bring it about.

After the union of the Canadas in 1841, a steady movement for the improvement of the elementary, public, or common schools continued for years, and the services of the Reverend Egerton Ryerson were engaged as chief superintendent of education with signal advantage to the country. In 1850, when the Lafontaine-Baldwin government was in office, the results of the superintendent's studies of the systems of other countries were embodied in a bill based on the principle of local assessment, aided by legislative grants, for the carrying on of the public schools. This measure is the basis of the present admirable school system of Upper Canada, and to a large extent of that of the other English-speaking provinces. In Lower Canada the history of public schools must be always associated with the names of Dr. Meilleur and the Honourable Mr. Chauveau; but the system has never been as effective as in the upper province. In both provinces, separate or dissentient schools were eventually established for the benefit of the Roman Catholics in Upper or Protestant Canada, and of the Protestants in Lower or Catholic Canada. In the maritime provinces satisfactory progress was also made in the development of a sound school system. In Nova Scotia Dr. Tupper, when provincial secretary (1863-1867), laid the foundations of the excellent schools that the province now enjoys.

During this period the newspaper press increased remarkably in influence and circulation. The most important newspaper in the Dominion, the *Globe*, was established at Toronto in 1844 by Mr. George Brown, a Scotchman by birth, who became a power from that time among the Liberal politicians of Canada. No notable books were produced in the English-speaking provinces except "Acadian Geology," a work by Dr. Dawson, who became in 1855 principal of McGill University, and was, in later years, knighted by the Queen; but the polished verses of Crémazie and the lucid histories of Canada by Ferland and Garneau already showed that French Canada had both a history and a literature.

Towards the close of this memorable period of Canadian development, the Prince of Wales, heir-apparent to the throne, visited the British American provinces, where the people gave full expression to their loyal feelings. This was the third occasion on which these communities had been favoured by the presence of members of the royal family. Prince William Henry, afterward

William IV, visited Nova Scotia during the years 1786-1788, in command of a frigate. From 1791 until 1797 Prince Edward, Duke of Kent, father of the present sovereign, was in command of the imperial forces, first at Quebec, and later at Halifax. The year 1860 was an opportue time for a royal visit to provinces where the people were in the full enjoyment of the results of the liberal system of self-government extended to them at the commencement of the Queen's reign by the mother-country.

A quarter of a century had passed after the union of the Canadas when the necessities of the provinces of British North America forced them to a momentous constitutional change, which gave a greater scope to the statesmanship of their public men, and opened up a wider sphere of effort to capital and enterprise. In the following chapter I shall show the nature of the conditions which brought about this union.

CHAPTER VIII.

THE EVOLUTION OF CONFEDERATION (1789—1864).

SECTION 1—The beginnings of confederation.

The idea of a union of the provinces of British North America had been under discussion for half a century before it reached the domain of practical statesmanship. The eminent Loyalist, Chief Justice Smith of Quebec, so early as 1789, in a letter to Lord Dorchester, gave an outline of a scheme for uniting all the provinces of British North America "under one general direction." A quarter of a century later Chief Justice Sewell of Quebec, also a Loyalist, addressed a letter to the father of the present Queen, the Duke of Kent, in which he urged a federal union of the isolated provinces. Lord Durham was also of opinion in 1839 that a legislative union of all the provinces "would at once decisively settle the question of races," but he did not find it possible to carry it out at that critical time in the history of the Canadas.

Some ten years later, at a meeting of prominent public men in Toronto, known as the British American League, the project of a federal union was submitted to the favourable consideration of the provinces. In 1854 the subject was formally brought before the legislature of Nova Scotia by the Honourable James William Johnston, the able leader of the Conservative party, and found its most eloquent exposition in the speech of the Honourable Joseph Howe, one of the fathers of responsible government. The result of the discussion was the unanimous adoption of a resolution—the first formally adopted by any provincial legislature—setting forth that "the union or confederation of the British provinces, while calculated to perpetuate their connection with the parent state, will promote their advancement and prosperity, increase their strength, and influence and elevate their position." Mr. Howe, on that occasion, expressed himself in favour of a federation of the empire, of which he was always an earnest advocate until his death.

In the legislature of Canada Mr., afterwards Sir, Alexander Tilloch Galt was an able exponent of union, and when he became a member of the Cartier-Macdonald government in 1858 the question was made a part of the ministerial policy, and received special mention in the speech of Sir Edmund Head, the governor-general, at the end of the session. The matter was brought to the attention of the imperial government on more than one occasion during these years by delegates from Canada and Nova Scotia, but no definite conclusion could be reached in view of the fact that the question had not been taken up generally in the provinces.

The political condition of the Canadas brought about a union much sooner than was anticipated by its most sanguine promoters. In a despatch written to the colonial minister by the Canadian delegates,—members of the Cartier-Macdonald ministry—who visited England in 1858 and laid the question of union before the government, they represented that "very grave difficulties now present themselves in conducting the government of Canada"; that "the progress of population has been more rapid in the western province, and claims are now made on behalf of its inhabitants for giving them representation in the legislature in proportion to their numbers"; that "the result is shown by agitation fraught with great danger to the peaceful and harmonious working of our constitutional system, and, consequently, detrimental to the progress of the province" that "this state of things is yearly becoming worse"; and that "the Canadian government are impressed with the necessity for seeking such a mode of dealing with these difficulties as may for ever remove them." In addition to this expression of opinion on the part of the representatives of the Conservative government of 1858, the Reformers of Upper Canada held a large and influential convention at Toronto in 1859, and adopted a resolution in which it was emphatically set forth, "that the best practicable remedy for the evils now encountered in the government of Canada is to be found in the formation of two or more local governments to which shall be committed the control of all matters of a local and sectional character, and some general authority charged with such matters as are necessarily common to both sections of the provinces"—language almost identical with that used by the Quebec convention six years later in one of its resolutions with respect to the larger scheme of federation. Mr. George Brown brought this scheme before the assembly in 1860, but it was rejected by a large majority. At this time constitutional and political difficulties of a serious nature had arisen between the French and English speaking sections of the united Canadian provinces. A large and influential party in Upper Canada had become deeply dissatisfied with the conditions of the union of 1840, which maintained equality of representation to the two provinces when statistics clearly showed that the western section exceeded French Canada both in population and wealth.

A demand was persistently and even fiercely made at times for such a readjustment of the representation in the assembly as would do full justice to the more populous and richer province. The French Canadian leaders resented this demand as an attempt to violate the terms on which they were brought into the union, and as calculated, and indeed intended, to place them in a position of inferiority to the people of a province where such fierce and unjust attacks were systematically made on their language, religion, and institutions generally. With much justice they pressed the fact that at the commencement of, and for some years subsequent to, the union, the French Canadians were numerically in the majority, and yet had no larger representation in the assembly than the inhabitants of the upper province, then inferior in population. Mr. George Brown, who had under his control a powerful newspaper, the *Globe*, of Toronto, was remarkable for his power of invective and his tenacity of purpose, and he made persistent and violent attacks upon the conditions of the union, and upon the French and English Conservatives, who were not willing to violate a solemn contract.

The difficulties between the Canadian provinces at last became so intensified by the public opinion created by Mr. Brown in Upper Canada in favour of representation by population, that good and stable government was no longer possible on account of the close division of parties in the legislature. Appeals were made frequently to the people, and new ministries formed,—in fact, five within two years—but the sectional difficulties had obviously reached a point where it was not possible to carry on successfully the administration of public affairs. On the 14th June, 1864, a committee of the legislative assembly of Canada, of whom Mr. Brown was chairman, reported that "a strong feeling was found to exist among the members of the committee in favour of changes in the direction of a federal system, applied either to Canada alone or to the whole of the

British North American provinces." On the day when this report was presented, the Conservative government, known as the Taché-Macdonald ministry, suffered the fate of many previous governments for years, and it became necessary either to appeal at once to the people, or find some other practical solution of the political difficulties which prevented the formation of a stable government. Then it was that Mr. Brown rose above the level of mere party selfishness, and assumed the attitude of a statesman, animated by patriotic and noble impulses which must help us to forget the spirit of sectionalism and illiberality which so often animated him in his career of heated partisanship. Negotiations took place between Mr. John A. Macdonald, Mr. Brown, Mr. Cartier, Mr. Galt, Mr. Morris, Mr. McDougall, Mr. Mowat, and other prominent members of the Conservative and Reform parties, with the result that a coalition government was formed on the distinct understanding that it would "bring in a measure next session for the purpose of removing existing difficulties by introducing the federal principle into Canada, coupled with such provisions as will permit the maritime provinces and the north-west territories to be incorporated into the same system of government." The Reformers who entered the government with Macdonald and Cartier on this fundamental condition were Mr. Brown, Mr. Oliver Mowat, and Mr. William McDougall, who stood deservedly high in public estimation.

While these events were happening in the Canadas, the maritime provinces were taking steps in the direction of their own union. In 1861 Mr. Howe, the leader of a Liberal government in Nova Scotia, carried a resolution in favour of such a scheme. Three years later the Conservative ministry of which Dr., now Sir, Charles Tupper, was premier, took measures in the legislature of Nova Scotia to carry out the proposition of his predecessor; and a conference was arranged at Charlottetown between delegates from the three provinces of Nova Scotia, New Brunswick, and Prince Edward Island By a happy forethought the government of Canada, immediately on hearing of this important conference, decided to send a delegation, composed of Messrs J.A. Macdonald, Brown, Cartier, Galt, McGee, Langevin, McDougall, and Campbell. The result of the conference was favourable to the consideration of the larger question of the union of all the provinces; and it was decided to hold a further conference at

Quebec in October for the purpose of discussing the question as fully as its great importance demanded.

SECTION 2.—The Quebec convention of 1864.

Thirty-three delegates met in the parliament house of this historic city. They were all men of large experience in the work of administration or legislation in their respective provinces. Not a few of them were noted lawyers who had thoroughly studied the systems of government in other countries. Some were gifted with rare eloquence and power of argument. At no time, before or since, has the city of Quebec been visited by an assemblage of notables with so many high qualifications for the foundation of a nation. Descendants of the pioneers of French Canada, English Canadians sprung from the Loyalists of the eighteenth century, eloquent Irishmen and astute Scotchmen, all, thoroughly conversant with Canadian interests, met in a convention summoned to discharge the greatest responsibilities ever entrusted to any body of men in Canada.

The chairman was Sir Etienne Paschal Taché, who had proved in his youth his fidelity to England on the famous battlefield of Chateauguay, and had won the respect of all classes and parties by the display of many admirable qualities. Like the majority of his compatriots he had learned to believe thoroughly in the government and institutions of Great Britain, and never lost an opportunity of recognising the benefits which his race derived from British connection. He it was who gave utterance to the oft-quoted words: "That the last gun that would be fired for British supremacy in America would be fired by a French Canadian." He lived to move the resolutions of the Quebec convention in the legislative council of Canada, but he died a few months before the union was formally established in 1867, and never had an opportunity of experiencing the positive advantages which his race, of whose interests he was always an earnest exponent, derived from a condition of things which gave additional guarantees for the preservation of their special institutions. But there were in the convention other men of much greater political force, more deeply versed in constitutional knowledge, more capable of framing a plan of union than the esteemed and discreet president. Most prominent among these was

Mr., afterwards Sir, John A. Macdonald, who had been for years one of the most conspicuous figures in Canadian politics, and had been able to win to a remarkable degree the confidence not only or the great majority of the French Canadians but also of a powerful minority in the western province where his able antagonist, Mr. Brown, until 1864 held the vantage ground by his persistency in urging its claims to greater weight in the administration of public affairs. Mr. Macdonald had a great knowledge of men and did not hesitate to avail himself of their weaknesses in order to strengthen his political power. His greatest faults were those of a politician anxious for the success of his party. His strength lay largely in his ability to understand the working of British institutions, and in his recognition of the necessity of carrying on the government in a country of diverse nationalities, on principles of justice and compromise. He had a happy faculty of adapting himself to the decided current of public opinion even at the risk of leaving himself open to a charge of inconsistency, and he was just as ready to adopt the measures of his opponents as he was willing to enter their ranks and steal away some prominent men whose support he thought necessary to his political success.

So early as 1861 he had emphatically expressed himself on the floor of the assembly in favour of the main principles of just such a federal union as was initiated at Quebec. The moment he found that the question of union was likely to be something more than a mere subject for academic discussion or eloquent expression in legislative halls, he recognised immediately the great advantages it offered, not only for the solution of the difficulties of his own party, but also for the consolidation of British American as well as imperial interests on the continent of North America From the hour when he became convinced of this fact he devoted his consummate ability not merely as a party leader, but as a statesman of broad national views, to the perfection of a measure which promised so much for the welfare and security of the British provinces. It was his good fortune, after the establishment of the federation, to be the first premier of the new Dominion and to mould its destinies with a firm and capable hand. He saw it extended to the Pacific shores long before he died, amid the regrets of all classes and creeds and races of a country he loved and in whose future he had the most perfect confidence.

The name of the Right Honourable Sir John Macdonald, to give him the titles he afterwards received from the crown, naturally brings up that of Mr., afterwards Sir, George Etienne Cartier, who was his faithful colleague and ally for many years in the legislature of old Canada, and for a short time after the completion of the federal union, until his death. This able French Canadian had taken an insignificant part in the unfortunate rising of 1837, but like many other men of his nationality he recognised the mistakes of his impetuous youth, and, unlike Papineau after the union of 1840, endeavoured to work out earnestly and honestly the principles of responsible government. While a true friend of his race, he was generous and fair in his relations with other nationalities, and understood the necessity of compromise and conciliation in a country of diverse races, needs, and interests. Sir John Macdonald appreciated at their full value his statesmanlike qualities, and succeeded in winning his sympathetic and faithful co-operation during the many years they acted together in opposition to the war of nationalities which would have been the eventual consequence of Mr. Brown's determined agitation if it had been carried to its logical and natural conclusion—conclusion happily averted by the wise stand taken by Mr. Brown himself with respect to the settlement of provincial troubles. In the settlement of the terms of union, we can see not only the master hand of Sir John Macdonald in the British framework of the system, but also the successful effort of Sir George Cartier to preserve intact the peculiar institutions of his native province.

All those who have studied Mr. Brown's career know something of his independent and uncompromising character; but for some time after he entered the coalition government his speeches in favour of federation assumed a dignified style and a breadth of view which stand out in great contrast with his bitter arguments as leader of the Clear Grits. In the framing of the Quebec resolutions his part was chiefly in arranging the financial terms with a regard to the interests of his own province.

Another influential member of the Canadian delegation was Mr., afterwards Sir, Alexander Galt, the son of the creator of that original character in fiction, Laurie Todd, who had been a resident for many years in Western Canada, where a pretty city perpetuates his name. His able son had been for a long time a prominent figure in Canadian politics, and was distinguished for his intelligent advocacy of railway construction and political union as measures essential to the material and political development of the provinces. His earnest and eloquent exposition of the necessity of union had no doubt much to do with creating a wide-spread public sentiment in its favour, and with preparing the way for the formation of the coalition government of 1864, on the basis of such a political measure. His knowledge of financial and commercial questions was found to be invaluable in the settlement of the financial basis of the union, while his recognised position as a representative of the Protestant English-speaking people in French Canada gave him much weight when it was a question of securing their rights and interests in the Quebec resolutions.

The other members of the Canadian delegation were men of varied accomplishments, some of whom played an important part in the working out of the federal system, the foundations of which they laid. There was a brilliant Irishman, Thomas D'Arcy McGee, poet, historian and orator, who had been in his rash youth obliged to fly from Ireland to the United States on account of his connection with the rebellious party known as Young Ireland during the troubles of 1848. When he removed from the United States in 1857 he advocated with much force a union of the provinces in the *New Era*, of which he was editor during its short existence. He was elected to parliament in 1858, and became a notable figure in Canadian politics on account of his eloquence and *bonhomie*. His most elaborate addresses had never the easy flow of Joseph Howe's speeches, but were laboured essays, showing too obviously the results of careful compilation in libraries, while brightened by touches of natural humour. He had been president of the council in the Sandfield Macdonald government of 1862—a moderate Reform ministry—but later he joined the Liberal-Conservative party as less sectional in its aspirations and more generous in its general policy than the one led by Mr. Brown. Mr. McGee was during his residence in Canada a firm friend of the British connection, having observed the beneficent character of British rule in his new Canadian home, with whose interests he so thoroughly identified himself.

Mr. William McDougall, the descendant of a Loyalist, had been long connected with the advocacy of Reform principles in the press and on the floor of parliament, and was distinguished for his clear, incisive style of debating. He had been for years a firm believer in the advantages of union, which he had been the first to urge at the Reform convention of 1859. Mr., afterwards Sir, Alexander Campbell, who had been for some years a legal partner of Sir John Macdonald, was gifted with a remarkably clear intellect, great common sense, and business capacity, which he displayed later as leader of the senate and as minister of the crown. Mr., afterwards Sir, Oliver Mowat, who had been a student of law in Sir John Macdonald's office at Kingston, brought to the discharge of the important positions he held in later times as minister, vice-chancellor, and premier of the province of Ontario, great legal learning, and admirable judgment. Mr., now Sir, Hector Langevin was considered a man of promise, likely to exercise in the future much influence among his countrymen. For some years after the establishment of the new Dominion he occupied important positions in the government of the country, and led the French Conservative party after the death of Sir George Cartier. Mr. James Cockburn was an excellent lawyer, who three years later was chosen speaker of the first house of commons of the federal parliament—a position which his sound judgment, knowledge of parliamentary law, and dignity of manner enabled him to discharge with signal ability. Mr. J.C. Chapais was a man of sound judgment, which made him equal to the administrative duties entrusted to him from time to time.

Of the five men sent by Nova Scotia, the two ablest were Dr., now Sir, Charles Tupper, who was first minister of the Conservative government, and Mr., later Sir, Adams G. Archibald, who was leader of the Liberal opposition in the assembly. The former was then as now distinguished for his great power as a debater and for the forcible expression of his opinions on the public questions on which he had made up his mind. When he had a great end in view he followed it with a tenacity of purpose that generally gave him success. Ever since he entered public life as an opponent of Mr. Howe, he has been a dominant force in the politics of Nova Scotia. While Conservative in name he entertained broad Liberal views which found expression in the improvement of the school system, at a very low ebb when he came into office, and in the readiness and energy with which he identified himself with the cause of the union of the provinces. Mr. Archibald was noted for his dignified demeanour, sound legal attainments, and clear plausible style of oratory, well calculated to instruct a learned audience. Mr. William A. Henry was a lawyer of considerable ability, who was at a later time elevated to the bench of the supreme court of Canada. Mr. Jonathan J. McCully, afterwards a judge in Nova Scotia, had never sat in the assembly, but he exercised influence in the legislative council on the Liberal side and was an editorial writer of no mean ability. Mr. Dickey was a leader of the Conservatives in the upper house and distinguished for his general culture and legal knowledge.

New Brunswick sent seven delegates, drawn from the government and opposition. The Loyalists who founded this province were represented by four of the most prominent members of the delegation, Tilley, Chandler, Gray, and Fisher. Mr., afterwards Sir, Samuel Leonard Tilley had been long engaged in public life and possessed admirable ability as an administrator. He had for years taken a deep interest in questions of intercolonial trade, railway intercourse and political union. He was a Reformer of pronounced opinions, most earnest in the advocacy of temperance, possessed of great tact and respected for his high character in all the relations of life. In later times he became finance minister of the Dominion and lieutenant-governor of his native province.

Mr. John Hamilton Gray, later a judge in British Columbia, was one of the most eloquent and accomplished men in the convention, and brought to the consideration of legal and constitutional questions much knowledge and experience. Mr. Fisher, afterwards a judge in his province, was also a well equipped lawyer and speaker who displayed a cultured mind. Like all the delegates from New Brunswick he was animated by a great love for British connection and institutions. Mr. Peter Mitchell was a Liberal, conspicuous for the energy he brought to the administration of public affairs, both in his own province and at a later time in the new Dominion as a minister of the crown. Mr. Edward Barron Chandler had long been a notable figure in the politics of New Brunswick, and was universally respected for his probity and worth. He had the honour of being at a later time the lieutenant-governor of the province with which he had been so long and honourably associated. Mr. John Johnson and Mr. William H. Steeves were also fully qualified to deal intelligently with the questions submitted to the convention.

Of the seven members of the Prince Edward Island delegation, four were members of the government and the rest were prominent men in one or other branch of the legislature. Colonel Gray—a descendant of a Virginia Loyalist—was prime minister of the island. Mr. George Coles was one of the fathers of responsible government in the island, and long associated with the advocacy and passage of many progressive measures, including the improvement of the educational system. Mr. Edward Whelan was a journalist, an Irishman by birth, and endowed, like so many of his countrymen, with a natural gift of eloquence. Mr. Thomas Heath Haviland, afterwards lieutenant-governor of the island, was a man of culture, and Mr. Edward Palmer was a lawyer of good reputation. Mr. William H. Pope and Mr. Andrew Archibald Macdonald were also thoroughly capable of watching over the special interests of the island.

Newfoundland had the advantage of being represented by Mr. Frederick B.T. Carter, then speaker of the house of assembly, and by Mr. Ambrose Shea, also a distinguished politician of the great island. Both were knighted at later times; the former became chief justice of his own province, and the latter governor of the Bahamas.

SECTION 3.—Confederation accomplished.

The Quebec convention sat with closed doors for eighteen days, and agreed to seventy-two resolutions, which form the basis of the Act of Union, subsequently passed by the imperial parliament. These resolutions set forth at the outset that in a federation of the British American provinces "the system of government best adapted under existing circumstances to protect the diversified interests of the several provinces, and secure harmony and permanency in the working of the union, would be a general government charged with matters of common interest to the whole country, and local governments for each of the Canadas, and for the provinces of Nova Scotia, New Brunswick, and Prince Edward Island, charged with the control of local matters in their respective sections" In another paragraph the resolutions declared that "in forming a constitution for a general government, the conference, with a view to the perpetuation of our connection with the mother-country, and the promotion of the best interests of the people of these provinces, desire to follow the model of the British constitution so far as our circumstances permit" In a subsequent paragraph it was set forth: "the executive authority or government shall be vested in the sovereign of the United Kingdom of Great Britain and Ireland, and be administered according to the well-understood principles of the British constitution, by a sovereign personally, or by the representative of the sovereign duly authorised."

In these three paragraphs of the Quebec resolutions we see clearly expressed the leading principles on which the Canadian federation rests—a federation, with a central government having jurisdiction over matters of common interest to the whole country comprised in the union, and a number of provincial governments having the control and management of certain local matters naturally and conveniently belonging to them, each government being administered in accordance with the well-understood principles of the British system of parliamentary institutions.

The resolutions also defined in express terms the respective powers of the central and provincial governments. Any subject that did not fall within the enumerated powers of the provincial legislatures was placed under the control of the general parliament. The convention recognised the necessity of preventing, as far as possible, the difficulties that had arisen in the working of the constitution of the United States, where the residuary power of legislation is given to the people of the respective states and not to the federal government. In a subsequent chapter I give a brief summary of these and other details of the system of government, generally laid down in the Quebec resolutions and practically embodied in an imperial statute three years later.

Although we have no official report of the discussions of the Quebec convention, we know on good authority that the question of providing revenues for the provinces was one that gave the delegates the greatest difficulty. In all the provinces the sources of revenue were chiefly customs and excise-duties which had to be set apart for the general government of the federation. Some of the delegates from Ontario, where there had existed for many years an admirable system of municipal government, which provided funds for education and local improvements, recognised the advantages of direct taxation; but the representatives of the other provinces would not consent to such a system, especially in the case of Nova Scotia, New Brunswick, and Prince Edward Island, where there were no municipal institutions, and the people depended almost exclusively on the annual votes of the legislature for the means to meet their local necessities. All of the delegates, in fact, felt that to force the maritime provinces to resort to direct taxes as the only method of carrying on their government, would be probably fatal to the success of the scheme, and it was finally decided that the central government should grant annual subsidies, based on population, relative debts, financial position, and such other facts as should be fairly brought into the consideration of the case.

It is unfortunate that we have no full report of the deliberations and debates of this great conference. We have only a fragmentary record from which it is difficult to form any adequate conclusions as to the part taken by the several delegates in the numerous questions which necessarily came under their purview.[4] Under these circumstances, a careful writer hesitates to form any positive opinion based upon these reports of the discussions, but no one can doubt that the directing spirit of the conference was Sir John Macdonald. Meagre as is the record of what he said, we can yet see that his words were those of a man who rose above the level of the mere politician, and grasped the magnitude of the questions involved. What he aimed at especially was to follow as closely as possible the fundamental principles of English parliamentary government, and to engraft them upon the general system of federal union. Mr. George Brown took a prominent part in the deliberations. His opinions read curiously now. He was in favour of having the lieutenant-governors appointed by the general government, and he was willing to give them an effective veto over provincial legislation. He advocated the election of a legislative chamber on a fixed day every third year, not subject to a dissolution during its term—also an adaptation of the American system. He went so far as to urge the advisability of having the executive council elected for three years—by the assembly, we may assume, though the imperfect report before us does not state so—and also of giving the lieutenant-governor the right of dismissing any of its members when the house was not sitting. Mr. Brown consequently appears to have been the advocate, so far as the provinces were concerned, of principles that prevail in the federal republic across the border. He opposed the introduction of responsible government, as it now obtains, in all the provinces of the Dominion, while conceding its necessity for the central government.

[4: Mr. Joseph Pope, for years the able confidential secretary of Sir John Macdonald, has edited and published all the official documents bearing on the origin and evolution of the British North America Act of 1867; but despite all the ability and fidelity he has devoted to the task the result is most imperfect and unsatisfactory on account of the absence of any full or exact original report of proceedings.]

We gather from the report of discussions that the Prince Edward Island delegates hesitated from the beginning to enter a union where their province would necessarily have so small a numerical representation—one of the main objections which subsequently operated against the island coming into the confederation. With respect to education we see that it was Mr., afterwards Sir, Alexander Galt, who was responsible for the provision in the constitution which gives the general government and parliament a certain control over provincial legislation in case the rights of a Protestant or a Roman Catholic minority are prejudicially affected. The minutes on this point are defective, but we have the original motion on the subject, and a note of Sir John Macdonald himself that it was passed, with the assent of all the provinces, at the subsequent London conference in 1867. The majority of the delegates appear from the outset to have supported strenuously the principle which lies at the basis of the confederation, that all powers not expressly reserved to the provinces should appertain to the general government, as against the opposite principle, which, as Sir John Macdonald pointed out, had led to great difficulties in the working of the federal system in the United States. Sir John Macdonald also, with his usual sagacity, showed that, in all cases of conflict of jurisdiction, recourse would be necessarily made to the courts, as was the practice even then whenever there was a conflict between imperial and Canadian statutes.

Addresses to the Queen embodying the Quebec resolutions were submitted to the legislature of Canada during the winter of 1865, and passed in both houses by large majorities after a very full discussion of the merits of the scheme. The opposition in the assembly came chiefly from Mr. Antoine A. Dorion, Mr. Luther H. Holton, Mr. Dunkin, Mr. Lucius Seth Huntington, Mr. John Sandfield Macdonald, and other able Liberals who were not disposed to follow Mr. Brown and his two colleagues in their patriotic abandonment of "partyism."

The vote on the address was, in the council—Contents 45, Non-contents 15. In the assembly it stood—Yeas 91, Nays 33. The minority in the assembly comprised 25 out of 65 representatives of French Canada, and only 8 out of the 65 from Upper Canada. With the speaker in the chair there were only 5 members absent on the taking of the final vote.

Efforts were made both in the council and assembly to obtain an unequivocal expression of public opinion at the polls before the address was submitted to the imperial government for final action. It was argued with much force that the legislature had had no special mandate from the people to carry out so vital a change in the political condition of the provinces, but this argument had relatively little weight in either house in view of the dominant public sentiment which, as it was obvious to the most superficial observer, existed in the valley of the St. Lawrence in favour of a scheme which seemed certain to settle the difficulties so long in the way of stable government, and offered so many auspicious auguries for the development of the provinces embraced in federation.

Soon after the close of the session Messrs Macdonald, Galt, Cartier, and Brown went to England to confer with the imperial authorities on various matters of grave public import. The British government agreed to guarantee a loan for the construction of the Intercolonial Railway and gave additional assurances of their deep interest in the proposed confederation. An understanding was reached with respect to the mutual obligations of the parent state and the dependency to provide for the defences of the country. Preliminary steps were taken in the direction of acquiring the north-west from the Hudson's Bay Company on equitable terms whenever their exact legal rights were ascertained. The report of the delegates was laid before the Canadian parliament during a very short session held in August and September of 1865. It was then that parliament formally ratified the Civil Code of Lower Canada, with which must be always honourably associated the name of Mr. Cartier.

In the maritime provinces, however, the prospect for some months was far from encouraging. Much dissatisfaction was expressed with the financial terms, and the haste with which the maritime delegates had yielded to the propositions of the Canadian government and given their adhesion to the larger scheme, when they were only authorised in the first instance by their respective legislatures to consider the feasibility of a union of Nova Scotia, New Brunswick, and Prince Edward Island. In New Brunswick Mr. Tilley found himself in a minority as a result of an appeal to the people on the question in 1865, but his successor Mr., afterwards Sir, Albert Smith, minister of marine in the Mackenzie government of 1873-78, was forced to resign a year later on some question purposely raised by Lieutenant-Governor Hamilton Gordon, then very anxious to carry the union before he left the province. A new government was immediately formed by Mr. Peter Mitchell, a very energetic Liberal politician—the first minister of marine in the first Dominion ministry—who had notoriously influenced the lieutenant-governor in his arbitrary action of practically dismissing the Smith cabinet. On an appeal to the people Mr. Mitchell was sustained, and the new legislature gave its approval to the union by a large majority. The opinion then generally prevailed in New Brunswick that a federation was essential to the security of the provinces, then threatened by the Fenians, and would strengthen the hands of the parent state on the American continent. In Nova Scotia the situation was aggravated by the fact that the opposition was led by Mr. Howe, who had always been the idol of a large party in the country, and an earnest and consistent supporter of the right of the people to be first consulted on every measure immediately affecting their interests. He succeeded in creating a powerful sentiment against the terms of the measure—especially the financial conditions—and it was not possible during 1865 to carry it in the legislature. It was not attempted to submit the question to the polls, as was done in New Brunswick, indeed such a course would have been fatal to its progress; but it was eventually sanctioned by a large vote of the two houses. A strong influence was exerted by the fact that confederation was approved by the imperial government, which sent out Sir Fenwick Williams of Kars as lieutenant-governor with special instructions that, both Canada and New Brunswick having given their consent, it was proposed to make such changes in the financial terms as would be more favourable to the maritime provinces. In Prince Edward Island and Newfoundland it was not possible for the advocates of federation to move successfully in the matter. The opposition to the scheme of union, as proposed at Quebec, was so bitter in these two provinces that the delegates found it useless to press the matter in their legislatures.

In the meantime, while confederation was on the eve of accomplishment, the people of Canada were subjected to an attack which supplied the strongest possible evidence of the necessity for a union enabling them to combine for purposes of general defence as well as other matters of national importance. In the month of April, 1866, the Fenians, an Irish organisation in the United States, made an insignificant demonstration on the New Brunswick frontier, which had no other effect than to excite the loyal action of the people of the province and strengthen the hands of the advocates of confederation. In the beginning of June a considerable body of the same order, under the command of one O'Neil, crossed from Buffalo into the Niagara district of Upper Canada and won a temporary success near Ridgeway, where the Queen's Own, a body of Toronto Volunteers, chiefly students and other young men, were badly handled by Colonel Booker. Subsequently Colonel Dennis and a small detachment of militia were surprised at Fort Erie by O'Neil. The knowledge that a large force of regulars and volunteers were marching against him under Colonel Peacock forced O'Neil and his men to disperse and find their way back to the United States, where a number were arrested by the orders of the Washington government. The Eastern Townships of Lower Canada were also invaded but the raiders retreated before a Canadian force with greater rapidity than they had shown in entering the province, and found themselves prisoners as soon as they crossed the frontier. Canada was kept in a state of anxiety for some months after these reckless invasions of a country where the Irish like all other nationalities have always had the greatest possible freedom; but the vigilance of the authorities and the readiness of the people of Canada to defend their soil prevented any more hostile demonstrations from the United States. The prisoners taken in the Niagara district were treated with a degree of clemency which their shameless conduct did not merit from an outraged people. No persons were ever executed, though a number were confined for a while in Kingston penitentiary. The invasion had the effect of stimulating the patriotism of the Canadian people to an extraordinary degree, and of showing them the necessity that existed for improving their home forces, whose organisation and equipment proved sadly defective during the invasion.

In the summer of 1866 the Canadian legislature met for the last time under the provisions of the Union Act of 1840, and passed addresses to the Queen, setting forth constitutions for the new provinces of Upper and Lower Canada, afterwards incorporated in the imperial act of union. A conference of delegates from the provinces of Nova Scotia, New Brunswick, and Canada was held in the December of 1866 at the Westminster Palace Hotel in the City of London. The members on behalf of Canada were Messrs Macdonald, Cartier, Galt, McDougall, Langevin, and W.P. Howland (in the place of Mr. Brown); on behalf of Nova Scotia, Messrs Tupper, Henry, McCully, Archibald, and J.W. Ritchie (who took Mr. Dickey's place); of New Brunswick, Messrs Tilley, Johnson, Mitchell, Fisher, and R.D. Wilmot. The last named, who took the place of Mr. Steeves, was a Loyalist by descent, and afterwards became speaker of the senate and a lieutenant-governor of his native province. Their deliberations led to some changes in the financial provisions of the Quebec plan, made with the view of satisfying the opposition as far as possible in the maritime provinces but without disturbing the fundamental basis to which Canada had already pledged itself in the legislative session of 1865. All the difficulties being now removed the Earl of Carnarvon, then secretary of state for the colonies, submitted to the house of lords on the 17th of February, 1867, a bill intituled, "An act for the union of Canada, Nova Scotia, and New Brunswick, and the government thereof; and for purposes connected therewith." It passed the two houses with very little discussion, and the royal assent was given to it on the 29th of March of the same year as "The British North America Act, 1867." It is interesting to know that in the original draft of the bill the united provinces were called the "Kingdom of Canada," but when it came eventually before parliament they were designated as the "Dominion of Canada"; and the writer had it from Sir John Macdonald himself that this amendment did not emanate from the colonial delegates but from the imperial ministry, one of whose members was afraid of wounding the susceptibilities of United States statesmen.

During the same session the imperial parliament passed a bill to guarantee a loan of three million pounds sterling for the construction of an intercolonial railway between Quebec and the coast of the maritime provinces—a work recognised as indispensable to the success of the new federation. Her Majesty's proclamation, giving effect to the Union Act, was issued on the 22nd May, 1867, declaring that "on and after the first of July, 1867, the provinces of Canada, Nova Scotia, and New Brunswick, shall form and be one Dominion, under the name of Canada."

CHAPTER IX.

CONFEDERATION. 1867—1900.

SECTION I—The first parliament of the Dominion of Canada. 1867—1872.

The Dominion of Canada took its place among the federal states of the world on the first of July, 1867. Upper and Lower Canada now became known as Ontario and Quebec, while Nova Scotia and New Brunswick retained their original historic names. The first governor-general was Viscount Monk, who had been head of the executive government of Canada throughout all the stages of confederation. He was an Irish nobleman, who had been a junior lord of the treasury in Lord Palmerston's government. He was a collateral descendant of the famous general of the commonwealth, created Duke of Albemarle after the Restoration. Without being a man of remarkable ability he was gifted with much discretion, and gave all the weight of his influence to bring about a federation, whose great benefits from an imperial as well as a colonial point of view he fully recognised.

The prime minister of the first federal government was naturally Sir John Macdonald, who chose as his colleagues Sir George E. Cartier, Sir S.L. Tilley,—to give them all their later titles—Sir A.T. Galt, Sir W.P. Howland, Mr. William McDougall, Mr. P. Mitchell, Sir A.G. Archibald, Mr. A.F. Blair, Sir A. Campbell, Sir H.L. Langevin, Sir E. Kenny, and Mr. J.C. Chapais. Mr. Brown had retired from the coalition government of 1864 some months before the union, nominally on a disagreement with his colleagues as to the best mode of conducting negotiations for a new reciprocity treaty with the United States. The ministry had appointed delegates to confer with the Washington government on the subject, but, while Mr. Brown recognised the desirability of reciprocal trade relations with the United States on equitable conditions, he did not deem it expedient to appear before American statesmen "as suitors for any terms they might be pleased to grant." A general impression, however, prevailed that this difference of opinion was not the real reason of Mr. Brown's resignation, but that the animating motive was his intense jealousy of Sir John Macdonald, whose dominant influence in the government he could no longer brook.

The governments of the four provinces were also regularly constituted at this time in accordance with the act of union. The first lieutenant-governor of Ontario was Lieutenant-General Stisted, of Quebec, Sir Narcisse Belleau; of Nova Scotia, Lieutenant-General Sir Fenwick Williams, the hero of Kars; of New Brunswick, Major-General Doyle, but only for three months. With the exception of the case of Quebec, these appointments were only temporary. It was considered prudent to select military men in view of the continuous reports of Fenian aggression. Sir William Howland became, a year later, lieutenant-governor of Ontario, Major-General Sir Francis Hastings Doyle of Nova Scotia in the fall of 1867, and Hon. L.A. Wilmot, of New Brunswick in July 1868. The first prime minister of Ontario was Mr. John Sandfield Macdonald, who had been leader of a Canadian ministry before confederation. He had been a moderate Liberal in politics, and opposed at the outset to the federal union, but before 1867 he became identified with the Liberal-Conservative party and gave his best assistance to the success of the federation. In Quebec, Mr. Pierre Chauveau, a man of high culture, formed the first government, which was also associated with the Liberal-Conservative party. In New Brunswick, Attorney-General Wetmore was the first prime minister, but he was appointed a judge in 1870, and Mr. George E. King, a judge of the supreme court of Canada some years later, became his successor. In Nova Scotia, Mr. Hiram Blanchard, a Liberal and unionist, formed a government, but it was defeated at the elections by an overwhelming majority by the anti-unionists, and Mr. Annand, the old friend of Mr. Howe, became first minister.

The elections for the Dominion house of commons took place in the summer of 1867, and Sir John Macdonald's government was sustained by nearly three-fourths of the entire representation. The most notable incident in this contest was the defeat of Mr. Brown. Soon after his resignation in 1866 he assumed his old position of hostility to Sir John Macdonald and the Conservatives. At a later date, when the Liberals were in office, he accepted a seat in the senate, but in the meantime he continued to manage the *Globe* and denounce his too successful and wily antagonist in its columns with his usual vehemence.

The first parliament of the new Dominion met in the autumn of 1867 in the new buildings at Ottawa—also chosen as the seat of government of the federation—and was probably the ablest body of men that ever assembled for legislative purposes within the limits of old or new Canada. In the absence of the legislation which was subsequently passed both in Ontario and Quebec against dual representation—or the election of the same representatives to both the Dominion parliament and the local legislatures—it comprised the leading public men of all parties in the two provinces in question. Such legislation had been enacted in the maritime provinces before 1867, but it did not prevent the ablest men of New Brunswick from selecting the larger and more ambitious field of parliamentary action. In Nova Scotia Sir Charles Tupper was the only man who emerged from the battle in which so many unionists were for the moment defeated. Even Sir Adams Archibald, the secretary of state, was defeated in a county where he had been always returned by a large majority. Mr. Howe came in at the head of a strong phalanx of anti-unionists—"Repealers" as they called themselves for a short time.

The legislation of the first parliament during its five years of existence was noteworthy in many respects. The departments of government were reorganised with due regard to the larger interests now intrusted to their care. The new department of marine and fisheries, rendered necessary by the admission of the maritime provinces, was placed under the direction of Mr. Peter Mitchell, then a member of the senate, who had done so much to bring New Brunswick into the union. An act was passed to provide for the immediate commencement of the Intercolonial Railway, which was actually completed by the 1st of July, 1876, under the supervision of Mr., now Sir, Sandford Fleming, as chief government engineer; and the provinces of Ontario and Quebec were at last directly connected with the maritime sections of the Dominion.

The repeal agitation in Nova Scotia received its first blow by the defection of Mr. Howe, who had been elected to the house of commons. He proceeded to England in 1868 with an address from the assembly of Nova Scotia, demanding a repeal of the union, but he made no impression whatever on a government and parliament convinced of the necessity of the measure from an imperial as well as colonial point of view. Dr. Tupper was present on behalf of the Dominion government to answer any arguments that the Repealers might advance against the union. The visit to England convinced Mr. Howe that further agitation on the question might be injurious to British connection, and that the wisest course was to make the union as useful as possible to the provinces. Then, as always, he was true to those principles of fidelity to the crown and empire which had forced his father to seek refuge in Nova Scotia, and which had been ever the mainspring of his action, even in the trying days when he and others were struggling for responsible government. He believed always in constitutional agitation, not in rebellion. He now agreed to enter the ministry as president of the council on condition that the financial basis, on which Nova Scotia had been admitted to the federation, was enlarged by the parliament of Canada. These "better terms" were brought before the Canadian parliament in the session of 1869, and provided for the granting of additional allowances to the provinces, calculated on increased amounts of debt as compared with the maximum fixed by the terms of the British North America Act of 1867. They met with strong opposition from Edward Blake, a very eminent lawyer and Reformer of Ontario, on the ground that they violated the original compact of union as set forth in the British North America Act; but despite the opposition of the western Reformers they were ratified by a large majority, who recognised the supreme necessity of conciliating Nova Scotia. On account of his decision to yield to the inevitable, Mr. Howe incurred the bitter antagonism of many men who had been his staunch followers in all the political contests of Nova Scotia, and it was with the greatest difficulty that he was re-elected for the county of Hants as a minister of the crown. He remained in the government until May, 1873, when he was appointed lieutenant-governor of Nova Scotia. The worries of a long life of political struggles, and especially the fatigue and exposure of the last election in Hants, had impaired his health and made it absolutely necessary that he should retire from active politics. Only a month after his appointment, the printer, poet and politician died in the famous old government house, admittance to which had been denied him in the stormy days when he fought Lord Falkland. It was a fit ending, assuredly, to the life of the statesman, who, with eloquent pen and voice, in the days when his opinions were even offensive to governors and social leaders, ever urged the right of his countrymen to a full measure of self-government.

Canada and all other parts of the British empire were deeply shocked on an April day of 1868 by the tragic announcement of the assassination of the brilliant Irishman, Thomas D'Arcy McGee on his return late at night from his parliamentary duties. He had never been forgiven by the Irish enemies of England for his strenuous efforts in Canada to atone for the indiscretion of his thoughtless youth. His remains were buried with all the honours that the state could give him, and proper provision was made for the members of his family by that parliament of which he had been one of the most notable figures. The murderer, Thomas Whelan, a member of the secret society that had ordered his death, was executed at Ottawa on the 11th February, 1869.

SECTION 2.—Extension of the Dominion from the Atlantic to the Pacific Ocean. 1869-1873.

The government and parliament, to whom were entrusted the destinies of the federation of four provinces, had a great work to accomplish in the way of perfecting and extending the Dominion, which was necessarily incomplete whilst its western territorial limits were confined to the boundaries of Ontario, and the provinces of British Columbia on the Pacific coast and of Prince Edward Island in the Gulf of the St. Lawrence remained in a position of isolation. The provisions of the British North America Act of 1867 provided in general terms for the addition of the immense territories which extend from the head of Lake Superior in a north-westerly direction as far as the Rocky Mountains. Three great basins divide these territories; Hudson Bay Basin, with probably a drainage of 2,250,000 square miles; the Winnipeg sub-basin tributary to the former, with nearly 400,000 square miles; the Mackenzie River basin with nearly 700,000 square miles. The Winnipeg basin covers a great area of prairie lands, whose luxuriant grasses and wild flowers were indented for centuries only by the tracks of herds of innumerable buffaloes on their way to the tortuous and sluggish streams which flow through that wide region. This plain slopes gently towards the arctic seas into which its waters flow, and is also remarkable for rising gradually from its eastern limits in three distinct elevations or steppes as far as the foot hills of the Rocky Mountains. Forests of trees, small for the most part, are found only when the prairies are left and we reach the more picturesque undulating country through which the North Saskatchewan flows. An extraordinary feature of this great region is the continuous chain of lakes and rivers which stretch from the basin of the St. Lawrence as far as the distant northern sea into which the Mackenzie, the second largest river in North America, carries its enormous volume of waters. As we stand on the rugged heights of land which divides the Winnipeg from the Laurentian basin we are within easy reach of rivers which flow, some to arctic seas, some to the Atlantic, and some to the Gulf of Mexico. If we ascend the Saskatchewan River, from Lake Winnipeg to the Rocky Mountains, we shall find ourselves within a measurable distance not only of the sources of the Mackenzie, one of whose tributaries reaches the head waters of the Yukon, a river of golden promise like the Pactolus of the eastern lands—but also within reach of the head waters of the rapid Columbia, and the still more impetuous Fraser, both of which pour into the Pacific Ocean, as well as of the Missouri, which here accumulates strength for its alliance with the Mississippi, that great artery of a more southern land. It was to this remarkable geographical feature that Oliver Wendell Holmes referred in the following well-known verses:

> "Yon stream whose sources run
>   Turned by a pebble's edge,
> Is Athabaska rolling toward the Sun
>   Through the cleft mountain ledge."

> "The slender rill had strayed,
>   But for the slanting stone,
> To evening's ocean, with the tangled braid
>   Of foam-flecked Oregon."

A great company claimed for two centuries exclusive trading privileges over a large portion of these territories, known as Rupert's Land, by virtue of a charter given by King Charles II, on the 2nd May, 1670, to Prince Rupert, the Duke of Albemarle, and other

Canada Under British Rule 1760-1900

Englishmen of rank and wealth. The early operations of this Company of Adventurers of England were confined to the vicinity of Hudson and James Bays. The French of Canada for many years disputed the rights of the English company to this great region, but it was finally ceded to England by the Treaty of Utrecht. Twenty years after the Treaty of Paris (1763) a number of wealthy and enterprising merchants, chiefly Scotch, established at Montreal the North-West Company for the purpose of trading in those north-western territories to which French traders had been the first to venture. This new company carried on its operations with such activity that in thirty years' time it employed four thousand persons and occupied sixty posts in different parts of the territories.

The Hudson's Bay Company's headquarters was York Factory, on the great bay to which British ships, every summer, brought out supplies for the posts. The North-West Company followed the route of the old French traders from Lachine by way of the Ottawa or the lakes to the head of Lake Superior, and its principal depot was Fort William on the Kaministiquia River. The servants of the North-West Company became indefatigable explorers of the territories as far as the Pacific Ocean and arctic seas. Mr., afterwards Sir, Alexander Mackenzie first followed the river which now bears his name, to the Arctic Ocean, into which it pours its mighty volume of water. He was also the first to cross the Rocky Mountains and reach the Pacific coast. Simon Fraser, another employee of the company, discovered, in 1808, the river which still recalls his exploits; and a little later, David Thompson, from whom a river is named, crossed further south and reached Oregon by the Columbia River. The energetic operations of the North-west Company so seriously affected the business of the Hudson's Bay Company that in some years the latter declared no dividends. The rivalry between the two companies reached its highest between 1811 and 1818, when Thomas Douglas, fifth Earl of Selkirk, who was an enthusiastic promoter of colonisation in British North America, obtained from the Hudson's Bay Company an immense tract of land in the Red River country and made an earnest effort to establish a Scotch settlement at Kildonan. But his efforts to people Assiniboia—the Indian name he gave to his wide domain—were baulked by the opposition of the employees of the North-west Company, who regarded this colonising scheme as fatal to the fur trade. In the territory conveyed to Lord Selkirk, the Montreal Company had established posts upon every river and lake, while the Hudson's Bay Company had only one fort of importance, Fort Douglas, within a short distance of the North-west Company's post of Fort Gibraltar, at the confluence of the Red and Assiniboine Rivers, where the city of Winnipeg now stands. The quarrel between the Scotch settlers who were under the protection of the Hudson's Bay Company and the North-westers, chiefly composed of French Canadians and French half-breeds, or *Métis* culminated in 1816, in the massacre of Governor Semple and twenty-six other persons connected with the new colony by a number of half-breeds. Two years later, a number of persons who had been arrested for this murder were tried at York in Upper Canada, but the evidence was so conflicting on account of the false swearing on the part of the witnesses that the jury were forced to acquit the accused. Lord Selkirk died at Pau, in 1820, but not before he had made an attempt to assist his young settlement, almost broken up by the shameful attack of 1816.

The little colony managed to exist, but its difficulties were aggravated from time to time by the ravages of clouds of grasshoppers which devastated the territories and brought the people to the verge of starvation. In March, 1821, the North-west Company made over all their property to the older company, which now reigned supreme throughout the territories. All doubts as to their rights were set at rest by an act of parliament giving them a monopoly of trade for twenty-one years in what were then generally known as the Indian territories, that vast region which lay beyond the confines of Rupert's Land, and was not strictly covered by the charter of 1670. This act was re-enacted in 1838 for another twenty-one years. No further extension, however, was ever granted, as an agitation had commenced in Canada by 1859 for the surrender of the company's privileges and the opening up of the territories, so long a great "lone land," to enterprise and settlement. When the two rival companies were united, Mr., afterwards Sir, George Simpson, became governor, and he continued to occupy that position until 1860, when he died in his residence at Lachine, near Montreal. This energetic man largely extended the geographical knowledge of the wide dominions entrusted to his charge, though like all the servants of the company, he discouraged settlement and minimised the agricultural capabilities of the country, when examined in 1857 before a committee of the English house of commons. In 1837 the company purchased from Lord Selkirk's heirs all their rights in Assiniboia. The Scotch settlers and the French half-breeds were now in close contiguity to each other on the Red and Assiniboine Rivers. The company established a simple form of government for the maintenance of law and order. In the course of time, their council included not only their principal factors and officials, but a few persons selected from the inhabitants. On the whole, law and order prevailed in the settlements, although there was always latent a certain degree of sullen discontent against the selfish rule of a mere fur company, invested with such great powers. The great object of the company was always to keep out the pioneers of settlement, and give no information of the value of the land and resources of their vast domain.

Some years before the federation of the British-American provinces the public men of Canada had commenced an agitation against the company, with the view of relieving from its monopoly a country whose resources were beginning to be known. Colonial delegates on several occasions interviewed the imperial authorities on the subject, but no practical results were obtained until federation became an accomplished fact. Then, at length, the company recognised the necessity of yielding to the pressure that was brought to bear upon them by the British government, at a time when the interests of the empire as well as of the new Dominion demanded the abolition of a monopoly so hostile to the conditions of modern progress in British North America. In 1868 successful negotiations took place between a Canadian delegation—Sir George Cartier and the Hon. William Macdougall—and the Hudson's Bay Company's representatives for the surrender of their imperial domain. Canada agreed to pay £300,000 sterling, and to reserve certain lands for the company. The terms were approved by the Canadian parliament in 1869, and an act was passed for the temporary government of Rupert's Land and the North-west territory when regularly transferred to Canada. In the summer of that year, surveyors were sent under Colonel Dennis to make surveys of townships in Assiniboia; and early in the autumn Mr. Macdougall was appointed lieutenant-governor of the territories, with the understanding that he should not act in an official capacity until he was authoritatively informed from Ottawa of the legal transfer of the country to the Canadian government. Mr. Macdougall left for Fort Garry in September, but he was unable to reach Red River on account of a rising of the half-breeds. The cause of the troubles is to be traced not simply to the apathy of the Hudson's Bay Company's officials, who took no steps to prepare the settlers for the change of government, nor to the fact that the Canadian authorities neglected to consult the wishes of the inhabitants, but chiefly to the belief that prevailed among the ignorant French half-breeds that it was proposed to take their lands from them. Sir John Macdonald admitted, at a later time, that much of the trouble arose "from the lack of conciliation, tact and prudence shown by the surveyors during the summer of 1869." Mr. Macdougall also appears to have disobeyed his instructions, for he attempted to set up his government by a *coup-de-main* on the 1st December, though he had no official information of the transfer of the country to Canada, and was not legally entitled to perform a single official act.

The rebellious half-breeds of the Red River settlement formed a provisional government, in which one Louis Riel was the controlling spirit from the beginning until the end of the revolt. He was a French Canadian half-breed, who had been educated in one of the French Canadian colleges, and always exercised much influence over his ignorant, impulsive, easily-deluded countrymen. The total population living in the settlements of Assiniboia at that time was about twelve thousand, of whom nearly one-half were *Métis* or half-breeds, mostly the descendants of the *coureurs-de-bois* and *voyageurs* of early times. So long as the buffalo ranged the prairies in large numbers, they were hunters, and cared nothing for the relatively tame pursuit of agriculture. Their small farms generally presented a neglected, impoverished appearance. The great majority had adopted the habits of their Indian lineage, and would neglect their farms for weeks to follow the scarce buffalo to their distant feeding grounds. The Scotch half-breed, the offspring of the marriage of Scotchmen with Indian women, still illustrated the industry and energy of his paternal race, and rose superior to Indian surroundings. It was among the French half-breeds that Riel found

Canada Under British Rule 1760-1900

his supporters. The Scotch and English settlers had disapproved of the sudden transfer of the territory in which they and their parents had so long lived, without any attempt having been made to consult their feelings as to the future government of the country. Though they took no active part in the rebellion, they allowed matters to take their course with indifference and sullen resignation. The employees of the Hudson's Bay Company were dissatisfied with the sale of the company's rights, as it meant, in their opinion, a loss of occupation and influence. The portion of the population that was always quite ready to hasten the acquisition of the territory by Canada, and resolutely opposed Riel from the outset, was the small Canadian element, which was led by Dr. Schultz, an able, determined man, afterwards lieutenant-governor of Manitoba. Riel imprisoned and insulted several of the loyal party who opposed him. At last he ruthlessly ordered the execution of one Thomas Scott, an Ontario man, who had defied him.

While these events were in progress, the Canadian government enlisted in the interests of law and order the services of Mr. Donald Smith, now Lord Strathcona, who had been long connected with the Hudson's Bay Company, and also of Archbishop Taché, of St. Boniface—the principal French settlement in the country—who returned from Rome to act as mediator between the Canadian authorities and his deluded flock. Unhappily, before the Archbishop could reach Fort Garry, Scott had been murdered, and the Dominion government could not consider themselves bound by the terms they were ready to offer to the insurgents under a very different condition of things. The murder of Scott had clearly brought Riel and his associates under the provisions of the criminal law; and public opinion in Ontario would not tolerate an amnesty, as was hastily promised by the Archbishop, in his zeal to bring the rebellion to an end. A force of 1200 regulars and volunteers was sent to the Red River towards the end of May, 1870, under the command of Colonel Wolseley, now a field-marshal and a peer of the realm. Riel fled across the frontier before the troops, after a tedious journey of three months from the day they left Toronto, reached Fort Garry. Peace was restored once more to the settlers of Assiniboia. The Canadian government had had several interviews with delegates from the discontented people of Red River, who had prepared what they called "a Bill of Rights," and it was therefore able intelligently to decide on the best form of governing the territories. The imperial government completed the formal transfer of the country to Canada, and the Canadian parliament in 1870 passed an act to provide for the government of a new province of Manitoba. Representation was given to the people in both houses of the Canadian parliament, and provision was made for a provincial government on the same basis that existed in the old provinces of the Dominion. The lieutenant-governor of the province was also, for the present, to govern the unorganised portion of the North-west with the assistance of a council of eleven persons. The first legislature of Manitoba was elected in the early part of 1871, and a provincial government was formed, with Mr. Albert Boyd as provincial secretary. The first lieutenant-governor was Sir Adams Archibald, the eminent Nova Scotian, who had been defeated in the elections of 1867. Mr. Macdougall had returned from the North-west frontier a deeply disappointed man, who would never admit that he had shown any undue haste in commencing the exercise of his powers as governor. Some years later he disappeared from active public life, after a career during which he had performed many useful services for Canada.

In another chapter on the relations between Canada and the United States I shall refer to the results of the international commission which met at Washington in 1870, to consider the Alabama difficulty, the fishery dispute, and other questions, the settlement of which could be no longer delayed. In 1870, while the Red River settlements were still in a troublous state, the Fenians made two attempts to invade the Eastern Townships, but they were easily repulsed and forced to cross the frontier. They were next heard of in 1871, when they attempted, under the leadership of the irrepressible O'Neil, who had also been engaged in 1870, and of O'Donohue, one of Riel's rebellious associates, to make a raid into Manitoba by way of Pembina, but their prompt arrest by a company of United States troops was the inglorious conclusion of the last effort of a dying and worthless organisation to strike a blow at England through Canada.

The Dominion government was much embarrassed for some years by the complications that arose from Riel's revolt and the murder of Scott. An agitation grew up in Ontario for the arrest of the murderers; and when Mr. Blake succeeded Mr. Sandfield Macdonald as leader of the Ontario government, a large reward was offered for the capture of Riel and such of his associates as were still in the territories. On the other hand, Sir George Cartier and the French Canadians were in favour of an amnesty. The Macdonald ministry consequently found itself on the horns of a dilemma; and the political tension was only relieved for a time when Riel and Lepine left Manitoba, on receiving a considerable sum of money from Sir John Macdonald. Although this fact was not known until 1875, when a committee of the house of commons investigated the affairs of the North-west, there was a general impression after 1870 throughout Ontario—an impression which had much effect on the general election of 1872—that the government had no sincere desire to bring Riel and his associates to justice.

In 1871 the Dominion welcomed into the union the great mountainous province of British Columbia, whose picturesque shores recall the memories of Cook, Vancouver and other maritime adventurers of the last century, and whose swift rivers are associated with the exploits of Mackenzie, Thompson, Quesnel, Fraser and other daring men, who first saw the impetuous waters which rush through the cañons of the great mountains of the province until at last they empty themselves into the Pacific Ocean. For many years Vancouver Island and the mainland, first known as New Caledonia, were under the control of the Hudson's Bay Company. Vancouver Island was nominally made a crown colony in 1849; that is, a colony without representative institutions, in which the government is carried on by a governor and council, appointed by the crown. The official authority continued from 1851 practically in the hands of the company's chief factor, Sir James Douglas, a man of signal ability, who was also the governor of the infant colony. In 1856 an assembly was called, despite the insignificant population of the island. In 1858 New Caledonia was organised as a crown colony under the name of British Columbia, as a consequence of the gold discoveries which brought in many people. Sir James Douglas was also appointed governor of British Columbia, and continued in that position until 1864. In 1866, the colony was united with Vancouver Island under the general designation of British Columbia. When the province entered the confederation of Canada in 1871 it was governed by a lieutenant-governor appointed by the crown, a legislature composed of heads of the public departments and several elected members. With the entrance of this province, so famous now for its treasures of gold, coal and other minerals in illimitable quantities, must be associated the name of Sir Joseph Trutch, the first lieutenant-governor under the auspices of the federation. The province did not come into the union with the same constitution that was enjoyed by the other provinces, but it was expressly declared in the terms of union that "the government of the Dominion will readily consent to the introduction of responsible government when desired by the inhabitants of British Columbia." Accordingly, soon after its admission, the province obtained a constitution similar to that of other provinces: a lieutenant-governor, a responsible executive council and an elective assembly. Representation was given it in both houses of the Dominion parliament, and the members took their seats during the session of 1872. In addition to the payment of a considerable subsidy for provincial expenses, the Dominion government pledged itself to secure the construction of a railway within two years from the date of union to connect the seaboard of British Columbia with the railway system of Canada, to commence the work simultaneously at both ends of the line, and to complete it within ten years from the admission of the colony to the confederation.

In 1872 a general election was held in the Dominion, and while the government was generally sustained, it came back with a minority from Ontario. The Riel agitation, the Washington Treaty, and the undertaking to finish the Pacific railway in so short a time, were questions which weakened the ministry. The most encouraging feature of the elections was the complete defeat of the anti-unionists in Nova Scotia,—the prelude to their disappearance as a party—all the representatives, with the exception of one member, being pledged to support a government whose chief merit was its persistent effort to cement the union and extend it from ocean to ocean. Sir Francis Hincks, finance minister since 1870, was defeated in Ontario and Sir George Cartier in Montreal. Both these gentlemen found constituencies elsewhere, but Sir George Cartier never took his seat, as his health had been seriously impaired, and he died in England in 1873. The state gave a public funeral to this great French

Canadian, always animated by a sincere desire to weld the two races together on principles of compromise and justice. Sir Francis Hincks also disappeared from public life in 1873, and died at Montreal in 1885 from an attack of malignant small-pox. The sad circumstances of his death forbade any public or even private display, and the man who filled so many important positions in the empire was carried to the grave with those precautions which are necessary in the case of those who fall victims to an infectious disease.

But while these two eminent men disappeared from the public life of Canada, two others began now to occupy a more prominent place in Dominion affairs. These were Mr. Edward Blake and Mr. Alexander Mackenzie, who had retired from the Ontario legislature when an act was passed, as in other provinces, against dual representation, which made it necessary for them to elect between federal and provincial politics. Sir Oliver Mowat, who had retired from the bench, was chosen prime minister of Ontario on the 25th October, 1872, and continued to hold the position with great success and profit to the province until 1896, when he became minister of justice in the Liberal government formed by Sir Wilfrid Laurier.

In 1873 Prince Edward Island yielded to the influences which had been working for some years in the direction of union, and allied her fortunes with those of her sister provinces. The public men who were mainly instrumental in bringing about this happy result, after much discussion in the legislature and several conferences with the Dominion government, were the following: Mr. R.P. Haythorne, afterwards a senator; Mr. David Laird, at a later time minister in Mr. Mackenzie's government and a lieutenant-governor of the Northwest territories; Mr. James C. Pope, who became a member of Sir John Macdonald's cabinet in 1879; Mr. T.H. Haviland, and Mr. G.W. Howlan, who were in later years lieutenant-governors of the island. The terms of union made not only very favourable financial arrangements for the support of the provincial government, but also allowed a sum of money for the purpose of extinguishing the claims of the landlords to whom the greater portion of the public domain had been given by the British government more than a hundred years before. The constitution of the executive authority and the legislature remained as before confederation. Adequate representation was allowed to the island in the Canadian parliament, and the members accordingly took their places in the senate and the house of commons during the short October session of 1873, when Sir John Macdonald's government resigned on account of transactions arising out of the first efforts to construct the Canadian Pacific railway.

The Dominion was now extended for a distance of about 3,500 miles, from the island of Prince Edward in the east to the island of Vancouver in the west. The people of the great island of Newfoundland, the oldest colony of the British crown in North America, have, however, always shown a determined opposition to the proposed federation, from the time when their delegates returned from the Quebec convention of 1864. Negotiations have taken place more than once for the entrance of the island into the federal union, but so far no satisfactory arrangement has been attained. The advocates of union, down to the present time, have never been able to create that strong public opinion which would sustain any practical movement in the direction of carrying Newfoundland out of its unfortunate position of insular, selfish isolation, and making it an active partner in the material, political, and social progress of the provinces of the Canadian Dominion. Financial and political difficulties have steadily hampered the development of the island until very recently, and the imperial government has been obliged to intervene for the purpose of bringing about an adjustment of questions which, more than once, have rendered the operation of local self-government very troublesome. The government of the Dominion, on its side, while always ready to welcome the island into the confederation, has been perplexed by the difficulty of making satisfactory financial arrangements for the admission of a colony, heavily burdened with debt, and occupying a position by no means so favourable as that of the provinces now comprised within the Dominion. Some Canadians also see some reason for hesitation on the part of the Dominion in the existence of the French shore question, which prejudicially affects the territorial interests of a large portion of the coast of the island, and affords a forcible example of the little attention paid to colonial interests in those old times when English statesmen were chiefly swayed by considerations of European policy.

SECTION 3.—Summary of noteworthy events from 1873 until 1900.

On the 4th November, 1873, Sir John Macdonald placed his resignation in the hands of the governor-general, the Earl of Dufferin; and the first ministry of the Dominion came to an end after six years of office. The circumstances of this resignation were regrettable in the extreme. In 1872 two companies received charters for the construction of the Canadian Pacific railway—one of them under the direction of probably the wealthiest man in Canada, Sir Hugh Allan of Montreal, and the other under the presidency of the Honourable David Macpherson, a capitalist of Toronto. The government was unwilling for political reasons to give the preference to either of these companies, and tried to bring about an amalgamation. While negotiations were proceeding with this object in view, the general elections of 1872 came on, and Sir Hugh Allan made large contributions to the funds of the Conservative party. The facts were disclosed in 1873 before a royal commission appointed by the governor-general to inquire into charges made in the Canadian house of commons by a prominent Liberal, Mr. Huntington. An investigation ordered by the house when the charges were first brought forward, had failed chiefly on account of the legal inability of the committee to take evidence under oath; and the government then advised the appointment of the commission in question. Parliament was called together in October, 1873, to receive the report of the commissioners, and after a long and vehement debate Sir John Macdonald, not daring to test the opinion of the house by a vote, immediately resigned. In justice to Sir John Macdonald it must be stated that Sir Hugh Allan knew, before he subscribed a single farthing, that the privilege of building the railway could be conceded only to an amalgamated company. When it was shown some months after the elections that the proposed amalgamation could not be effected, the government issued a royal charter to a new company in which all the provinces were fairly represented, and in which Sir Hugh Allan appears at first to have had no special influence, although the directors of their own motion, subsequently selected him as president on account of his wealth and business standing in Canada. Despite Sir John Macdonald's plausible explanations to the governor-general, and his vigorous and even pathetic appeal to the house before he resigned, the whole transaction was unequivocally condemned by sound public opinion. His own confidential secretary, whom he had chosen before his death as his biographer, admits that even a large body of his faithful supporters "were impelled to the conclusion that a government which had benefited politically by large sums of money contributed by a person with whom it was negotiating on the part of the Dominion, could no longer command their confidence or support, and that for them the time had come to choose between their conscience and their party."

The immediate consequence of this very unfortunate transaction was the formation of a Liberal government by Mr. Alexander Mackenzie, the leader of the opposition, who had entered the old parliament of Canada in 1861, and had been treasurer in the Ontario ministry led by Mr. Blake until 1872. He was Scotch by birth, and a stonemason by trade. He came to Canada in early manhood, and succeeded in raising himself above his originally humble position to the highest in the land. His great decision of character, his clear, logical intellect, his lucid, incisive style of speaking, his great fidelity to principle, his inflexible honesty of purpose, made him a force in the Liberal party, who gladly welcomed him as the leader of a government. When he appealed to the country in 1874, he was supported by a very large majority of the representatives of the people. His administration remained in office until the autumn of 1878, and passed many measures of great usefulness to the Dominion. The North-west territories were separated from the government of Manitoba, and first organised under a lieutenant-governor and council, appointed by the governor-general of Canada. In 1875, pending the settlement of the western boundary of Ontario, it was necessary to create a separate territory out of the eastern part of the North-west, known as the district of Keewatin, which was placed under the jurisdiction of the lieutenant-governor of Manitoba. This boundary dispute was not settled until 1884, when the judicial committee of the privy council, to whose decision the question had been referred, materially altered the limits of Keewatin and extended the western boundaries of Ontario. In 1878, in response to an address of the Canadian parliament, an imperial order in council was passed to annex to the Dominion all British possessions in North America not then included within the confederation—an order intended to place beyond question the right of Canada to all British North America except

Newfoundland. In the course of succeeding years a system of local government was established in the North-west territories and a representation allowed them in the senate and house of commons.

As soon as the North-west became a part of the Dominion, the Canadian government recognised the necessity of making satisfactory arrangements with the Indian tribes. The policy first laid down in the proclamation of 1763 was faithfully carried out in this great region. Between 1871 and 1877 seven treaties were made by the Canadian government with the Crees, Chippewas, Salteaux, Ojibways, Blackfeet, Bloods and Piegans, who received certain reserves of land, annual payments of money and other benefits, as compensation for making over to Canada their title to the vast country where they had been so long the masters. From that day to this the Indians have become the wards of the government, who have always treated them with every consideration. The Indians live on reserves allotted to them in certain districts where schools of various classes have been provided for their instruction. They are systematically taught farming and other industrial pursuits; agents and instructors visit the reserves from time to time to see that the interests of the Indians are protected; and the sale of spirits is especially forbidden in the territories chiefly with the view of guarding the Indians from such baneful influences. The policy of the government for the past thirty years has been on the whole most satisfactory from every point of view. In the course of a few decades the Indians of the prairies will be an agricultural population, able to support themselves.

The Mackenzie ministry established a supreme court, or general court of appeal, for Canada. The election laws were amended so as to abolish public nominations and property qualification for members of the house of commons, as well as to provide for vote by ballot and simultaneous polling at a general election—a wise provision which had existed for some years in the province of Nova Scotia. An act passed by Sir John Macdonald's government for the trial of controverted elections by judges was amended, and a more ample and effective provision made for the repression and punishment of bribery and corruption at elections. A force of mounted police was organised for the maintenance of law and order in the North-west territories. The enlargement of the St. Lawrence system of canals was vigorously prosecuted in accordance with the report of a royal commission, appointed in 1870 by the previous administration to report on this important system of waterways. A Canada temperance act—known by the name of Senator Scott, who introduced it when secretary of state—was passed to allow electors in any county to exercise what is known as "local option"; that is to say, to decide by their votes at the polls whether they would permit the sale of intoxicating liquors within their respective districts. This act was declared by the judicial committee of the privy council to be constitutional and was extended in the course of time to very many counties of the several provinces; but eventually it was found quite impracticable to enforce the law, and the great majority of those districts of Ontario and Quebec, which had been carried away for a time on a great wave of moral reform to adopt the act, decided by an equally large vote to repeal it. The agitation for the extension of this law finally merged into a wide-spread movement among the temperance people of the Dominion for the passage of a prohibitory liquor law by the parliament of Canada. In 1898 the question was submitted to the electors of the provinces and territories by the Laurier government. The result was a majority of only 14,000 votes in favour of prohibition out of a total vote of 543,049, polled throughout the Dominion. The province of Quebec declared itself against the measure by an overwhelming vote. The temperance people then demanded that the Dominion government should take immediate action in accordance with this vote; but the prime minister stated emphatically to the house of commons as soon as parliament opened in March, 1899, "that the voice of the electorate, which has been pronounced in favour of prohibition—only twenty-three per cent. of the total electoral vote of the Dominion—is not such as to justify the government in introducing a prohibitory law." In the premier's opinion the government would not be justified in following such a course "unless at least one-half of the electorate declared itself at the polls in its favour." In the province of Manitoba, where the people have pronounced themselves conclusively in favour of prohibition, the Macdonald government are now moving to give effect to the popular wishes and restrain the liquor traffic so far as it is possible to go under the provisions of the British North

America act of 1867 and the decisions of the courts as to provincial powers.

For two years and even longer, after its coming into office, the Mackenzie government was harassed by the persistent effort that was made in French Canada for the condonation of the serious offences committed by Riel and his principal associates during the rebellion of 1870. Riel had been elected by a Manitoba constituency in 1874 to the Dominion house of commons and actually took the oath of allegiance in the clerk's office, but he never attempted to sit, and was subsequently expelled as a fugitive from criminal justice. Lepine was convicted of murder at Winnipeg and sentenced to be hanged, when the governor-general, Lord Dufferin, intervened and commuted the sentence to two years' imprisonment, with the approval of the imperial authorities, to whom, as an imperial officer entrusted with large responsibility in the exercise of the prerogative of mercy, he had referred the whole question. Soon afterwards the government yielded to the strong pressure from French Canada and relieved the tension of the public situation by obtaining from the representative of the crown an amnesty for all persons concerned in the North-west troubles, with the exception of Riel and Lepine, who were banished for five years, when they also were to be pardoned. O'Donohue was not included, as his first offence had been aggravated by his connection with the Fenian raid of 1871, but he was allowed in 1877 the benefit of the amnesty. The action of Lord Dufferin in pardoning Lepine and thereby relieving his ministers from all responsibility in the matter was widely criticised, and no doubt had much to do with bringing about an alteration in the terms of the governor-general's commission and his instructions with respect to the prerogative of mercy. Largely through the instrumentality of Mr. Blake, who visited England for the purpose, in 1875, new commissions and instructions have been issued to Lord Dufferin's successors, with a due regard to the larger measure of constitutional freedom now possessed by the Dominion of Canada. As respects the exercise of the prerogative of mercy, the independent judgment of the governor-general may be exercised in cases of imperial interest, but only after consultation with his responsible advisers, while he is at liberty to yield to their judgment in all cases of local concern.

One of the most important questions with which the Mackenzie government was called upon to deal was the construction of the Canadian Pacific railway. It was first proposed to utilise the "water-stretches" on the route of the railroad, and in that way lessen its cost, but the scheme was soon found to be impracticable. The people of British Columbia were aggrieved at the delay in building the railway, and several efforts were made to arrange the difficulty through the intervention of the Earl of Carnarvon, colonial secretary of state, of the governor-general when he visited the province in 1876, and of Mr., afterwards Sir, James Edgar, who was authorised to treat with the provincial government on the subject. At the instance of the secretary of state the government agreed to build immediately a road from Esquimalt to Nanaimo on Vancouver Island, to prosecute the surveys with vigour, and make arrangements for the completion of the railway in 1890. Mr. Blake opposed these terms, and in doing so no doubt represented the views of a large body of the Liberal party, who believed that the government of Canada had in 1871 entered into the compact with British Columbia without sufficient consideration of the gravity of the obligation they were incurring. The commons, however, passed the Esquimalt and Nanaimo bill only to hear of its rejection in the senate, where some Liberals united with the Conservative majority to defeat it. When the surveys were all completed, the government decided to build the railway as a public work; but by the autumn of 1878, when Mr. Mackenzie was defeated at a general election, only a few miles of the road had been completed, and the indignation of British Columbia had become so deep that the legislature passed a resolution for separation from the Dominion unless the terms of union were soon fulfilled.

During the existence of the Mackenzie government there was much depression in trade throughout the Dominion, and the public revenues showed large deficits in consequence of the falling-off of imports. When the elections took place in September, 1878, the people were called upon to give their decision on a most important issue. With that astuteness which always enabled him to gauge correctly the tendency of public opinion, Sir John Macdonald recognised the fact that the people were prepared to accept any new fiscal policy which promised to relieve the country from the great depression which had too long hampered internal and external trade. In the session of 1878 he brought forward a resolution, declaring emphatically that the welfare of Canada required "the adoption of a national policy which, by a judicious readjustment of the tariff will benefit the agricultural, the mining, the manufacturing and other interests of the Dominion ... will retain in Canada thousands of our fellow-countrymen now obliged to expatriate themselves in search of the employment denied them at home ... will restore prosperity to our struggling industries now so sadly depressed ... will prevent Canada from being made a sacrifice market ... will encourage and develop an interprovincial trade ... and will procure eventually for this country a reciprocity of trade with the United States." This ingenious resolution was admirably calculated to captivate the public mind, though it was defeated in the house of commons by a large majority. Mr. Mackenzie was opposed to the principle of protection, and announced the determination of the government to adhere to a revenue tariff instead of resorting to any protectionist policy, which would, in his opinion, largely increase the burdens of the people under the pretence of stimulating manufactures. As a consequence of his unbending fidelity to the principles of his life, Mr. Mackenzie was beaten at the general election by an overwhelming majority. If he had possessed even a little of the flexibility of his astute opponent he would have been more successful as a leader of a party.

One of Lord Dufferin's last official acts in October, 1878, was to call upon Sir John Macdonald to form a new administration on the resignation of Mr. Mackenzie. The new governor-general, the Marquess of Lorne, and the Princess Louise, arrived in Canada early in November and were everywhere received with great enthusiasm. The new protective policy—"the National Policy" as the Conservatives like best to name it—was laid before parliament in the session of 1879, by Sir Leonard Tilley, then finance minister; and though it has undergone some important modifications since its introduction it has formed the basis of the Canadian tariff for twenty years. The next important measure of the government was the vigorous prosecution of the Canadian Pacific railway. During the Mackenzie administration the work had made little progress, and the people of British Columbia had become very indignant at the failure to carry out the terms on which they had entered the confederation. In the session of 1880-81 Sir Charles Tupper, minister of railways, announced that the government had entered into a contract with a company of capitalists to construct the railway from Montreal to Burrard's Inlet. Parliament ratified the contract by a large majority despite the vigorous opposition made by Mr. Blake, then leader of the Liberal party, who had for years considered this part of the agreement with British Columbia as extremely rash. Such remarkable energy was brought to the construction of this imperial highway that it was actually in operation at the end of five years after the commencement of the work—only one-half of the time allowed in the charter for its completion. The financial difficulties which the company had to encounter in the progress of the work were very great, and they were obliged in 1884 to obtain a large loan from the Dominion government. The loan was secured on the company's property, and was paid off by 1887. The political fortunes of the Conservative administration, in fact, were indissolubly connected with the success of this national enterprise, and from the moment when the company commenced the work Sir John Macdonald never failed to give it his complete confidence and support.

One of the delicate questions which the Macdonald government was called upon to settle soon after their coming into office was what is known as "the Letellier affair." In March, 1878, the lieutenant-governor of the province of Quebec, Mr. Letellier de Saint-Just, who had been previously a member of the Mackenzie Liberal government, dismissed the Boucherville Conservative ministry on the ground that they had taken steps in regard to both administrative and legislative measures not only contrary to his representations, but even without previously advising him of what they proposed to do. At his request Mr., now Sir, Henry Joly de Lotbinière formed a Liberal administration, which appealed to the country. The result was that the two parties came back evenly balanced. The Conservatives of the province were deeply irritated at this action of the lieutenant-governor, and induced Sir John Macdonald, then leader of the opposition, to make a motion in the house of commons, declaring Mr. Letellier's conduct "unwise and subversive of the sound principles of responsible government." This motion was made as an amendment on the proposal to go into committee of supply, and under a peculiar usage of the Canadian commons it was not permitted to move a second amendment at this stage. Had such a course been regular, the Mackenzie government would have proposed an amendment similar to that which was moved in the senate, to the effect that it was inexpedient to offer any opinion on the action of the lieutenant-governor of Quebec for the reason that "the federal and provincial governments, each in its own sphere, enjoyed responsible government equally, separately, and independently"—in other words, that the wisest constitutional course to follow under the circumstances was to allow each province to work out responsible government without any undue interference on the part of the Dominion government or parliament. As it happened, however, Mr. Mackenzie and his colleagues had no alternative open to them but to vote down the motion proposed in the commons; while in the Conservative senate the amendment, which could not be submitted to the lower house under the rules, was defeated, and the motion condemning the lieutenant-governor carried by a large party vote.

In 1879, when the Macdonald government was in office, the matter was again brought before the house of commons and the same motion of censure that had been defeated in 1878 was introduced in the same way as before, and carried by a majority of 85. The prime minister then informed Lord Lorne that in the opinion of the government Mr. Letellier's "usefulness was gone," and he recommended his removal from office; but the governor-general was unwilling to agree hastily to such a dangerous precedent as the removal of a lieutenant-governor, and as an imperial officer he referred the whole matter to her Majesty's government for their consideration and instructions. The colonial secretary did not hesitate to state "that the lieutenant-governor of a province has an indisputable right to dismiss his ministers if, from any cause, he feels it incumbent to do so," but that, in deciding whether the conduct of a lieutenant-governor merits removal from his office, as in the exercise of other powers vested in him by the imperial state the governor-general "must act by and with the advice of his ministers." After further consideration of the subject, the Canadian government again recommended the dismissal of Mr. Letellier, and the governor-general had now no alternative except to act on the advice of his responsible ministers. It was unfortunate that the constitutional issue was obscured, from the outset, by the political bitterness that was imported into it, and that the procedure, followed in two sessions, of proposing an amendment, condemnatory of the action of the lieutenant-governor, on the motion of going into committee of supply, prevented the house from coming to a decision squarely on the true constitutional issue—actually raised in the senate in 1878—whether it was expedient for the parliament or government of Canada to interfere in a matter of purely provincial concern.

In 1891 another case of the dismissal of a ministry, having a majority in the assembly, occurred in the province of Quebec, but the intervention of parliament was not asked for the purpose of censuring the lieutenant-governor for the exercise of his undoubted constitutional power. It appears that, in 1891, the evidence taken before a committee of the senate showed that gross irregularities had occurred in connection with the disbursement of certain government subsidies which had been voted by parliament for the construction of the Bay des Chaleurs railway, and that members of the Quebec cabinet were compromised in what was clearly a misappropriation of public money. In view of these grave charges, Lieutenant-governor Angers forced his prime minister, Mr. Honoré Mercier, to agree to the appointment of a royal commission to hold an investigation into the transaction in question. When the lieutenant-governor was in possession of the evidence taken before this commission, he came to the conclusion that it was his duty to relieve Mr. Mercier and his colleagues of their functions as ministers "in order to protect the dignity of the crown and safeguard the honour and interest of the province in danger." Mr. de Boucherville was then called upon to form a ministry which would necessarily assume full responsibility for the action of the lieutenant-governor under the circumstances, and after some delay the new ministry went to the country and were sustained by a large majority. It is an interesting coincidence that the lieutenant-governor who dismissed the Mercier government and the prime minister who assumed full responsibility for the dismissal of the Mercier administration, were respectively attorney-general and premier in the cabinet who so deeply resented a similar action in 1878. But Mr. Letellier was then dead—

notoriously as a result of the mental strain to which he had been subject in the constitutional crisis which wrecked his political career—and it was left only for his friends to feel that the whirligig of time brings its revenge even in political affairs[5].

[5: Since this chapter was in type, the Dominion government have found it necessary to dismiss Mr. McInnes from the lieutenant-governorship of British Columbia, on the ground—as set forth in an order-in-council—that "his official conduct had been subversive of the principles of responsible government," and that his "usefulness was gone." While Mr. McInnes acted as head of the executive at Victoria, the political affairs of the province became chaotic. He dismissed ministries in the most summary manner. When the people were at last appealed to at a general election by Mr. Martin, his latest adviser, he was defeated by an overwhelming majority, and the Ottawa government came to the conclusion—to quote the order-in-council—"that the action of the lieutenant-governor in dismissing his ministers has not been approved by the people of British Columbia," and it was evident, "that the government of the province cannot be successfully carried on in the manner contemplated by the constitution under the administration of the present incumbent of the office." Consequently, Mr. McInnes was removed from office, and the Dominion government appointed in his place Sir Henri Joly de Lotbinière, who has had large experience in public affairs, and is noted for his amiability and discretion.]

A very important controversy involving old issues arose in 1888 in connection with an act passed by the Mercier government of Quebec for the settlement of the Jesuits' estates, which, so long ago as 1800, had fallen into the hands of the British government, on the death of the last surviving member of the order in Canada, and had been, after some delay, applied to the promotion of public instruction in the province of Quebec. The bishops of the Roman Catholic Church always contended that the estates should have been vested in them "as the ordinaries of the various dioceses in which this property was situated." After confederation, the estates became the property of the government of Quebec and were entirely at the disposal of the legislature. The Jesuits in the meantime had become incorporated in the province, and made, as well as the bishops, a claim to the estates.

Eventually, to settle the difficulty and strengthen himself with the ecclesiastics of the province, Mr. Mercier astutely passed a bill through the legislature, authorising the payment of $400,000 as compensation to the Jesuits in lieu of all the lands held by them prior to the conquest and subsequently confiscated by the crown. It was expressly set forth in the preamble of the act—and it was this proposition which offended the extreme Protestants—that the amount of compensation was to remain as a special deposit until the Pope had made known his wishes respecting the distribution. Some time later the Pope divided the money among the Jesuits, the archbishops and bishops of the province, and Laval University. The whole matter came before the Dominion house of commons in 1888, when a resolution was proposed to the effect that the government should have at once disallowed the act as beyond the power of the legislature, because, among other reasons, "it recognizes the usurpation of a right by a foreign authority, namely his Holiness the Pope, to claim that his consent was necessary to dispose of and appropriate the public funds of a province." The very large vote in support of the action of the government-188 against 13-was chiefly influenced by the conviction that, to quote the minute of council, "the subject-matter of the act was one of provincial concern, only having relation to a fiscal matter entirely within the control of the legislature of Quebec." The best authorities agree in the wisdom of not interfering with provincial legislation except in cases where there is an indisputable invasion of Dominion jurisdiction or where the vital interests of Canada as a whole may imperatively call for such interference.

In March, 1885, Canada was startled by the news that the half-breeds of the Saskatchewan district in the North-west had risen in rebellion against the authority of the Dominion government. It is difficult to explain clearly the actual causes of an uprising which, in all probability, would never have occurred had it not been for the fact that Riel had been brought back from Montana by his countrymen to assist them in obtaining a redress of certain grievances. This little insurrection originated in the Roman Catholic mission of St. Laurent, situated between the north and south branches of the Saskatchewan River, and contiguous to the British settlement of Prince Albert. Within the limits of this mission there was a considerable number of half-breeds, who had for the most part migrated from Manitoba after selling the "scrip[6]" for lands generously granted to them after the restoration of order in 1870 to the Red River settlements. Government surveyors had been busily engaged for some time in laying out the Saskatchewan country in order to keep pace with the rapidly increasing settlement. When they came to the mission of St. Laurent they were met with the same distrust that had done so much harm in 1870. The half-breeds feared that the system of square blocks followed by the surveyors would seriously interfere with the location of the farms on which they had "squatted" in accordance with the old French system of deep lots with a narrow frontage on the banks of the rivers. The difficulties arising out of these diverse systems of surveys caused a considerable delay in the issue of patents for lands, and dissatisfied the settlers who were anxious to know what land their titles covered. The half-breeds not only contended that their surveys should be respected, but that they should be also allowed scrip for two hundred and forty acres of land, as had been done in the case of their compatriots in Manitoba. Many of the Saskatchewan settlers had actually received this scrip before they left the province, but nevertheless they hoped to obtain it once more from the government, and to sell it with their usual improvidence to the first speculators who offered them some ready money.

[6: A certificate from the government that a certain person is entitled to receive a patent from the crown for a number of acres of the public lands—a certificate legally transferable to another person by the original holder.]

The delay of the government in issuing patents and scrip and the system of surveys were no doubt the chief grievances which enabled Riel and Dumont—the latter a resident of Batoche—to excite the half-breeds against the Dominion authorities at Ottawa. When a commission was actually appointed by the government in January, 1885, to allot scrip to those who were entitled to receive it, the half-breeds were actually ready for a revolt under the malign influence of Riel and his associates. Riel believed for some time after his return in 1884 that he could use the agitation among his easily deluded countrymen for his own selfish purposes. It is an indisputable fact that he made an offer to the Dominion government to leave the North-west if they would pay him a considerable sum of money. When he found that there was no likelihood of Sir John Macdonald repeating the mistake which he had made at the end of the first rebellion, Riel steadily fomented the agitation among the half-breeds, who were easily persuaded to believe that a repetition of the disturbances of 1870 would obtain them a redress of any grievances they might have. It is understood that one of the causes that aggravated the agitation at its inception was the belief entertained by some white settlers of Prince Albert that they could use the disaffection among the half-breeds for the purpose of repeating the early history of Manitoba, and forcing the Dominion government to establish a new province in the Saskatchewan country, though its entire population at that time would not have exceeded ten thousand persons, of whom a large proportion were half-breeds. Riel for a time skilfully made these people believe that he would be a ductile instrument in their hands, but when his own plans were ripe for execution he assumed despotic control of the whole movement and formed a provisional government in which he and his half-breed associates were dominant, and the white conspirators of Prince Albert were entirely ignored. The loyal people of Prince Albert, who had always disapproved of the agitation, as well as the priests of the mission, who had invariably advised their flock to use only peaceful and constitutional methods of redress, were at last openly set at defiance and insulted by Riel and his associates. The revolt broke out on the 25th March, 1885, when the half-breeds took forcible possession of the government stores, and made prisoners of some traders at Duck Lake. A small force of Mounted Police under the command of Superintendent Crozier was defeated near the same place by Dumont, and the former only saved his men from destruction by a skilful retreat to Fort Carleton. The half-breed leaders circulated the news of this victory over the dreaded troops of the government among the Indian bands of the Saskatchewan, a number of whom immediately went on the war-path. Fort Carleton had to be given up by the mounted police, who retired to Prince Albert, the key of the district. The town of Battleford was besieged by the Indians, but they were successfully kept in check for weeks until the place was relieved. Fort Pitt was evacuated by Inspector

Canada Under British Rule 1760-1900

Dickens, a son of the great novelist, who succeeded in taking his little force of police into Battleford. Two French missionaries and several white men were ruthlessly murdered at Frog Lake by a band of Crees, and two women were dragged from the bodies of their husbands and carried away to the camp of Big Bear. Happily for them some tender-hearted half-breeds purchased them from the Indians and kept them in safety until they were released at the close of the disturbances.

The heart of Canada was now deeply stirred and responded with great heartiness to the call of the government for troops to restore order to the distracted settlements. The minister of militia, Mr. Adolphe Caron—afterwards knighted for his services on this trying occasion—showed great energy in the management of his department. Between four and five thousand men were soon on the march for the territories under Major-General Middleton, the English officer then in command of the Canadian militia. Happily for the rapid transport of the troops the Canadian Pacific Railway was so far advanced that, with the exception of 72 miles, it afforded a continuous line of communication from Montreal to Qu'Appelle. The railway formed the base from which three military expeditions could be despatched to the most important points of the Saskatchewan country—one direct to Batoche, a second to Battleford, and a third for a flank movement to Fort Edmonton, where a descent could be made down the North Saskatchewan for the purpose of recapturing Fort Pitt and attacking the rebellious Indians under Big Bear. On the 24th of April General Middleton fought his first engagement with the half-breeds, who were skilfully concealed in rifle pits in the vicinity of Fish Creek, a small erratic tributary of the South Saskatchewan. Dumont for the moment succeeded in checking the advance of the Canadian forces, who fought with much bravery but were placed at a great disadvantage on account of Middleton not having taken sufficient precautions against a foe thoroughly acquainted with the country and cunningly hidden. The Canadian troops were soon able to continue their forward movement and won a decisive victory at Batoche, in which Colonels Williams, Straubenzie, and Grasett notably distinguished themselves. Riel was soon afterwards captured on the prairie, but Dumont succeeded in crossing the frontier of the United States. While Middleton was on his way to Batoche, Lieutenant-Colonel Otter of Toronto, an able soldier who was, fifteen years later, detached for active service in South Africa, was on the march for the relief of Battleford, and had on the first of May an encounter with a large band of Indians under Poundmaker on the banks of Cut Knife Creek, a small tributary of the Battle River. Though Otter did not win a victory, he showed Poundmaker the serious nature of the contest in which he was engaged against the Canadian government, and soon afterwards, when the Cree chief heard of the defeat of the half-breeds at Batoche, he surrendered unconditionally. Another expedition under the command of Lieutenant-Colonel Strange also relieved Fort Pitt; and Big Bear was forced to fly into the swampy fastnesses of the prairie wilderness, but was eventually captured near Fort Carleton by a force of Mounted Police.

This second rebellion of the half-breeds lasted about three months, and cost the country upwards of five million dollars. Including the persons murdered at Frog Lake, the loyal population of Canada lost thirty-six valuable lives, among whom was Lieutenant-Colonel Williams, a gallant officer, and a member of the house of commons, who succumbed to a serious illness brought on by his exposure on the prairie. The casualties among the half-breeds were at least as large, if not greater. Five Indian chiefs suffered the extreme penalty of the law, while Poundmaker, Big Bear, and a number of others were imprisoned in the territories for life or for a term of years, according to the gravity of their complicity in the rebellion. Any hopes that Riel might have placed in the active sympathy of the French Canadian people of Quebec were soon dispelled. He was tried at Regina in July and sentenced to death, although the able counsel allotted to him by the government exhausted every available argument in his defence, even to the extent of setting up a plea of insanity, which the prisoner himself deeply resented. The most strenuous efforts were made by the French Canadians to force the government to reprieve him, but Sir John Macdonald was satisfied that the loyal sentiment of the great majority of the people of Canada demanded imperatively that the law should be vindicated. The French Canadian representatives in the cabinet, Langevin, Chapleau, and Caron, resisted courageously the storm of obloquy which their determination to support the prime minister raised against them;

and Riel was duly executed on the 16th November. For some time after his death attempts were made to keep up the excitement which had so long existed in the province of Quebec on the question. The Dominion government was certainly weakened for a time in Quebec by its action in this matter, while Mr. Honoré Mercier skilfully used the Riel agitation to obtain control of the provincial government at the general election of 1886, but only to fall five years later, under circumstances which must always throw a shadow over the fame of a brilliant, but unsafe, political leader (see p. 247). The attempt to make political capital out of the matter in the Dominion parliament had no other result than to weaken the influence in Ontario of Mr. Edward Blake, the leader of the opposition since the resignation of Mr. Mackenzie in 1880. He was left without the support of the majority of the Liberal representatives of the province in the house of commons when he condemned the execution of Riel, principally on the ground that he was insane—a conclusion not at all justified by the report of the medical experts who had been chosen by the government to examine the condemned man previous to the execution. The energy with which this rebellion was repressed showed both the half-breeds and the Indians of the west the power of the Ottawa government. From that day to this order has prevailed in the western country, and grievances have been redressed as far as possible. The readiness with which the militia force of Canada rallied to the support of the government was conclusive evidence of the deep national sentiment that existed throughout the Dominion. In Ottawa, Port Hope, and Toronto monuments have been raised in memory of the brave men who gave up their lives for the Dominion, but probably the most touching memorial of this unfortunate episode in Canadian history is the rude cairn of stone which still stands among the wild flowers of the prairie in memory of the gallant fellows who were mown down by the unerring rifle shots of the half-breeds hidden in the ravines of Fish Creek.

In 1885 parliament passed a general franchise law for the Dominion in place of the system—which had prevailed since 1867—of taking the electoral lists of the several provinces as the lists for elections to the house of commons. The opposition contested this measure with great persistency, but Sir John Macdonald pressed it to a successful conclusion, mainly on the ground that it was necessary in a country like Canada, composed of such diverse elements, to have for the Dominion uniformity of suffrage, based on a small property qualification, instead of having diverse systems of franchise—in some provinces, universal franchise, to which he and other Conservatives generally were strongly opposed.

Between 1880 and 1894 Canada was called upon to mourn the loss of a number of her ablest and brightest statesmen—one of them the most notable in her political history. It was on a lovely May day of 1880 that the eminent journalist and politician, George Brown, died from the effects of a bullet wound which he received at the hand of one Bennett, a printer, who had been discharged by the *Globe* for drunkenness and incapacity. The Conservative party in 1888 suffered a great loss by the sudden decease of Mr. Thomas White, minister of the interior in the Macdonald ministry, who had been for the greater part of his life a prominent journalist, and had succeeded in winning a conspicuous and useful position in public affairs as a writer, speaker, and administrator. Three years later, the Dominion was startled by the sad announcement, on the 6th June, 1891, that the voice of the great prime minister, Sir John Macdonald, who had so long controlled the affairs of Canada, would never more be heard in that federal parliament of which he had been one of the fathers. All classes of Canadians vied with one another in paying a tribute of affection and respect to one who had been in every sense a true Canadian. Men forgot for the moment his mistakes and weaknesses, the mistakes of the politician and the weaknesses of humanity, "only to remember"—to quote the eloquent tribute paid to him by Mr. Laurier, then leader of the opposition—"that his actions always displayed great originality of view, unbounded fertility of resources, a high level of intellectual conception, and above all, a far-reaching vision beyond the event of the day, and still higher, permeating the whole, a broad patriotism, a devotion to Canada's welfare, Canada's advancement, and Canada's glory." His obsequies were the most stately and solemn that were ever witnessed in the Dominion; his bust was subsequently unveiled in the crypt of St. Paul's Cathedral by the Earl of Rosebery, when prime minister of England; noble monuments were raised to his memory in the cities of Hamilton, Toronto, Ottawa, and Montreal; and the Queen addressed a letter full of gracious sympathy to his widow and conferred on her the dignity of a peeress of the United Kingdom under the title of Baroness of Earnscliffe, as a mark of her Majesty's gratitude "for the devoted and faithful services which he rendered for so many years to his sovereign and his Dominion."

Mr. Alexander Mackenzie, stonemason, journalist, and prime minister, died in April, 1892, a victim to the paralysis which had been steadily creeping for years over his enfeebled frame, and made him a pitiable spectacle as he sat like a Stoic in the front seats of the opposition, unable to speak or even to rise without the helping arm of some attentive friend. On the 30th October, 1893, Sir John Abbott, probably the ablest commercial lawyer in Canada, who had been premier of Canada since the death of Sir John Macdonald, followed his eminent predecessors to the grave, and was succeeded by Sir John Thompson, minister of justice in the Conservative government since September, 1885. A great misfortune again overtook the Conservative party on the 12th December, 1894, when Sir John Thompson died in Windsor Castle, whither he had gone at her Majesty's request to take the oath of a privy councillor of England — high distinction conferred upon him in recognition of his services on the Bering Sea arbitration. Sir John Thompson was gifted with a rare judicial mind, and a remarkable capacity for the lucid expression of his thoughts, which captivated his hearers even when they were not convinced by arguments clothed in the choicest diction. His remains were brought across the Atlantic by a British frigate, and interred in his native city of Halifax with all the stately ceremony of a national funeral. The governor-general, Lord Stanley of Preston, now the Earl of Derby, called upon the senior privy councillor in the cabinet, Sir Mackenzie Bowell, to form a new ministry. He continued in office until April, 1896, when he retired in favour of Sir Charles Tupper, who resigned the position of high commissioner for Canada in England to enter public life as the recognised leader of the Liberal-Conservative party. This eminent Canadian had already reached the middle of the eighth decade of his life, but age had in no sense impaired the vigour or astuteness of his mental powers. He has continued ever since, as leader of the Liberal-Conservative party, to display remarkable activity in the discussion of political questions, not only as a leader of parliament, but on the public platform in every province of the Dominion.

During the session of 1891 the political career of Sir Hector Langevin, the leader of the Liberal-Conservative party in French Canada, was seriously affected by certain facts disclosed before the committee of privileges and elections. This committee had been ordered by the house of commons to inquire into charges made by Mr. Israel Tarte against another member of the house, Mr. Thomas McGreevy, who was accused of having used his influence as a commissioner of the Quebec harbour, a government appointment, to obtain fraudulently from the department of public works, presided over by Sir Hector for many years, large government contracts in connection with the Quebec harbour and other works. The report of the majority of the committee found Mr. McGreevy guilty of fraudulent acts, and he was not only expelled from the house but was subsequently imprisoned in the Ottawa common gaol after his conviction on an indictment laid against him in the criminal court of Ontario. With respect to the complicity of the minister of public works in these frauds the committee reported that it was clear that, while the conspiracy had been rendered effective by reason of the confidence which Sir Hector Langevin placed in Mr. McGreevy and in the officers of the department, yet the evidence did not justify them in concluding that Sir Hector knew of the conspiracy or willingly lent himself to its objects. A minority of the committee, on the other hand, took the opposite view of the transactions, and claimed that the evidence showed the minister to be cognisant of the facts of the letting of the contracts, and that in certain specified cases he had been guilty of the violation of a public trust by allowing frauds to be perpetrated. The report of the majority was carried by a party vote, with the exception of two Conservative members who voted with the minority. Sir Hector Langevin had resigned his office in the government previous to the inquiry, and though he continued in the house for the remainder of its constitutional existence, he did not present himself for re-election in 1896 when parliament was dissolved.

Unhappily it was not only in the department of public works that irregularities were discovered. A number of officials in several departments were proved before the committee of public accounts to have been guilty of carelessness or positive misconduct in the discharge of their duties, and the government was obliged, in the face of such disclosures, to dismiss or otherwise punish several persons in whom they had for years reposed too much confidence.

On the 20th and 21st of June, 1893, a convention of the most prominent representative Liberals of the Dominion was held in the city of Ottawa; and Sir Oliver Mowat, the veteran premier of Ontario, was unanimously called upon to preside over this important assemblage. Resolutions were passed with great enthusiasm in support of tariff reform, a fair measure of reciprocal trade with the United States, a sale of public lands only to actual settlers upon reasonable terms of settlement, an honest and economical administration of government, the right of the house of commons to inquire into all matters of public expenditure and charges of misconduct against ministers, the reform of the senate, the submission of the question of prohibition to a vote of the people, and the repeal of the Dominion franchise act passed in 1885, as well as of the measure of 1892, altering the boundaries of the electoral districts and readjusting the representation in the house of commons. This convention may be considered the commencement of that vigorous political campaign, which ended so successfully for the Liberal party in the general election of 1896.

In the summer of 1894 there was held in the city of Ottawa a conference of delegates from eight self-governing colonies in Australasia, South Africa, and America, who assembled for the express purpose of discussing questions which affected not merely their own peculiar interests, but touched most nearly the unity and development of the empire at large The imperial government was represented by the Earl of Jersey, who had been a governor of one of the Australian colonies. After very full discussion the conference passed resolutions in favour of the following measures:

(1) Imperial legislation enabling the dependencies of the empire to enter into agreements of commercial reciprocity, including the power to make differential tariffs with Great Britain or with one another. (2) The removal of any restrictions in existing treaties between Great Britain and any foreign power, which prevent such agreements of commercial reciprocity. (3) A customs arrangement between Great Britain and her colonies by which trade within the empire might be placed on a more favourable footing than that

which is carried on with foreign countries. (4) Improved steamship communication between Canada, Australasia, and Great Britain. (5) Telegraph communication by cable, free from foreign control, between Canada and Australia. These various resolutions were brought formally by the Earl of Jersey to the notice of the imperial government, which expressed the opinion, through the Marquess of Ripon, then secretary of state for the colonies, that the "general economic results" of the preferential trade recommended by the conference "would not be beneficial to the empire." Lord Ripon even questioned the desirability of denouncing at that time the treaties with Belgium and Germany—a subject which had engaged the attention of the Canadian parliament in 1892, when the government, of which Sir John Abbott was premier, passed an address to the Queen, requesting that immediate steps be taken to free Canada from treaty restrictions "incompatible with the rights and powers conferred by the British North America act of 1867 for the regulation of the trade and commerce of the Dominion." Any advantages which might be granted by Great Britain to either Belgium or the German Zollverein under these particular treaties, would also have to be extended to a number of other countries which had what is called the "favoured nations clause" in treaties with England. While these treaty stipulations with regard to import duties did not prevent differential treatment by the United Kingdom in favour of British colonies, or differential treatment by British colonies in favour of each other, they did prevent differential treatment by British colonies in favour of the United Kingdom. As we shall presently see, when I come to review the commercial policy of the new Dominion government three years later, the practical consequence of these treaties was actually to force Canada to give for some months not only to Germany and Belgium, but to a number of other countries, the same commercial privileges which they extended in 1897 to the parent state.

Among the difficult questions, which have agitated the Dominion from time to time and perplexed both Conservative and Liberal politicians, are controversies connected with education. By the British North America act of 1867 the legislature of each province may exclusively make laws in relation to education, but at the same time protection is afforded to denominational or dissentient schools by giving authority to the Dominion government to disallow an act clearly infringing the rights or privileges of a religious minority, or to obtain remedial legislation from parliament itself according to the circumstances of the case. From 1871 until 1875 the government of the Dominion was pressed by petitions from the Roman Catholic inhabitants of New Brunswick to disallow an act passed by the provincial legislature in relation to common schools on the ground that it was an infringement of certain rights which they enjoyed as a religious body at the time of confederation. The question not only came before the courts of New Brunswick and the Canadian house of commons, but was also submitted to the judicial committee of the imperial privy council; but only with the result of showing beyond question that the objectionable legislation was clearly within the jurisdiction of the legislature of New Brunswick, and could not be constitutionally disallowed by the Dominion government on the ground that it violated any right or privilege enjoyed by the Roman Catholics at the time of union. A solution of the question was, however, subsequently reached by an amicable arrangement between the Roman Catholics and Protestants, which has ever since worked most satisfactorily in that province.

The Manitoba school question, which agitated the country from 1890 until 1896, was one of great gravity on account of the issues involved. The history of the case shows that, prior to the formation of Manitoba in 1870, there was not in the province any public system of education, but the several religious denominations had established such schools as they thought fit to maintain by means of funds voluntarily contributed by members of their own communion. In 1871 the legislature of Manitoba established an educational system distinctly denominational. In 1890 this law was repealed, and the legislature established a system of strictly non-sectarian schools. The Roman Catholic minority of the province was deeply aggrieved at what they considered a violation of the rights and privileges which they enjoyed under the terms of union adopted in 1870. The first subsection of the twenty-second section of the act of 1870 set forth that the legislature of the province could not pass any law with regard to schools which might "prejudicially affect any right or privilege with respect to denominational schools which any class of persons have, by law or practice, in the province at the time of union." The dispute was brought before the courts of Canada, and finally before the judicial committee of the privy council, which decided that the legislation of 1890 was constitutional inasmuch as the only right or privilege which the Roman Catholics then possessed "by law or practice" was the right or privilege of establishing and maintaining for the use of members of their own church such schools as they pleased. The Roman Catholic minority then availed themselves of another provision of the twenty-second section of the Manitoba act, which allows an appeal to the governor-in-council "from any act or decision of the legislature of the province or of any provincial authority, affecting any right or privilege of the Protestant or Roman Catholic minority of the Queen's subjects in relation to education."

The ultimate result of this reference was a judgment of the judicial committee to the effect that the appeal was well founded and that the governor-in-council had jurisdiction in the premises, but the committee added that "the particular course to be pursued must be determined by the authorities to whom it has been committed by the statute." The third subsection of the twenty-second section of the Manitoba act—a repetition of the provision of the British North America act with respect to denominational schools in the old provinces—provides not only for the action of the governor-in-council in case a remedy is not supplied by the proper provincial authority for the removal of a grievance on the part of a religious minority, but also for the making of "remedial laws" by the parliament of Canada for the "due execution" of the provision protecting denominational schools. In accordance with this provision Sir Mackenzie Bowell's government passed an order-in-council on the 21st March, 1895, calling upon the government of Manitoba to take the necessary measures to restore to the Roman Catholic minority such rights and privileges as were declared by the highest court of the empire to have been taken away from them. The Manitoba government not only refused to move in the matter but expressed its determination "to resist unitedly by every constitutional means any such attempt to interfere with their provincial autonomy." The result was the introduction of a remedial bill by Mr. Dickey, minister of justice, in the house of commons during the session of 1896; but it met from the outset very determined opposition during the most protracted sittings—one of them lasting continuously for a week—ever known in the history of the Canadian or any other legislature of the empire. On several divisions the bill was supported by majorities ranging from 24 to 18—several French members of the opposition having voted for it and several Conservative Protestant members against its passage. The bill was introduced on the 11th February, and the motion for its second reading was made on the 3rd March, from which date it was debated continuously until progress was reported from a committee of the whole house on the 16th April, after the house had sat steadily from Monday afternoon at 3 o'clock until 2 o'clock on the following Thursday morning. It was then that Sir Charles Tupper, leader of the government in the house, announced that no further attempt would be made to press the bill that session. He stated that it was absolutely necessary to vote money for the urgent requirements of the public service and pass other important legislation during the single week that was left before parliament would be dissolved by the efflux of time under the constitutional law, which fixes the duration of the house of commons "for five years from the day of the return of the writs for choosing the house and no longer."

In the general election of 1896 the Manitoba school question was an issue of great importance. From the commencement to the close of the controversy the opponents of denominational schools combined with the supporters of provincial rights to defeat the government which had so determinedly fought for what it considered to be the legal rights of the Roman Catholic minority of Manitoba. It had looked confidently to the support of the great majority of the French Canadians, but the result of the elections was most disappointing to the Conservative party. Whilst in the provinces, where the Protestants predominated, the Conservatives held their own to a larger extent than had been expected even by their sanguine friends, the French province gave a great majority to Mr. Launer, whose popularity among his countrymen triumphed over all influences, ecclesiastical and secular, that could be used in favour of denominational schools in Manitoba.

The majority against Sir Charles Tupper was conclusive, and he did not attempt to meet parliament as the head of a government. Before his retirement from office, immediately after his defeat at the elections, he had some difference of opinion with the governor-general, the Earl of Aberdeen, who refused, in the exercise of his discretionary power, to sanction certain appointments to the senate and the judicial bench, which the prime minister justified by reference to English and Canadian precedents under similar conditions—notably of 1878 when Mr. Mackenzie resigned. Soon after the general election, and Lord Dufferin was governor-general, Sir Charles Tupper considered the subject of sufficient constitutional importance to bring it before the house of commons, where Sir Wilfrid Laurier, then premier, defended the course of the governor-general. The secretary of state for the colonies also approved in general terms of the principles which, as the governor-general explained in his despatches, had governed his action in this delicate matter.

On Sir Charles Tapper's defeat at the elections, Mr. Laurier became first minister of a Liberal administration, in which positions were given to Sir Oliver Mowat, so long premier of Ontario, to Mr. Blair, premier of New Brunswick, to Mr. Fielding, premier of Nova Scotia, and eventually to Mr. Sifton, the astute attorney-general of Manitoba. Sir Richard Cartwright and Sir Louis Davies—to give the latter the title conferred on him in the Diamond Jubilee year—both of whom had been in the foremost rank of the Liberal party for many years, also took office in the new administration; but Mr. Mills, versed above most Canadian public men in political and constitutional knowledge, was not brought in until some time later, when Sir Oliver Mowat, the veteran minister of justice, was appointed to the lieutenant-governorship of Ontario. A notable acquisition was Mr. Tarte, who had acquired much influence in French Canada by his irrepressible energy, and who was placed over the department of public works.

When the school question came to be discussed in 1897, during the first session of the new parliament, the premier explained to the house that, whilst he had always maintained "that the constitution of this country gave to this parliament and government the right and power to interfere with the school legislation of Manitoba, it was an extreme right and reserved power to be exercised only when other means had been exhausted." Believing then that "it was far better to obtain concessions by negotiation than by coercion," he had, as soon as he came into office, communicated with the Manitoba government on the subject, and had "as a result succeeded in making arrangements which gave the French Catholics of the province religious teaching in their schools and the protection of their language," under the conditions set forth in a statute expressly passed for the purpose by the legislature of Manitoba[7]. The premier at the same time admitted that "the settlement was not acceptable to certain dignitaries of the church to which he belonged"; but subsequently the Pope published an encyclical advising acceptance of the concessions made to the Manitoba Catholics, while claiming at the same time that these concessions were inadequate, and expressing the hope that full satisfaction would be obtained ere long from the Manitoba government. Since the arrangement of this compromise, no strenuous or effective effort has been made to revive the question as an element of political significance in party contests. Even in Manitoba itself, despite the defeat of the Greenway government, which was responsible for the Manitoba school act of 1890, and the coming into office of Mr. Hugh John Macdonald, the son of the great Conservative leader, there has been no sign of the least intention to depart from the legislation arranged by Sir Wilfrid Laurier in 1897 as, in his opinion, the best possible compromise under the difficult conditions surrounding a most embarrassing question.

[7: This statute provides that religious teaching by a Roman Catholic priest, or other person duly authorised by him, shall take place at the close of the hours devoted to secular instruction; that a Roman Catholic teacher may be employed in every school in towns and cities where the average attendance of Roman Catholic children is forty or upwards, and in villages and rural districts where the attendance is twenty-five or upwards; and that French as well as English shall be taught in any school where ten pupils speak the French language.]

In the autumn of 1898 Canada bade farewell with many expressions of regret to Lord and Lady Aberdeen, both of whom had won the affection and respect of the Canadian people by their earnest efforts to support every movement that might promote the social, intellectual and moral welfare of the people. Lord Aberdeen was the seventh governor-general appointed by the crown to administer public affairs since the union of the provinces in 1867. Lord Monck, who had the honour of initiating confederation, was succeeded by Sir John Young, who was afterwards raised to the peerage as Baron Lisgar—a just recognition of the admirable discretion and dignity with which he discharged the duties of his high position. His successor, the Earl of Dufferin, won the affection of the Canadian people by his grace of demeanour, and his Irish gift of eloquence, which he used in the spirit of the clever diplomatist to flatter the people of the country to their heart's content. The appointment of the Marquess of Lorne, now the Duke of Argyll, gave to Canada the honour of the presence of a Princess of the reigning family. He showed tact and discretion in some difficult political situations that arose during his administration, and succeeded above all his predecessors in stimulating the study of art, science and literature within the Dominion. The Marquess of Lansdowne and Lord Stanley of Preston—both inheritors of historic names, trained in the great school of English administration—also acquired the confidence and respect of the Canadian people. On the conclusion of Lord Aberdeen's term of office in 1898, he was succeeded by the Earl of Minto, who had been military secretary to the Marquess of Lansdowne, when governor-general, from the autumn of 1883 until the end of May, 1888, and had also acted as chief of staff to General Middleton during the North-west disturbances of 1885.

Since its coming into office, the Laurier administration has been called upon to deal with many questions of Canadian as well as imperial concern. One of its first measures—to refer first to those of Canadian importance—was the repeal of the franchise act of 1885, which had been found so expensive in its operation that the Conservative government had for years taken no steps to prepare new electoral lists for the Dominion under its own law, but had allowed elections to be held on old lists which necessarily left out large numbers of persons entitled to vote. In accordance with the policy to which they had always pledged themselves as a party, the Liberal majority in parliament passed an act which returned to the electoral lists of the provinces. An attempt was also made in 1899 and 1900 to amend the redistribution acts of 1882 and 1892, and to restore so far as practicable the old county lines which had been deranged by those measures. The bill was noteworthy for the feature, novel in Canada, of leaving to the determination of a judicial commission the rearrangement of electoral divisions, but it was rejected in the senate on the ground that the British North America act provides only for the readjustment of the representation after the taking of each Decennial census, and that it is "a violation of the spirit of the act" to deal with the question until 1901, when the official figures of the whole population will be before parliament. The government was also called upon to arrange the details of a provisional government for the great arctic region of the Yukon, where remarkable gold discoveries were attracting a considerable population from all parts of the world. An attempt to build a short railway to facilitate communication with that wild and distant country was defeated in the senate by a large majority. The department of the interior has had necessarily to encounter many difficulties in the administration of the affairs of a country so many thousand miles distant. These difficulties have formed the subject of protracted debates in the house of commons and have led to involved political controversies which it would not be possible to explain satisfactorily within the limits of this chapter.

In accordance with the policy laid down in 1897 by Mr. Fielding, the finance minister, when presenting the budget, the Laurier government has not deemed it prudent to make such radical changes in the protective or "National Policy" of the previous administration as might derange the business conditions of the Dominion, which had come to depend so intimately upon it in the course of seventeen years, but simply to amend and simplify it in certain particulars which would remove causes of friction between the importers and the customs authorities, and at the same time make it, as they stated, less burdensome in its operation. The question of reciprocal trade between Canada and the United States had for some time been disappearing in the background and was no longer a dominant feature of the commercial policy of the Liberal party as it had been until 1891, when its leaders were prepared under existing conditions to enter into the fullest trade arrangements possible with the country to the south. The illiberality of the tariff of the United States with respect to Canadian products had led the Canadian people to look to new markets, and especially to those of Great Britain, with whom they were desirous, under the influence of a steadily growing imperial spirit, to have the closest commercial relations practicable. Consequently the most important feature of the Laurier government's policy, since 1897, has been the preference given to British products in Canada—a preference which now allows a reduction in the tariff of 33-1/3 per cent. on British imports compared with foreign goods. In their endeavour, however, to give a preference to British imports, the government was met at the outset by difficulties arising from the operation of the Belgian and German treaties; and after very full consultation with the imperial government, and a reference of the legal points involved to the imperial law officers of the crown, Canada was obliged to admit Belgian and German goods on the same terms as the imports of Great Britain, and also to concede similar advantages to twenty-two foreign countries which were by treaty entitled to any commercial privileges that Great Britain or her colonies might grant to a third power. Happily for Canada at this juncture the colonial secretary of state was Mr. Chamberlain, who was animated by aspirations for the strengthening of the relations between the parent state and her dependencies, and who immediately recognised the imperial significance of the voluntary action of the Canadian government. The result was the "denunciation" by the imperial authorities of the Belgian and German treaties, which consequently came to an end on the 31st July, 1898. Down to that date Canada was obliged to give to the other countries mentioned the preference which she had intentionally given to Great Britain alone, and at the same time to refund to importers the duties which had been collected in the interval from the countries in question. With the fall, however, of the Belgian and German treaties Canada was at last free to model her tariff with regard to imperial as well as Canadian interests. It was a fortunate coincidence that the government should have adopted this policy at a time when the whole British empire was celebrating the sixtieth anniversary of the accession of her Majesty Queen Victoria to the throne. In the magnificent demonstration of the unity and development of the empire that took place in London in June, 1897, Canada was represented by her brilliant prime minister, who then became the Right Honourable Sir W. Laurier, G.C.M.G., and took a conspicuous place in the ceremonies that distinguished this memorable episode in British and colonial history.

A few months later the relations between Canada and Great Britain were further strengthened by the reduction of letter postage throughout the empire—Australia excepted—largely through the instrumentality of Mr. Mulock, Canadian postmaster-general. The Canadian government and parliament also made urgent representations to the imperial authorities in favour of the immediate construction of a Pacific cable; and it may now be hoped that the pecuniary aid offered to this imperial enterprise by the British, Australasian and Canadian governments will secure its speedy accomplishment. I may add here that debates have taken place in the Canadian house of commons for several sessions on the desirability of obtaining preferential treatment in the British market for Canadian products The Conservative party, led by Sir Charles Tupper, have formulated their opinions in parliament by an emphatic declaration that "no measure of preference, which falls short of the complete realisation of such a policy, should be considered final or satisfactory." The Laurier government admits the desirability of such mutual trade preference, but at the same time it recognises the formidable difficulties that lie in the way of its realisation so long as Great Britain continues bound to free trade, and under these circumstances declares it the more politic and generous course to continue giving a special preference to British products with the hope that it may eventually bring about a change in public opinion in the parent state which will operate to the decided commercial or other advantage of the dependency.

This chapter may appropriately close with a reference to the remarkable evidences of attachment to the empire that have been given by the Canadian people at the close of the nineteenth century. From the mountains of the rich province washed by the Pacific Sea, from the wheat-fields and ranches of the western prairies, from the valley of the great lakes and the St. Lawrence where French and English Canadians alike enjoy the blessings of British rule, from the banks of the St John where the United Empire Loyalists first made their homes, from the rugged coasts of Acadia and Cape Breton, from every part of the wide Dominion men volunteered with joyous alacrity to fight in South Africa in support of the unity of the empire. As I close these pages Canadians are fighting side by side with men from the parent Isles, from Australasia and from South Africa, and have shown that they are worthy descendants of the men who performed such gallant deeds on the ever memorable battlefields of Chateauguay, Chrystler's Farm, and Lundy's Lane. Not the least noteworthy feature of this significant event in the annals of Canada and the empire is the fact that a French Canadian premier has had the good fortune to give full expression to the dominant imperial sentiment of the people, and consequently to offer an additional guarantee for the union of the two races and the security of British interests on the continent of America.

SECTION 4.—Political and social conditions of Canada under confederation.

At the present time, a population of probably five million four hundred thousand souls inhabit a Dominion of seven regularly organised provinces, and of an immense fertile territory stretching from Manitoba to British Columbia. This Dominion embraces an area of 3,519,000 square miles, including its water surface, or very little less than the area of the United States with Alaska, and measures 3500 miles from east to west; and 1400 miles from north to south.

No country in the world gives more conclusive evidences of substantial development and prosperity than the Dominion under the beneficial influences of federal union and the progressive measures of governments for many years. The total trade of the country has grown from over $131,000,000 in the first year of confederation to over $321,000,000 in 1899, while the national revenue has risen during the same period from $14,000,000 to $47,000,000, and will probably be $50,000,000 in 1900. The railways, whose expansion so closely depends on the material conditions of the whole country, stretch for 17,250 miles compared with 2278 miles in 1868; while the remarkable system of canals, which extend from the great lakes to Montreal, has been enlarged so as to give admirable facilities for the growing trade of the west. The natural resources of the country are inexhaustible, from the fisheries of Nova Scotia to the wheat-fields of the north-west, from the coal-mines of

Cape Breton to the gold deposits of the dreary country through which the Yukon and its tributaries flow.

No dangerous questions like slavery, or the expansion of the African race in the southern states, exist to complicate the political and social conditions of the confederation, and, although there is a large and increasing French Canadian element in the Dominion, its history so far need not create fear as to the future, except perhaps in the minds of gloomy pessimists. While this element naturally clings to its national language and institutions, yet, under the influence of a complete system of local self-government, it has always taken as active and earnest a part as the English element in establishing and strengthening the confederation. It has steadily grown in strength and prosperity under the generous and inspiring influence of British institutions, which have given full scope to the best attributes of a nationality crushed by the depressing conditions of French rule for a century and a half.

The federal union gives expansion to the national energies of the whole Dominion, and at the same time affords every security to the local interests of each member of the federal compact. In all matters of Dominion concern, Canada is a free agent. While the Queen is still head of the executive authority, and can alone initiate treaties with foreign nations (that being an act of complete sovereignty), and while appeals are still open to the privy council of England from Canadian courts within certain limitations, it is an admitted principle that the Dominion is practically supreme in the exercise of all legislative rights and privileges granted by the imperial parliament,—rights and privileges set forth explicitly in the British North America act of 1867,—so long as her legislative action does not conflict with the treaty obligations of the parent state, or with imperial legislation directly applicable to Canada with her own consent.

The crown exercises a certain supervision over the affairs of the Dominion through a governor-general, who communicates directly with an imperial secretary of state; but in every matter directly affecting Canada—as for instance, in negotiations respecting the fisheries, the Bering Sea, and other matters considered by several conferences at Washington—the Canadian government is consulted and its statements are carefully considered, since they represent the sentiments and interests of the Canadian people, who, as citizens of the empire, are entitled to as much weight as if they lived in the British Isles.

In the administration of Canadian affairs the governor-general is advised by a responsible council representing the majority of the house of commons. As in England, the Canadian cabinet, or ministry, is practically a committee of the dominant party in parliament and is governed by the rules, conventions and usages of parliamentary government which have grown up gradually in the parent state. Whenever it is necessary to form a ministry in Canada, its members are summoned by the governor-general to the privy council of Canada; another illustration of the desire of the Canadians to imitate the old institutions of England and copy her time-honoured procedure.

The parliament of Canada consists of the Queen, the senate, and the house of commons. In the formation of the upper house, three geographical groups were arranged in the first instance, Ontario, Quebec, and the maritime provinces, and each group received a representation of twenty-four members. More recently other provinces have been admitted into the Dominion without reference to this arrangement, and now seventy-eight senators altogether may sit in parliament. The remarkably long tenure of power enjoyed by the Conservative party—twenty-five years from 1867—enabled it in the course of time to fill the upper house with a very large numerical majority of its own friends, and this fact, taken in connection with certain elements of weakness inherent in a chamber which is not elected by the people and has none of the ancient privileges or prestige of a house of lords, long associated with the names of great statesmen and the memorable events of English history, has created an agitation among the Liberal party for radical changes in its constitution which would bring it, in their opinion, more in harmony with the people's representatives in the popular branch of the general legislature. While some extremists would abolish the chamber, Sir Wilfrid Launer and other prominent Liberals recognise its necessity in our parliamentary system. In all probability death will ere long solve difficulties arising out of the political composition of the body, if the Liberal party remain in power.

The house of commons, the great governing body of the Dominion, has been made, so far as circumstances will permit, a copy of the English house. Its members are not required to have a property qualification, and are elected by the votes of the electors of the several provinces where, in a majority of cases, universal suffrage, under limitations of citizenship and residence, prevails.

In each province there is a lieutenant-governor, appointed by the Dominion government for five years, an executive council, and a legislature consisting of only one house, except in Nova Scotia and Quebec where a legislative council appointed by the crown still continues. The principles of responsible government exist in all the provinces, and practically in the North-west territory.

In the enumeration of the legislative powers, respectively given to the Dominion and provincial legislatures, an effort was made to avoid the conflicts of jurisdiction that have so frequently arisen between the national and state governments of the United States. In the first place we have a recapitulation of those general or national powers that properly belong to the central authority, such as customs and excise duties, regulation of trade and commerce, militia and defence, post-office, banking and coinage, railways and public works "for the general advantage," navigation and shipping, naturalisation and aliens, fisheries, weights and measures, marriage and divorce, penitentiaries, criminal law, census and statistics. On the other hand, the provinces have retained control over municipal institutions, public lands, local works and undertakings, incorporation of companies with provincial objects, property and civil rights, administration of justice, and generally "all matters of a merely local and private nature in the province." The *residuary* power rests with the general parliament of Canada.

The parliament of Canada, in 1875, established a supreme court, or general court of appeal, for Canada, whose highest function is to decide questions as to the respective legislative powers of the Dominion and provincial parliaments, which are referred to it in due process of law by the subordinate courts of the provinces. The decisions of this court are already doing much to solve difficulties that impede the successful operation of the constitution. As a rule cases come before the supreme court on appeal from the lower courts, but the law regulating its powers provides that the governor in council may refer any matter to this court on which a question of constitutional jurisdiction has been raised. But the supreme court of Canada is not necessarily the court of last resort of Canada. The people have an inherent right as subjects of the Queen to appeal to the judicial committee of the privy council of the United Kingdom.

But it is not only by means of the courts that a check is imposed upon hasty, or unconstitutional, legislation. The constitution provides that the governor-general may veto or reserve any bill passed by the two houses of parliament when it conflicts with imperial interests or imperial legislation. It is now understood that the reserve power of disallowance which her Majesty's government possesses under the law is sufficient to meet all possible cases. This sovereign power is never exercised except in the case of an act clearly in conflict with an imperial statute or in violation of a treaty affecting a foreign nation. The Dominion government also supervises all the provincial legislation and has in a few cases disallowed provincial acts. This power is exercised very carefully, and it is regarded with intense jealousy by the provincial governments, which have more than once attempted to set it at defiance. In practice it is found the wisest course to leave to the courts the decision in cases where doubts exist as to constitutional authority or jurisdiction.

The organised districts of the North-west—Assiniboia, Alberta, Athabaska, and Saskatchewan—are governed by a lieutenant-governor appointed by the government of Canada and aided by a council chosen by himself from an assembly elected by the people under a very liberal franchise. These territories have also representatives in the two houses of the parliament of Canada. The Yukon territory in the far north-west, where rich discoveries of gold have attracted a large number of people within the past two years, is placed under a provisional government, composed of a commissioner and council appointed by the Dominion government[8], and acting under instructions given from time to time by the same authority or by the minister of the interior.

[8: Since this sentence was in type the Dominion government has given effect to a provision of a law allowing the duly qualified electors of the Yukon to choose two members of the council.]

The public service enjoys all the advantages that arise from permanency of tenure and appointment by the crown. It has on the whole been creditable to the country and remarkably free from political influences. The criminal law of England has prevailed in all the provinces since it was formerly introduced by the Quebec act of 1774. The civil law of the French regime, however, has continued to be the legal system in French Canada since the Quebec act, and has now obtained a hold in that province which insures its permanence as an institution closely allied with the dearest rights of the people. Its principles and maxims have been carefully collected and enacted in a code which is based on the famous code of Napoleon. In the other provinces and territories the common law of England forms the basis of jurisprudence on which a large body of Canadian statutory law has been built in the course of time.

At the present time all the provinces, with the exception of Prince Edward Island, have an excellent municipal system, which enables every defined district, large or small, to carry on efficiently all those public improvements essential to the comfort, convenience and general necessities of the different communities that make up the province at large. Even in the territories of the north-west, every proper facility is given to the people in a populous district, or town, to organise a system equal to all their local requirements.

Every Englishman will consider it an interesting and encouraging fact that the Canadian people, despite their neighbourhood to a prosperous federal commonwealth, should not even in the most critical and gloomy periods of their history have shown any disposition to mould their institutions directly on those of the United States and lay the foundation for future political union. Previous to 1840, which was the commencement of a new era in the political history of the provinces, there was a time when discontent prevailed throughout the Canadas, but not even then did any large body of the people threaten to sever the connection with the parent state. The Act of Confederation was framed under the direct influence of Sir John Macdonald and Sir George Cartier, and although one was an

English Canadian and the other a French Canadian, neither yielded to the other in the desire to build up a Dominion on the basis of English institutions, in the closest possible connection with the mother country. While the question of union was under consideration it was English statesmen and writers alone who predicted that this new federation, with its great extent of territory, its abundant resources, and ambitious people, would eventually form a new nation independent of Great Britain. Canadian statesmen never spoke or wrote of separation, but regarded the constitutional change in their political condition as giving them greater weight and strength in the empire. The influence of British example on the Canadian Dominion can be seen throughout its governmental machinery, in the system of parliamentary government, in the constitution of the privy council and the houses of parliament, in an independent judiciary, in appointed officials of every class—in the provincial as well as Dominion system—in a permanent and non-political civil service, and in all elements of sound administration. During the thirty-three years that have passed since 1867, the attachment to England and her institutions has gained in strength, and it is clear that those predictions of Englishmen to which we have referred are completely falsified. On the contrary, the dominant sentiment is for strengthening the ties that have in some respects become weak in consequence of the enlargement of the political rights of the Dominion, which has assumed the position of a semi-independent power, since England now only retains her imperial sovereignty by declaring peace or war with foreign nations, by appointing a governor-general, by controlling colonial legislation through the Queen in council and the Queen in parliament—but not so as to diminish the rights of local self-government conceded to the Dominion—and by requiring that all treaties with foreign nations should be made through her own government, while recognising the right of the dependency to be consulted and directly represented on all occasions when its interests are immediately affected.

In no respect have the Canadians followed the example of the United States, and made their executive entirely separate from the legislative authority. On the contrary, there is no institution which works more admirably in the federation—in the general as well as provincial governments—than the principle of making the ministry responsible to the popular branch of the legislature, and in that way keeping the executive and legislative departments in harmony with each other, and preventing that conflict of authorities which is a distinguishing feature of the very opposite system that prevails in the federal republic. If we review the amendments made of late years in the political constitutions of the States, and especially those ratified not long since in New York, we see in how many respects the Canadian system of government is superior to that of the republic. For instance, Canada has enjoyed for years, as results of responsible government, the secret ballot, stringent laws against bribery and corruption at all classes of elections, the registration of voters, strict naturalisation laws, infrequent political elections, separation of municipal from provincial or national contests, appointive and permanent officials in every branch of the civil service, a carefully devised code of private bill legislation, the printing of all public as well as private bills before their consideration by the legislative bodies; and yet all these essentials of safe administration and legislation are now only in part introduced by constitutional enactment in so powerful and progressive a state as New York.

Of course, in the methods of party government we can see in Canada at times an attempt to follow the example of the United States, and to introduce the party machine with its professional politicians and all those influences that have degraded politics since the days of Jackson and Van Buren. Happily, so far, the people of Canada have shown themselves fully capable of removing those blots that show themselves from time to time on the body politic. Justice has soon seized those men who have betrayed their trust in the administration of public affairs. Although Canadians may, according to their political proclivities, find fault with some methods of governments and be carried away at times by political passion beyond the bounds of reason, it is encouraging to find that all are ready to admit the high character of the judiciary for learning, integrity and incorruptibility. The records of Canada do not present a single instance of the successful impeachment or removal of a judge for improper conduct on the bench since the days of responsible government; and the three or four petitions laid before parliament, in the course of a quarter of a century, asking for an investigation into vague charges against some judges, have never required a judgment of the house. Canadians have built wisely when, in the formation of their constitution, they followed the English plan of retaining an intimate and invaluable connection between the executive and legislative departments, and of keeping the judiciary practically independent of the other authorities of government. Not only the life and prosperity of the people, but the satisfactory working of the whole system of federal government rests more or less on the discretion and integrity of the judges. Canadians are satisfied that the peace and security of the whole Dominion do not more depend on the ability and patriotism of statesmen in the legislative halls than on that principle of the constitution, which places the judiciary in an exalted position among all the other departments of government, and makes law as far as possible the arbiter of their constitutional conflicts. All political systems are very imperfect at the best; legislatures are constantly subject to currents of popular prejudice and passion; statesmanship is too often weak and fluctuating, incapable of appreciating the true tendency of events, and too ready to yield to the force of present circumstances or dictates of expediency; but law, as worked out on English principles in all the dependencies of the empire and countries of English origin, as understood by Blackstone, Dicey, Story, Kent, and other great masters of constitutional and legal learning, gives the best possible guarantee for the security of institutions in a country of popular government.

In an Appendix to this history I have given comparisons in parallel columns between the principal provisions of the federal constitutions of the Canadian Dominion, and the Australian Commonwealth. In studying carefully these two systems we must be impressed by the fact that the constitution of Canada appears more influenced by the spirit of English ideas than the constitution of Australia, which has copied some features of the fundamental law of the United States. In the preamble of the Canadian British North America act we find expressly stated "the desire of the Canadian provinces to be federally united into one Dominion under the crown of the United Kingdom of Great Britain and Ireland, with a constitution similar in principle to that of the United Kingdom," while the preamble of the Australian constitution contains only a bald statement of an agreement "to unite in one indissoluble federal Commonwealth under the crown," When we consider the use of "Commonwealth"—a word of republican significance to British ears—as well as the selection of "state" instead of "province," of "house of representatives" instead of "house of commons," of "executive council" instead of "privy council," we may well wonder why the Australians, all British by origin and aspiration, should have shown an inclination to deviate from the precedents established by the Canadian Dominion, which, though only partly English, resolved to carve the ancient historic names of the parent state on the very front of its political structure.

As the several States of the Commonwealth have full control of their own constitutions, they may choose at any moment to elect their own governors as in the States of the American Union, instead of having them appointed by the crown as in Canada. We see also an imitation of the American constitution in the principle which allots to the central government only certain enumerated powers, and leaves the residuary power of legislation to the States. Again, while the act provides for a high and other federal courts, the members of which are to be appointed and removed as in Canada by the central government, the States are still to have full jurisdiction over the State courts as in the United States. The Canadian constitution, which gives to the Dominion exclusive control over the appointment and removal of the judges of all the superior courts, offers a positive guarantee against the popular election of judges in the provinces. It is not going too far to suppose that, with the progress of democratic ideas in Australia—a country inclined to political experiments—we may find the experience of the United States repeated, and see elective judges make their appearance when a wave of democracy has suddenly swept away all dictates of prudence and given unbridled licence to professional political managers only anxious for the success of party. In allowing the British Parliament to amend the Act of Union on an address of the Canadian parliament, we have yet another illustration of the desire of Canadians to respect the supremacy of the sovereign legislature of the empire. On the other hand, the Australians make themselves entirely independent of the action of the imperial parliament, which might be invaluable in some crisis affecting deeply the integrity and unity of the Commonwealth, and give full scope to the will of democracy expressed at the polls. In also limiting the right of appeal to the Queen in council—by giving to the high court the power to prevent appeals in constitutional disputes—the Australians have also to a serious degree weakened one of the most important ties that now bind them to the empire, and afford additional illustration of the inferiority of the Australian constitution, from an imperial point of view, compared with that of the Canadian Dominion, where a reference to the judicial committee of the privy council is highly valued.

The Canadian people are displaying an intellectual activity commensurate with the expansion of their territory and their accumulation of wealth. The scientific, historical and political contributions of three decades, make up a considerable library which shows the growth of what may be called Canadian literature, since it deals chiefly with subjects essentially of Canadian interest. The attention that is now particularly devoted to the study and writing of history, and the collection of historical documents relating to the Dominion, prove clearly the national or thoroughly Canadian spirit that is already animating the cultured class of its people.

Of the numerous historical works that have appeared since 1867 two only demand special mention in this short review. One of these is *A History of the days of Montcalm and Lévis* by the Abbé Casgrain, who illustrates the studious and literary character of the professors of the great university which bears the name of the first bishop of Canada, Monseigneur Laval. A more elaborate general history of Canada, in ten octavo volumes, is that by Dr. Kingsford, whose life closed with his book. Whilst it shows much industry and conscientiousness on the part of the author, it fails too often to evoke our interest even when it deals with the striking and picturesque story of the French régime, since the author considered it his duty to be sober and prosaic when Parkman is bright and eloquent.

A good estimate of the progress of literary culture in Canada can be formed from a careful perusal of the poems of Bliss Carman, Archibald Lampman, Charles G.W. Roberts, Wilfred Campbell, Duncan Campbell Scott and Frederick George Scott. The artistic finish of their verse and the originality of their conception entitle them fairly to claim a foremost place alongside American poets since Longfellow, Emerson, Whittier, Bryant and Lowell have disappeared. Pauline Johnson, who has Indian blood in her veins,

Archbishop O'Brien of Halifax, Miss Machar, Ethelyn Weatherald, Charles Mair and several others might also be named to prove that poetry is not a lost art in Canada, despite its pressing prosaic and material needs.

Dr. Louis Fréchette is a worthy successor of Crémazie and has won the distinction of having his best work crowned by the French Academy. French Canadian poetry, however, has been often purely imitative of French models like Musset and Gautier, both in style and sentiment, and consequently lacks strength and originality. Fréchette has all the finish of the French poets and, while it cannot be said that he has yet originated fresh thoughts, which are likely to live among even the people whom he has so often instructed and delighted, yet he has given us poems like that on the discovery of the Mississippi which prove that he is capable of even better things if he would seek inspiration from the sources of the deeply interesting history of his own country, or enter into the inner mysteries and social relations of his picturesque compatriots.

The life of the French Canadian habitant has been admirably described in verse by Dr. Drummond, who has always lived among that class of the Canadian people and been a close observer of their national and personal characteristics. He is the only writer who has succeeded in giving a striking portraiture of life in the cabin, in the "shanty" (*chantier*), and on the river, where the French habitant, forester, and canoe-man can be seen to best advantage.

But if Canada can point to some creditable achievements of recent years in history, poetry and essays, there is one department in which Canadians never won any marked success until recently, and that is in the novel or romance. Even Mr. Kirby's *Le Chien d'Or* which recalls the closing days of the French régime—the days of the infamous Intendant Bigot who fattened on Canadian misery—does not show the finished art of the skilled novelist, though it has a certain crude vigour of its own, which has enabled it to live while so many other Canadian books have died. French Canada is even weaker in this particular, and this is the more surprising because there is abundance of material for the novelist or the writer of romance in her peculiar society and institutions. But this reproach has been removed by Mr. Gilbert Parker, now a resident in London, but a

Canadian by birth, education and sympathies, who is animated by a laudable ambition of giving form and vitality to the abundant materials that exist in the Dominion for the true story-teller. His works show great skill in the use of historic matter, more than ordinary power in the construction of a plot, and, above all, a literary finish which is not equalled by any Canadian writer in the same field of effort. Other meritorious Canadian workers in romance are Mr. William McLennan, Mrs. Coates (Sarah Jeannette Duncan), and Miss Dougall, whose names are familiar to English readers.

The name of Dr. Todd is well known throughout the British empire, and indeed wherever institutions of government are studied, as that of an author of most useful works on the English and Canadian constitutions. Sir William Dawson, for many years the energetic principal of McGill University, the scientific prominence of which is due largely to his mental bias, was the author of several geological books, written in a graceful and readable style. The scientific work of Canadians can be studied chiefly in the proceedings of English, American and Canadian societies, especially, of late years, in the transactions of the Royal Society of Canada, established over eighteen years ago by the Marquess of Lorne when governor-general of the Dominion. This successful association is composed of one hundred and twenty members who have written "memoirs of merit or rendered eminent services to literature or science."

On the whole, there have been enough good poems, histories, and essays, written and published in Canada during the last four or five decades, to prove that there has been a steady intellectual growth on the part of the Canadian people, and that it has kept pace at all events with the mental growth in the pulpit, or in the legislative halls, where, of late years, a keen practical debating style has taken the place of the more rhetorical and studied oratory of old times. The intellectual faculties of Canadians only require larger opportunities for their exercise to bring forth rich fruit. The progress in the years to come will be much greater than that Canadians have yet shown, and necessarily so, with the wider distribution of wealth, the dissemination of a higher culture, and a greater confidence in their own mental strength, and in the opportunities that the country offers to pen and pencil. What is now wanted is the cultivation of a good style and artistic workmanship.

Much of the daily literature of Canadians—indeed the chief literary aliment of large numbers—is the newspaper press, which illustrates necessarily the haste, pressure and superficiality of writings of that ephemeral class. Canadian journals, however, have not yet descended to the degraded sensationalism of New York papers, too many of which circulate in Canada to the public detriment. On the whole, the tone of the most ably conducted journals—the Toronto *Globe*, and the Montreal *Gazette* notably—is quite on a level with the tone of debate in the legislative bodies of the country.

Now, as in all times of Canada's history, political life claims many strong, keen and cultured intellects, though at the same time it is too manifest that the tendency of democratic conditions and heated party controversy is to prevent the most highly educated and sensitive organisations from venturing on the agitated and unsafe sea of political passion and competition. The speeches of Sir Wilfrid Laurier—the eloquent French Canadian premier, who in his mastery of the English tongue surpasses all his versatile compatriots—of Sir Charles Tupper, Mr. Foster and others who might be mentioned, recall the most brilliant period of parliamentary annals (1867—1873), when in the first parliament of the Dominion the most prominent men of the provinces were brought into public life, under the new conditions of federal union. The debating power of the provincial legislative bodies is excellent, and the chief defects are the great length and discursiveness of the speeches on local as well as on national questions. It is also admitted that of late years there has been a tendency to impair the dignity and to lower the tone of discussion.

Many Canadians have devoted themselves to art since 1867, and some Englishmen will recognise the names of L.R. O'Brien, Robert Harris, J.W.L. Forster, Homer Watson, George Reid—the painter of "The Foreclosure of the Mortgage," which won great praise at the World's Fair of Chicago—John Hammond, F.A. Verner, Miss Bell, Miss Muntz, W. Brymner, all of whom are Canadians by birth and inspiration. The establishment of a Canadian Academy of Art by the Princess Louise, and of other art associations, has done a good deal to stimulate a taste for art, though the public encouragement of native artists is still very inadequate, when we consider the excellence already attained under great difficulties in a relatively new country, where the great mass of people has yet to be educated to a perception of the advantages of high artistic effort.

Sculpture would be hardly known in Canada were it not for the work of the French Canadian Hebert, who is a product of the schools of Paris, and has given to the Dominion several admirable statues and monuments of its public men. While Canadian architecture has hitherto been generally wanting in originality of conception, the principal edifices of the provinces afford many good illustrations of effective adaptation of the best art of Europe. Among these may be mentioned the following:—the parliament and departmental buildings at Ottawa, admirable examples of Italian Gothic; the legislative buildings at Toronto, in the Romanesque style; the English cathedrals in Montreal and Fredericton, correct specimens of early English Gothic; the French parish church of Notre-Dame, in Montreal, attractive for its stately Gothic proportions; the university of Toronto, an admirable conception of Norman architecture; the Canadian Pacific railway station at Montreal and the Frontenac Hotel at Quebec, fine examples of the adaptation of old Norman architecture to modern necessities; the provincial buildings at Victoria, in British Columbia, the general design of which is Renaissance, rendered most effective by pearl-grey stone and several domes; the headquarters of the bank of Montreal, a fine example of the Corinthian order, and notable for the artistic effort to illustrate, on the walls of the interior, memorable scenes in Canadian history; the county and civic buildings of Toronto, an ambitious effort to reproduce the modern Romanesque, so much favoured by the eminent American architect, Richardson; Osgoode Hall, the seat of the great law courts of the province of Ontario, which in its general character recalls the architecture of the Italian Renaissance. Year by year we see additions to our public and private buildings, interesting from an artistic point of view, and illustrating the accumulating wealth of the country, as well as the growth of culture and taste among the governing classes.

The universities, colleges, academies, and high schools, the public and common schools of the Dominion, illustrate the great desire of the governments and the people of the provinces to give the greatest possible facilities for the education of all classes at the smallest possible cost to individuals. At the present time there are between 13,000 and 14,000 students attending 62 universities and colleges. The collegiate institutes and academies of the provinces also rank with the colleges as respects the advantages they give to young men and women. Science is especially prominent in McGill and Toronto Universities—which are the most largely attended—and the former affords a notable example of the munificence of the wealthy men of Montreal, in establishing chairs of science and otherwise advancing its educational usefulness. Laval University stands deservedly at the head of the Roman Catholic institutions of the continent, on account of its deeply interesting historic associations, and the scholarly attainments of its professors, several of whom have won fame in Canadian letters. Several universities give instructions in medicine and law, and Toronto has also a medical college for women. At the present time, at least one-fifth of the people of the Dominion is in attendance at the universities, colleges, public and private schools. The people of Canada contribute upwards of ten millions of dollars annually to the support of their educational establishments, in the shape of government grants, public taxes, or private fees. Ontario alone, in 1899, raised five millions and a half of dollars for the support of its public school system; and of this amount the people directly contributed ninety-one per cent, in the shape of taxes. On the other hand, the libraries of Canada are not numerous; and it is only in Ontario that there is a law providing for the establishment of such institutions by a vote of the taxpayers in the municipalities. In this province there are at least 420 libraries, of which the majority are connected with mechanics' institutes, and are made public by statute. The weakness of the public school system—especially in Ontario—is the constant effort to teach a child a little of everything, and to make him a mere machine. The consequences are superficiality—a veneer of knowledge—and the loss of individuality.

CHAPTER X.

CANADA'S RELATIONS WITH THE UNITED STATES AND HER INFLUENCE IN IMPERIAL COUNCILS (1783—1900).

I have deemed it most convenient to reserve for the conclusion of this history a short review of the relations that have existed for more than a century between the provinces of the Dominion and the United States, whose diplomacy and legislation have had, and must always have, a considerable influence on the material and social conditions of the people of Canada.—an influence only subordinate to that exercised by the imperial state. I shall show that during the years when there was no confederation of Canada—when there were to the north and north-east of the United States only a number of isolated provinces, having few common sympathies or interests except their attachment to the crown and empire—the United States had too often its own way in controversial questions affecting the colonies which arose between England and the ambitious federal republic. On the other hand, with the territorial expansion of the provinces under one Dominion, with their political development, which has assumed even national attributes, with the steady growth of an imperial sentiment in the parent state, the old condition of things that too often made the provinces the shuttlecock of skilful American diplomacy has passed away. The statesmen of the Canadian federation are now consulted, and exercise almost as much influence as if they were members of the imperial councils in London.

I shall naturally commence this review with a reference to the treaty of 1783, which acknowledged the independence of the United States, fixed the boundaries between that country and British North America, and led to serious international disputes which lasted until the middle of the following century. Three of the ablest men in the United States—Franklin, John Adams, and John Jay—succeeded by their astuteness and persistency in extending their country's limits to the eastern bank of the Mississippi, despite the insidious efforts of Vergennes on the part of France to hem in the new nation between the Atlantic and the Appalachian Range. The comparative value set upon Canada during the preliminary negotiations may be easily deduced from the fact that Oswald, the English plenipotentiary, proposed to give up to the United States the south-western and most valuable part of the present province of Ontario, and to carry the north-eastern boundary up to the River St. John. The commissioners of the United States did not accept this suggestion. Their ultimate object—an object actually attained—was to make the St. Lawrence the common boundary between the two countries by following the centre of the river and the great lakes as far as the head of Lake Superior. The issue of negotiations so stupidly conducted by the British commissioner, was a treaty which gave an extremely vague definition of the boundary in the north-east between Maine and Nova Scotia—which until 1784 included New Brunswick—and displayed at the same time a striking example of geographical ignorance as to the north-west. The treaty specified that the boundary should pass from the head of Lake Superior through Long Lake to the north-west angle of the Lake of the Woods, and thence to the Mississippi, when, as a matter of fact there was no Long Lake, and the source of the Mississippi was actually a hundred miles or so to the south of the Lake of the Woods. This curious blunder in the north-west was only rectified in 1842, when Lord Ashburton settled the difficulty by conceding to the United States an invaluable corner of British territory in the east (see below, p 299).

The only practical advantage that the people of the provinces gained from the Treaty of Ghent, which closed the war of 1812—15, was an acknowledgment of the undoubted fishery rights of Great Britain and her dependencies in the territorial waters of British North America. In the treaty of 1783 the people of the United States obtained the "right" to fish on the Grand and other banks of Newfoundland, and in the Gulf of St. Lawrence and at "all other places in the sea, where the inhabitants of both countries used at any time heretofore to fish", but they were to have only "the liberty" of taking fish on the coasts of Newfoundland and also of "all other of his Britannic Majesty's dominions in America; and also of drying and curing fish in any of the unsettled bays, harbours, and creeks of Nova Scotia (then including New Brunswick), Magdalen Islands, and Labrador, so long as the same shall remain unsettled." In the one case, it will be seen, there was a recognised right, but in the other only a mere "liberty" or privilege extended to the fishermen of the

United States. At the close of the war of 1812 the British government would not consent to renew the merely temporary liberties of 1783, and the United States authorities acknowledged the soundness of the principle that any privileges extended to the republic in British territorial waters could only rest on "conventional stipulation." The convention of 1818 forms the legal basis of the rights, which Canadians have always maintained in the case of disputes between themselves and the United States as to the fisheries on their own coasts, bays, and harbours of Canada. It provides that the inhabitants of the United States shall have for ever the liberty to take, dry, and cure fish on certain parts of the coast of Newfoundland, on the Magdalen Islands and on the southern shores of Labrador, but they "renounce for ever any liberty, heretofore enjoyed" by them to take, dry, and cure fish, "on or within three marine miles of any of the coasts, bays or creeks or harbours of his Britannic Majesty's other dominions in America"; provided, however, that the American fishermen shall be admitted to enter such bays and harbours, for the purpose of shelter, and of repairing damages therein, of purchasing wood, and of obtaining water, and "for no other purpose whatever."

In April, 1817, the governments of Great Britain and the United States came to an important agreement which ensured the neutrality of the great lakes. It was agreed that the naval forces to be maintained upon these inland waters should be confined to the following vessels: on Lakes Champlain and Ontario to one vessel, on the Upper Lakes to two vessels, not exceeding in each case a hundred tons burden and armed with only one small cannon. Either nation had the right to bring the convention to a termination by a previous notice of six months. This agreement is still regarded by Great Britain and the United States to be in existence, since Mr. Secretary Seward formally withdrew the notice which was given for its abrogation in 1864, when the civil war was in progress and the relations between the two nations were considerably strained at times.

The next international complication arose out of the seizure of the steamer *Caroline*, which was engaged in 1837 in carrying munitions of war between the United States and Navy Island, then occupied by a number of persons in the service of Mr. Mackenzie and other

Canadian rebels. In 1840 the authorities of New York arrested one Macleod on the charge of having murdered a man who was employed on the *Caroline*. The Washington government for some time evaded the whole question by throwing the responsibility on the state authorities and declaring that they could not interfere with a matter which was then within the jurisdiction of the state courts. The matter gave rise to much correspondence between the two governments, but happily for the peace of the two countries the American courts acquitted Macleod, as the evidence was clear that he had had nothing to do with the actual seizing of the *Caroline*; and the authorities at Washington soon afterwards acknowledged their responsibility in such affairs by passing an act directing that subjects of foreign powers, if taken into custody for acts done or committed under the authority of their own government, "the validity or effect whereof depends upon the law of nations, should be discharged." The dissatisfaction that had arisen in the United States on account of the cutting out of the *Caroline* was removed in 1842, when Sir Robert Peel expressed regret that "some explanation and apology for the occurrence had not been previously made," and declared that it was "the opinion of candid and honourable men that the British officers who executed this transaction, and their government who approved it, intended no insult or disrespect to the sovereign authority of the United States[9]."

[9: Hall's *Treatise on International Law* (3rd ed.), pp. 311—313]

In the course of time the question of the disputed boundary between Maine and New Brunswick assumed grave proportions. By the treaty of 1783, the boundary was to be a line drawn from the source of the St. Croix, directly north to the highlands "which divide the rivers which fall into the Atlantic ocean from those which fall into the river St. Lawrence;" thence along the said highlands to the north-easternmost head of the Connecticut River; and the point at which the due north line was to cut the highlands was also designated as the north-west angle of Nova Scotia. The whole question was the subject of several commissions, and of one arbitration, from 1783 until 1842, when it was finally settled. Its history appears to be that of a series of blunders on the part of England from the beginning to the end. The first blunder occurred in 1796 when the commissioners appointed to inquire into the question, declared that the Schoodic was the River St. Croix mentioned in the treaty. Instead, however, of following the main, or western, branch of the Schoodic to its source in the Schoodic Lakes, they went beyond their instructions and chose a northern tributary of the river, the Chiputnaticook, as the boundary, and actually placed a monument at its head as a basis for any future proceeding on the part of the two governments. The British government appear to have been very anxious at this time to settle the question, for they did not take exception to the arrangement made by the commissioners, but in 1798 declared the decision binding on both countries.

Still this mistake might have been rectified had the British government in 1835 been sufficiently alive to British interests in America to have accepted a proposal made to them by President Jackson to ascertain the true north-western angle of Nova Scotia, or the exact position of the highlands, in accordance with certain well-understood rules in practical surveying which have been always considered obligatory in that continent. It was proposed by the United States to discard the due north line, to seek to the west of that line the undisputed highlands that divide the rivers which empty themselves into the River St. Lawrence from those which fall into the Atlantic Ocean, to find the point in the 'watershed' of these highlands nearest to the north line, and to trace a direct course from it to the monument already established. "If this principle had been adopted," says Sir Sandford Fleming, the eminent Canadian engineer, "a straight line would have been drawn from the monument at the head of the Chiputnaticook to a point which could have been established with precision in the 'watershed' of the highlands which separate the sources of the Chaudière from those of the Penobscot,—this being the most easterly point in the only highlands agreeing beyond dispute with the treaty. The point is found a little to the north and west of the intersection of the 70th meridian west longitude and the 46th parallel of north latitude." Had this proposal been accepted England would have obtained without further difficulty eleven thousand square miles, or the combined areas of Massachusetts and Connecticut.

For several years after this settlement was suggested a most serious conflict went on between New Brunswick and the state of Maine. The authorities of Maine paid no respect whatever to the negotiations that were still in progress between the governments of Great Britain and the United States, but actually took possession of the disputed territory, gave titles for lands and constructed forts and roads within its limits. Collisions occurred between the settlers and the intruders, and considerable property was destroyed. The legislature of Maine voted $800,000 for the defence of the state, and the legislature of Nova Scotia amid great enthusiasm made a grant of $100,000 to assist New Brunswick in support of her rights. Happily the efforts of the United States and British governments prevented the quarrel between the province and the state from assuming international proportions; and in 1842 Mr. Alexander Baring, afterwards Lord Ashburton, was authorised by the ministry of the Earl of Aberdeen to negotiate with Mr. Daniel Webster, then secretary of state in the American cabinet, for the settlement of matters in dispute between the two nations. The result was the Ashburton Treaty, which, in fixing the north-eastern boundary between British North America and the United States, started due north from the monument incorrectly placed at the head of the Chiputnaticook instead of the source of the true St. Croix, and consequently at the very outset gave up a strip of land extending over some two degrees of latitude, and embracing some 3000 square miles of British territory. By consenting to carry the line due north from the misplaced monument Lord Ashburton ignored the other natural landmark set forth in the treaty: "the line of headlands which divide the waters flowing into the Atlantic from those which flow into the St. Lawrence." A most erratic boundary was established along the St. John, which flows neither into the St. Lawrence nor the Atlantic, but into the Bay of Fundy, far east of the St. Croix. In later years the historian Sparks found in Paris a map on which Franklin himself had marked in December, 1782, with a heavy red line, what was then considered the true natural boundary between the two countries. Mr. Sparks admitted in sending the map that it conceded more than Great Britain actually claimed, and that "the line from the St. Croix to the Canadian highlands is intended to exclude [from the territory of the United States] all the waters running into the St.

John." Canadians have always believed with reason that that portion of the present state of Maine, through which the Aroostook and other tributaries of the St. John flow, is actually British territory. If we look at the map of Canada we see that the state of Maine now presses like a huge wedge into the provinces of New Brunswick and Quebec as a sequence of the unfortunate mistakes of 1796, 1835, and 1842, on the part of England and her agents. In these later times a "Canadian short line" railway has been forced to go through Maine in order to connect Montreal with St. John, and other places in the maritime provinces. Had the true St. Croix been chosen in 1796, or President Jackson's offer accepted in 1835, this line could go continuously through Canadian territory, and be entirely controlled by Canadian legislation.

Another boundary question was the subject of much heated controversy between England and the United States for more than a quarter of a century, and in 1845 brought the two countries very close to war. In 1819 the United States obtained from Spain a cession of all her rights and claims north of latitude forty-two, or the southern boundary of the present state of Oregon. By that time the ambition of the United States was not content with the Mississippi valley, of which she had obtained full control by the cession of the Spanish claims and by the Louisiana purchase of 1803, but looked to the Pacific coast, where she made pretensions to a territory stretching from 42° to 54° 40' north latitude, or a territory four times the area of Great Britain and Ireland, or of the present province of Ontario. The claims of the two nations to this vast region rested on very contradictory statements with respect to priority of discovery, and that occupation and settlement which should, within reasonable limits, follow discovery; and as the whole question was one of great perplexity, it should have been settled, as suggested by England, on principles of compromise. But the people of the United States, conscious at last of the importance of the territory, began to bring their influence to bear on the politicians, until by 1845 the Democratic party declared 'for 54° 40' or fight,' Mr. Crittenden announced that "war might now be looked upon as almost inevitable." Happily President Polk and congress came to more pacific conclusions after a good deal of warlike talk; and the result was a treaty (1846) by which England accepted the line 49 degrees to the Pacific coast, and obtained the whole of Vancouver Island, which for a while seemed likely to be divided with the United States. But Vancouver Island was by no means a compensation for what England gave up, for, on the continent, she yielded all she had contended for since 1824, when she first proposed the Columbia River as a basis of division.

But even then the question of boundary was not finally settled by this great victory which had been won for the United States by the persistency of her statesmen. The treaty of 1846 continued the line of boundary westward along "the 49th parallel of north latitude to the middle of the channel which separates the continent from Vancouver Island, and thence southerly through the middle of the said channel and of Fuca's straits to the Pacific Ocean" Anyone reading this clause for the first time, without reference to the contentions that were raised afterwards, would certainly interpret it to mean the whole body of water that separates the continent from Vancouver, — such a channel, in fact, as divides England from France; but it appears there are a number of small channels separating the islands which lie in the great channel in question, and the clever diplomatists at Washington immediately claimed the Canal de Haro, the widest and deepest, as the canal of the treaty. Instead of at once taking the ground that the whole body of water was really in question, the English government claimed another channel, Rosario Strait, inferior in some respects, but the one most generally, and indeed only, used at the time by their vessels. The importance of this difference of opinion lay chiefly in the fact, that the Haro gave San Juan and other small islands, valuable for defensive purposes, to the United States, while the Rosario left them to England. Then, after much correspondence, the British government, as a compromise, offered the middle channel, or Douglas, which would still retain San Juan. If they had always adhered to the Douglas — which appears to answer the conditions of the treaty, since it lies practically in the middle of the great channel — their position would have been much stronger than it was when they came back to the Rosario. The British representatives at the Washington conference of 1871 suggested the reference of the question to arbitration, but the United States' commissioners, aware of their vantage ground, would consent to no other arrangement than to leave to the decision of the Emperor of

Germany the question whether the Haro or the Rosario channel best accorded with the treaty; and the Emperor decided in favour of the United States. However, with the possession of Vancouver in its entirety, Canada can still be grateful; and San Juan is now only remembered as an episode of skilful American diplomacy. The same may be said of another acquisition of the republic—insignificant from the point of view of territorial area, but still illustrative of the methods which have won all the great districts we have named — Rouse's Point at the outlet of Lake Champlain, "of which an exact survey would have deprived" the United States, according to Mr. Schouler in his excellent history.

During this period the fishery question again assumed considerable importance. The government at Washington raised the contention that the three miles' limit, to which their fishermen could be confined by the convention of 1818, should follow the sinuosities of the coasts, including the bays, the object being to obtain access to the valuable mackerel fisheries of the Bay of Chaleurs and other waters claimed to be exclusively within the territorial jurisdiction of the maritime provinces. The imperial government sustained the contention of the provinces—a contention practically supported by American authorities in the case of the Delaware, Chesapeake, and other bays on the coast of the United States—that the three miles' limit should be measured from a line drawn from headlands of all bays, harbours and creeks. In the case of the Bay of Fundy, however, the imperial government allowed a departure from this general principle, when it was urged by the Washington government that one of its headlands was in the territory of the United States, and that it was an arm of the sea rather than a bay. The result was that foreign fishing vessels were only shut out from the bays on the coasts of Nova Scotia and New Brunswick within the Bay of Fundy. All these questions were, however, placed in abeyance by the reciprocity treaty of 1854 (see p. 96), which lasted until 1866, when it was repealed by the action of the United States, in accordance with the provision bringing it to a conclusion after one year's notice from one of the parties interested.

The causes which led in 1866 to the repeal of a treaty so advantageous to the United States have been long well understood. The commercial classes in the eastern and western states were, on the whole, favourable to an enlargement of the treaty; but the real cause of its repeal was the prejudice in the northern states against Canada on account of its supposed sympathy for the confederate states during the Secession war. A large body of men in the north believed that the repeal of the treaty would sooner or later force Canada to join the republic; and a bill was actually introduced in the house of representatives providing for her admission—a mere political straw, it is true, but showing the current of opinion in some quarters in those days. When we review the history of those times, and consider the difficult position in which Canada was placed, it is remarkable how honourably her government discharged its duties of a neutral between the belligerents. In the case of the raid of some confederate refugees in Canada on the St. Alban's bank in Vermont, the Canadian authorities brought the culprits to trial and even paid a large sum of money in acknowledgment of an alleged responsibility when some of the stolen notes were returned to the robbers on their release on technical grounds by a Montreal magistrate. It is well, too, to remember how large a number of Canadians fought in the union armies—twenty against one who served in the south. No doubt the position of Canada was made more difficult at that critical time by the fact that she was a colony of Great Britain, against whom both north and south entertained bitter feelings by the close of the war; the former mainly on account of the escape of confederate cruisers from English ports, and the latter because she did not receive active support from England. The north had also been much excited by the promptness with which Lord Palmerston had sent troops to Canada when Mason and Slidell were seized on an English packet on the high seas, and by the bold tone held by some Canadian papers when it was doubtful if the prisoners would be released.

Before and since the union, the government of Canada has made repeated efforts to renew a commercial treaty with the government at Washington. In 1865 and 1866, Canadian delegates were prepared to make large concessions, but were reluctantly brought to the conclusion that the committee of ways and means in congress "no longer desired trade between the two countries to be carried on upon the principle of reciprocity." In 1866 Sir John Rose, while minister of finance, made an effort in the same direction, but he was met by the obstinate refusal of the republican party, then as always, highly protective.

All this while the fishery question was assuming year by year a form increasingly irritating to the two countries. The headland question was the principal difficulty, and the British government, in order to conciliate the United States at a time when the Alabama question was a subject of anxiety, induced the Canadian government to agree, very reluctantly it must be admitted, to shut out foreign fishing vessels only from bays less than six miles in width at their entrances. In this, however, as in all other matters, the Canadian authorities acknowledged their duty to yield to the considerations of imperial interests, and acceded to the wishes of the imperial government in almost every respect, except actually surrendering their territorial rights in the fisheries. They issued licenses to fish, at low rates, for several years, only to find eventually that American fishermen did not think it worth while to buy these permits when they could evade the regulations with little difficulty. The correspondence went on for several years, and eventually led to the Washington conference or commission of 1871, which was primarily intended to settle the fishery question, but which actually gave the precedence to the Alabama difficulty—then of most concern in the opinion of the London and Washington governments. The representatives of the United States would not consider a proposition for another reciprocity treaty on the basis of that of 1854. The questions arising out of the convention of 1818 were not settled by the commission, but were practically laid aside for ten years by an arrangement providing for the free admission of salt-water fish to the United States, on the condition of allowing the fishing vessels of that country free access to the Canadian fisheries. The free navigation of the St. Lawrence was conceded to the United States in return for the free use of Lake Michigan and of certain rivers in Alaska. The question of giving to the vessels of the Canadian provinces the privilege of trading on the coast of the United States—a privilege persistently demanded for years by Nova Scotia—was not considered; and while the canals of Canada were opened up to the United States on the most liberal terms, the Washington government contented itself with a barren promise in the treaty to use its influence with the authorities of the states to open up their artificial waterways to Canadians. The Fenian claims were abruptly laid aside, although, if the principle of "due diligence," which was laid down in the new rules for the settlement of the Alabama difficulty had been applied to this question, the government of the United States would have been mulcted in heavy damages. In this case it would be difficult to find a more typical instance of responsibility assumed by a state through the permission of open and notorious acts, and by way of complicity after the acts; however, as in many other negotiations with the United States, Canada felt she must make sacrifices for the empire, whose government wished all causes of irritation between England and the United States removed as far as possible by the treaty. One important feature of this commission was the presence, for the first time in the history of treaties, of a Canadian statesman. The astute prime minister of the Dominion, Sir John Macdonald, was chosen as one of the English high commissioners: and though he was necessarily tied down by the instructions of the imperial state, his knowledge of Canadian questions was of great service to Canada during the conference. If the treaty finally proved more favourable to the Dominion than it at first appeared to be, it was owing largely to the clause which provided for a reference to a later commission of the question, whether the United States would not have to pay the Canadians a sum of money, as the value of their fisheries over and above any concessions made them in the treaty. The result of this commission was a payment of five millions and a half of dollars to Canada and Newfoundland, to the infinite disappointment of the politicians of the United States, who had been long accustomed to have the best in all the bargains with their neighbours. Nothing shows more clearly the measure of the local self-government at last won by Canada and the importance of her position in the empire, than the fact that the English government recognised the right of the Dominion government to name the commissioner who represented Canada on an arbitration which decided a question of such deep importance to her interests.

The clauses of the Washington treaty relating to the fisheries and to trade with Canada lasted for fourteen years, and then were repealed by the action of the United States government. In the year 1874 the Mackenzie ministry attempted, through Mr. George Brown, to negotiate a new reciprocity treaty, but met with a persistent hostility from leading men in congress. The relations between Canada and the United States again assumed a phase of great uncertainty. Canada from 1885 adhered to the letter of the convention of 1818, and allowed no fishing vessels to fish within the three miles limit, to transship cargoes of fish in her ports, or to enter them for any purpose except for shelter, wood, water, and repairs. For the infractions of the treaty several vessels were seized, and more than one of them condemned. A clamour was raised in the United States on the ground that the Canadians were wanting in that spirit of friendly intercourse which should characterise the relations of neighbouring peoples. The fact is, the Canadians were bound to adhere to their legal rights—rights which had always been maintained before 1854; which had remained in abeyance between 1854 and 1866; which naturally revived after the repeal of the reciprocity treaty of 1854; which again remained in abeyance between 1871 and 1885; and were revived when the United States themselves chose to go back to the terms of the convention of 1818.

In 1887 President Cleveland and Mr. Secretary Bayard, acting in a statesmanlike spirit, obtained the consent of England to a special commission to consider the fishery question. Sir Sackville West, Mr. Joseph Chamberlain, and Sir Charles Tupper represented England; Mr. Bayard, then secretary of state, Mr. Putnam of Maine, and Mr. Angell of Michigan University, represented the United States. Sir Charles Tupper could not induce the American commissioners to consider a mutual arrangement providing for greater freedom of commercial intercourse between Canada and the United States. Eventually the commission agreed unanimously to a treaty which was essentially a compromise. Foreign fishermen were to be at liberty to go into any waters where the bay was more than ten miles wide at the mouth, but certain bays, including the Bay of Chaleurs, were expressly excepted in the interests of Canada from the operation of this provision. The United States did not attempt to acquire the right to fish on the inshore fishing-grounds of Canada— that is, within three miles of the coasts—but these fisheries were to be left for the exclusive use of the Canadian fishermen. More satisfactory arrangements were made for vessels obliged to resort to the Canadian ports in distress; and a provision was made for allowing American fishing-vessels to obtain supplies and other privileges in the harbours of the Dominion whenever congress allowed the fish of that country to enter free into the market of the United States, President Cleveland in his message, submitting the treaty to the senate, acknowledged that it "supplied a satisfactory, practical and final adjustment, upon a basis honourable and just to both parties, of the difficult and vexed questions to which it relates." The republican party, however, at that important juncture—just before a presidential election—had a majority in the senate, and the result was the failure in that body of a measure, which, although by no means too favourable to Canadian interests, was framed in a spirit of judicious statesmanship.

As a sequel of the acquisition of British Columbia, the Canadian government was called upon in 1886 to urge the interests of the Dominion in an international question that had arisen in Bering Sea. A United States cutter seized in the open sea, at a distance of more than sixty miles from the nearest land, certain Canadian schooners, fitted out in British Columbia, and lawfully engaged in the capture of seals in the North Pacific Ocean, adjacent to Vancouver Island, Queen Charlotte Islands, and Alaska—a portion of the territory of the United States acquired in 1867 from Russia. These vessels were taken into a port of Alaska, where they were subjected to forfeiture, and the masters and mates fined and imprisoned. Great Britain at once resisted the claim of the United States to the sole sovereignty of that part of Bering Sea lying beyond the westerly boundary of Alaska—a stretch of sea extending in its widest part some 600 or 700 miles beyond the mainland of Alaska, and clearly under the law of nations a part of the great sea and open to all nations. Lord Salisbury's government, from the beginning to the end of the controversy, sustained the rights of Canada as a portion of the British empire. After very protracted and troublesome negotiations it was agreed to refer the international question in dispute to a court of arbitration, in which Sir John Thompson, prime minister of Canada, was one of the British arbitrators. The arbitrators decided in favour of the British contention that the United States had no jurisdiction in Bering Sea outside of the three miles limit, and at the same time made certain regulations to restrict the wholesale slaughter of fur-bearing seals in the North Pacific Ocean. In 1897 two commissioners, appointed by the governments of the United States and Canada, awarded the sum of $463,454 as compensation to Canada for the damages sustained by the fishermen of British Columbia, while engaged in the lawful prosecution of their industry on that portion of the Bering Sea declared to be open to all nations. This sum was paid in the summer of 1898 by the United States.

In 1897 the Canadian government succeeded in obtaining the consent of the governments of Great Britain and the United States to the appointment of a joint high commission to settle various questions in dispute between Canada and the United States. Canada was represented on this commission by Sir Wilfrid Laurier, Sir Richard Cartwright, Sir Louis Davies, and Mr. John Charlton, M.P., Newfoundland by Sir James Winter; the United States by Messieurs C.W. Fairbanks, George Gray, J.W. Foster, Nelson Dingley Jr., J.A. Kasson, and T. Jefferson Coolidge. The eminent jurist, Baron Herschell, who had been lord chancellor in the last Gladstone ministry, was chosen chairman of this commission, which met in the historic city of Quebec on several occasions from the 23rd August until the 10th October, 1898, and subsequently at Washington from November until the 20th February, 1899, when it adjourned. Mr. Dingley died in January and was replaced by Mr. Payne, and Lord Herschell also unhappily succumbed to the effects of an accident soon after the close of the sittings of the commission. In an eulogy of this eminent man in the Canadian house of commons, the Canadian prime minister stated that during the sittings of the commission "he fought for Canada not only with enthusiasm, but with conviction and devotion." England happily in these modern times has felt the necessity of giving to the consideration of Canadian interests the services of her most astute and learned statesmen and diplomatists.

This commission was called upon to consider a number of international questions—the Atlantic and inland fisheries, the Alaska boundary, the alien labour law, the bonding privilege, the seal fishery in the Bering Sea, reciprocity of trade in certain products of the two countries, and other minor issues. For the reasons given in a previous part of this chapter (page 269), when referring to the commercial policy of the Laurier government, reciprocity was no longer the all-important question to be discussed, though the commissioners were desirous of making fiscal arrangements with

Canada Under British Rule 1760-1900

respect to lumber, coal, and some other Canadian products for which there is an increasing demand in the markets of the United States. The long and earnest discussions of the commission on the various questions before them were, however, abruptly terminated by the impossibility of reaching a satisfactory conclusion with respect to the best means of adjusting the vexed question of the Alaska boundary, which had become of great international import in consequence of the discovery of gold in the territory of Alaska and the district of Yukon in Canada.

The dispute between Great Britain and the United States has arisen as to the interpretation to be given to the Anglo-Russian treaty of 1825, which was made forty-two years before Russia sold her territorial rights in Alaska to the United States, that sale being subject of course to the conditions of the treaty in question. Under the third article of this treaty[10]—the governing clause of the contract between England and Russia—boundary line between Canada and Alaska commences at the south end of Prince of Wales Island, thence runs north through Portland Channel to the fifty-sixth degree of north latitude, thence follows the summit of the mountains situated parallel to the coast of the continent, to one hundred and forty-one west longitude and thence to the frozen ocean. That part of the line between fifty-six north latitude and one hundred and forty-one west longitude is where the main dispute arises. Great Britain on behalf of Canada contends that, by following the summits of the mountains between these two points, the true boundary would cross Lynn Canal, about half way between the headlands and tide-water at the head of the canal, and leave both Skagway and Dyea—towns built up chiefly by United States citizens—within British territory. The contention of Great Britain always has been that the boundary should follow the general contour of the coast line and not the inlets to their head waters. On the other hand the United States contend that the whole of Lynn Canal up to the very top, to the extent of tide-water, is a part of the ocean, and that the territory of the United States goes back for ten leagues from the head of the canal and consequently includes Skagway and Dyea. In other words the United States claim that the boundary should not follow the coast line but pass around the head of this important inlet, which controls access to the interior of the gold-bearing region.

[10: The following is the article in full: "The line of demarcation between the possessions of the high contracting parties upon the coast of the continent and the islands of America to the north-west, shall be drawn in the following manner: commencing from the southernmost point of the island called Prince of Wales Island, which point lies in the parallel of fifty-four degrees forty minutes north latitude, and between the one hundred and thirty-first and the one hundred and thirty-third degree of west longitude, the said line shall ascend to the north along the channel called Portland Channel as far as the point of the continent where it strikes the fifty-sixth degree of north latitude. From this last-mentioned point the line of demarcation shall follow the summit of the mountains situated parallel to the coast as far as the point of intersection of the one hundred and forty-first degree of west longitude (of the same meridian), and finally from the said point of intersection of the one hundred and forty-first degree in its prolongation as far as the frozen ocean, shall form the limit between the Russian and British possessions, on the continent of America to the north-west"]

The Canadian commissioners first offered as a compromise to leave Dyea and Skagway in the possession of the United States if the commissioners of that country would agree that Canada should retain Pyramid Harbour, which would give to Canadians a highway into the Yukon district. The acceptance of this compromise would have made a common water of the Lynn Canal, and at the same time left to the United States the greater portion of the territory in dispute. When the commissioners of the United States refused this fair compromise, the Canadians offered to refer the whole question to arbitration in order to ascertain the true boundary under the Anglo-Russian treaty. They proposed that the arbitrators should be three jurists of repute: one chosen for Great Britain by the judicial committee of the privy council, one appointed by the president of the United States, and the third a high international authority to act as an umpire. The commissioners of the United States positively refused to agree to this proposition and suggested the appointment of six jurists, three to be appointed by Great Britain, and the others by the United States. The Canadian representatives were unable to agree to the amendment suggested by their American colleagues, on the ground that it did not "provide a tribunal which would necessarily, and in the possible event of differences of opinion, finally dispose of the question," They also refused to agree to other propositions of the United States as "a marked and important departure from the rules of the Venezuelan boundary reference." The commissioners of the United States were not only unwilling to agree to the selection of an impartial European umpire, but were desirous of the appointment of an American umpire—from the South American Republics—over whom the United States would have more or less influence. Under these circumstances the Canadian commissioners were unwilling to proceed to the determination of other questions (on which a conclusion had been nearly reached) "until the boundary question had been disposed of either by agreement or reference to arbitration." The commission adjourned until August in the same year, but the negotiations that took place in the interval between the governments of Great Britain and the United States on the question at issue were not sufficiently advanced to enable a meeting at the proposed date. In these circumstances a *modus vivendi* was arranged between the United States and Canada, whose interests have been carefully guarded throughout the controversy by the government of the imperial state.

This review of Canada's relations with the United States and England for more than a century illustrates at once her weakness and her strength—her weakness in the days of provincial isolation and imperial indifference; her strength under the inspiring influences of federal union and of an imperial spirit which gives her due recognition in the councils of the empire. It may now be said that, in a limited sense, there is already a loose system of federation between Great Britain and her dependencies. The central government of Great Britain, as the guardian of the welfare of the whole empire, cooperates with the several governments of her colonial dependencies, and, by common consultation and arrangement, endeavours to come to such a determination as will be to the advantage of all the interests at stake. In other words, the conditions of the relations between Great Britain and Canada are such as to insure unity of policy so long as each government considers the interests of Great Britain and the dependency as identical, and keeps in view the obligations, welfare, and unity of the empire at large. Full consultation in all negotiations affecting Canada, representation in every arbitration and commission that may be the result of such negotiations, are the principles which, of late years, have been admitted by Great Britain in acknowledgement of the development of Canada and of her present position in the empire; and any departure from so sound a doctrine would be a serious injury to the imperial connection, and an insult to the ability of Canadians to take a part in the great councils of the world. The same mysterious Providence that has already divided the continent of North America, as far as Mexico, between Canada and the United States, and that in the past prevented their political fortunes from becoming one, still forces the Canadian communities with an irresistible power to press onward until they realise those high conceptions which some statesmen already imagine for them in a not very distant future. These conceptions are of a still closer union with the parent state, which shall increase their national responsibilities, and at the same time give the Dominion a recognised position in the central councils of the empire.

APPENDIX A.

COMPARISONS BETWEEN THE MAIN PROVISIONS OF THE CONSTITUTIONS OF THE DOMINION OF CANADA AND THE AUSTRALIAN COMMONWEALTH.

CANADA. AUSTRALIA.

Name. Name
The Dominion of Canada The Commonwealth of Australia.

How Constituted. How Constituted
Of provinces. Of states.

Seat of Government. Seat of Government
At Ottawa until the Queen Within federal territory in otherwise directs. New South Wales, at least 100 miles from Sydney

Executive Power. Executive Power Vested in the Queen. Vested in the Queen. Queen's representative, a Queen's representative, a governor-general, appointed by governor-general, appointed by the Queen in council. the Queen in council.

Salary of governor-general Not less than £10,000 paid £10,000 sterling, paid by Dominion by the commonwealth, fixed by government, alterable by parliament from time to time, the parliament of Canada, but not diminished during tenure of subject to the disallowance of a governor-general. the crown, as in 1868, when parliament passed a bill to reduce this salary.

CANADA. AUSTRALIA. Ministers called by governor-general Same—only for "privy to form a cabinet, first councillors" read "executive sworn in as privy councillors, councillors" hold office while they have the confidence of the popular house of parliament, in accordance with the conventions, understandings, and maxims of responsible or parliamentary government.

Privy councillors hold, as the Executive councillors administer crown may designate, certain such departments as departments of state, not limited governor-general from time to in name or number, but left to time establishes. Until other the discretionary action of provision is

Canada	Australia
made by parliament. Such officers, who departments shall not election on accepting office of emolument.	parliament. Number of such heads of may sit in parliament, these must seek a new exceed seven.

Command of Military and Naval Forces
Vested in the Queen.

Command of Military and Naval Forces
In the Queen's representative.

Parliament
The Queen.
Senate.
House of commons.
Session once at least every year.
Privileges, immunities and powers held by senate and house of commons, such as are defined by act of the parliament of Canada, but not to exceed those enjoyed at the passing of such act by the commons' house of parliament of Great Britain.

Parliament
The Queen.
Senate.
House of representatives.
The same.

Such as declared by the parliament of the commonwealth, and, until declared, such as are held by the commons' house of parliament of Great Britain at the date of the establishment of the commonwealth.

CANADA. AUSTRALIA

Senate composed of twenty-four members for each of the three following divisions (1) Ontario, (2) Quebec, and (3) maritime provinces of Nova Scotia, New Brunswick, and Prince Edward Island. Other provinces can be represented under the constitution, but the total number of senators shall not at any time exceed seventy-eight, except in the case of the admission of Newfoundland, when the maximum may be eighty-two. Senators

Senate composed of six senators for each state, directly chosen for six years by the people of the state voting as one electorate; half the number shall retire every three years, but shall be eligible for re-election. No property qualification is required, but senators must be British subjects of the full age of twenty-one years. In Queensland the people can vote in divisions, instead of in one electorate.

CANADA	AUSTRALIA
appointed by the crown for life, but removable for certain disabilities. They must have a property qualification and be of the full age of thirty years.	
Speaker of the senate appointed by the governor-general (in council).	President of the senate elected by that body.
Fifteen senators form a quorum until parliament of Canada otherwise provides.	One-third of whole number of senators form a quorum until parliament of commonwealth otherwise provides.
Non-attendance for two whole sessions vacates a senator's seat.	Non-attendance for two consecutive months of any session vacates a senator's seat.
Members of house of commons elected every five years, or whenever parliament is dissolved by the governor-general.	Every three years.
No property qualification, but must be British subjects of full age of twenty-one years.	The same.
The electors for the Dominion of electors for commons are the electors of the members of the house of several provinces, under the representatives is that limitations of a statute passed prescribed by the law of each by the Dominion parliament in state for the electors of the 1878. Qualifications vary, but more numerous house of the universal suffrage, qualified by parliament of the state. residence, generally prevails.	Qualification of electors for commons are the electors of the members of the house of representatives is that limitations of a prescribed by the law of each by the Dominion state for the electors of the 1878. Qualifications vary, more numerous house of the universal suffrage, qualified by parliament of the state. residence, generally prevails.
A fresh apportionment of representatives to be made after each census, or not longer than intervals of ten years.	The same.
Speaker of house of commons elected by the members of the house.	The same.
Quorum of house of commons —twenty members, of whom the speaker counts one.	Quorum of house of representatives —one-third of the whole number of members

	until otherwise provided by parliament.
No such provision.	Member vacates his seat when absent, without permission, for two months of a session.
No such provision.	Parliament to be called together not later than thirty days after that appointment for return of writs.

Allowance to each member of senate and commons $1,000 for a session of thirty days, and mileage expenses, 10 cents a mile going and returning.

Allowance of £400 to members of both houses until other provision is made by parliament. Not expressly provided for by constitution but by statute of parliament from time to time.

CANADA.	AUSTRALIA.
Canadian statutes disqualify contractors and certain persons holding office on receiving emoluments or fees from the crown while sitting in parliament.	Same classes disqualified in the constitution.
Each house determines the rules, and orders necessary for the regulation of its own proceedings; not in the constitution.	The constitution has a special provision on the subject.

Money And Tax Bills

	Money and Tax Bills
The same.	Money and tax bills can only originate in the house of representatives.
ǀSame by practice. The senate can reject, but not amend, taxation or appropriation bills.	

Not in Canadian constitution. The senate may return money and appropriation bills to the house of representatives, requesting the omission or amendment of any provision therein, but it is optional for the house to make such omissions or amendments.

No such provision. If bills, other than money bills, have twice been passed by the house of representatives and twice been rejected by the senate or passed by that body with amendments to which the house of representatives will not agree, the governor-general may dissolve the two houses simultaneously; and if, after the new election they continue to disagree, the governor-general may convene a joint sitting of the members of the two houses, who shall deliberate and vote upon the bill, which can only become law if passed by an absolute majority of the members sitting and voting.

Legislative Powers of the Parliament of the Dominion.	*Legislative Powers of the Parliament of the Commonwealth.*
Respective powers of the federal parliament and provincial legislatures are enumerated and defined in the constitution; the residuum of power rests with the central government in relation to all matters not coming within the classes of subjects by the British North America act of 1867 assigned exclusively to the legislatures.	The Legislative powers of the federal parliament are alone enumerated, and the states expressly retain all the powers vested in them by their respective constitutions at the establishment of the commonwealth as to matters not specified as being within the exclusive jurisdiction of the federal parliament.
The Provinces.	*The States.*
Legislatures may alter provincial constitutions except as regards the office of lieutenant-governor.	Constitutions may be altered under the authority of the parliaments thereof.
Lieutenant-governors are appointed by the governor-general-in-council, and removable by him within five years only for cause assigned and communicated by message to the two houses of parliament.	The constitution of each state continues (subject to the constitution) as at the establishment of the commonwealth, or as at the admission or establishment of the states, as the case may be, until altered in accordance with the constitution of the

CANADA	AUSTRALIA
	states. In other words, the powers of the states over their own constitutions are preserved.
Acts of the provincial legislatures may be disallowed by the governor-general-in-council one year after their receipt.	When a law of the state is inconsistent with one of the commonwealth, the latter shall, to the extent of such inconsistency, be invalid.
Education is within exclusive jurisdiction of the provinces, with conditions for the maintenance and protection of rights and privileges of religious bodies in a province with respect to denominational schools.	No special provisions in the constitution; education being one of the subjects exclusively within the powers of the state parliaments, under the clause leaving them in possession of all powers not expressly given to the federal parliament.
The federal parliament can alone impose duties or taxes on imports.	A state shall not impose any taxes or duties upon imports except such as are necessary for executing the inspection laws of a state, but the net produce of all charges so levied shall be for use of the, commonwealth, and such inspection laws may be annulled by the parliament of the commonwealth.
Similar power.	The parliament of the commonwealth may from time to time admit new states, and make laws for the provisional administration and government of any territory surrendered by any state to the commonwealth, or of any territory placed by the Queen under the commonwealth, or otherwise acquired by the same.
CANADA.	AUSTRALIA.
The Judiciary.	*The Judiciary.*

CANADA	AUSTRALIA
The same.	The parliament of the commonwealth can establish a federal supreme court, called the High Court of Australia, and other federal courts for the commonwealth; the judges to be appointed by the governor-general, to hold office during good behaviour, not to be removed except upon an address of both houses of parliament, but so that the salary paid to any judge shall not be diminished during his continuance in office.
No such provision with respect to diminution of salary during tenure of office.	
Similar provisions by statutory enactments of Dominion parliament.	The high court can adjudicate in cases arising out of the constitution, or controversies between states, or in which the commonwealth is a party.
No such stringent provision exists in the Canadian constitution, but appeals in all cases are allowed, by virtue of the exercise of the royal prerogative, from the provincial courts as well as from the supreme court of Canada to the Queen-in-council; however, the such appeals, but they must be reserved for her Majesty's pleasure.	Appeals only allowed to Queen-in-council from high court on constitutional issues between commonwealth and any state, or between two or more states, when high court gives leave to appeal. Otherwise, the royal prerogative to grant appeals is not impaired. Parliament may, however, make laws limiting *i.e.*, in practice, to the judicial committee of the privy council.

CANADA. AUSTRALIA.

CANADA	AUSTRALIA
Judges of the superior and county courts in the provinces (except those of probate in New Brunswick, Nova Scotia and Prince Edward Island) are appointed	Judges in the states are appointed and removable under existing state constitutions, which the state parliaments can change at will.

by the governor-general-in-council, and removable only by the same on the address of the two houses of parliament. Their salaries and allowances are fixed by the parliament of Canada.

Canada	Commonwealth / States
The provinces have jurisdiction over the administration of justice in a province, including the constitution, maintenance, and organisation of provincial courts, both of civil and criminal jurisdiction, and including the procedure in civil matters in those courts.	Similar powers in the states.
The enactment and amendment of the criminal law rest with the Dominion parliament.	With the states.
The enactment and amendment of all laws relating to property and civil rights rest with the provinces.	With the states.

Trade and Finance. *Trade* and *Finance.*

Canada	Commonwealth
Customs and excise, trade and commerce, are within exclusive jurisdiction of Dominion parliament.	The parliament of the commonwealth has sole power to impose uniform duties of customs and excise, and to grant bounties upon goods when it thinks it expedient. As soon as such duties or customs are imposed, trade and intercourse throughout the commonwealth, whether by internal carriage or ocean navigation, is to be free.
The Dominion government can veto any such unconstitutional law.	The parliament of the commonwealth may annul any state law interfering with the freedom of trade or commerce between the different parts of the

	commonwealth, or giving preference to the ports of one part over those of another.
The power of direct taxation is within the jurisdiction of both the Dominion parliament and provincial legislatures, the one for limits — but taxation, when exercised by the commonwealth, for provincial purposes. must be uniform.	Direct taxation may be imposed by the commonwealth and by each state within its own limits — but Dominion taxation, when solely exercised by the commonwealth, must be uniform.
Both Dominion and provincial governments have unlimited borrowing power under the authority of parliament and legislatures.	Same is true of commonwealth and states.
Certain money subsidies are paid annually to the provinces towards the support of their governments and legislatures.	Of the net revenue of the commonwealth from duties of customs and excise, not more than one-fourth shall be applied annually by the commonwealth towards its expenditure. The balance shall, in accordance with certain conditions of the constitution, be paid to the several states, or applied towards the payment of interest on debts of the several states. This arrangement is limited to ten years. Financial aid may be granted to any state upon such terms as the federal parliament may deem expedient. Western Australia may, subject to certain restrictions, impose duties on goods imported from other parts of the commonwealth.
No such provision; but the Dominion parliament and provincial legislatures could by the governor-general-in-council	For the administration of laws relating to interstate trade

legislation arrange a similar commission.	may appoint an interstate commission.

Canada is liable for the debts and liabilities of the provinces existing at the time of the union, under the conditions and terms laid down in the constitution.	amount of The parliament of the commonwealth may consolidate or take over state debts by general consent, but a state shall indemnify the commonwealth, and the amount of interest payable in respect to a debt shall be deducted from its share of the surplus revenue of the commonwealth.

Imperial Control over Legislation.	*Imperial Control over Australian Legislation.*	*Control over Dominion Legislation.*
As the old state constitutions continue in force until amended after receipt of any Dominion act, state legislation is still subject to power of disallowance by Queen in council.	The same.	Bills may be reserved by the governor-general for the Queen's pleasure, and her Majesty in council may within two years after receipt of any Dominion by the state, disallow the same.

No such provision.	The governor-general may return any "law" presented to him for the Queen's assent and suggest amendments therein, and the houses may deal with them as they think fit.

The recommendation of the crown is required before initiation of a money vote in parliament.	The same.

Amendments to the Constitution.	*Amendments to the Constitution.*
By the imperial parliament on an address of the houses of the Dominion parliament to the Queen.	Any proposed amendment to the constitution must be first passed by an absolute majority of each house of parliament, and submitted in each state to the electors qualified to vote for members of the house of representatives. If in majority of the states a majority of the

electors voting approve the proposed law, and if a majority of all the electors voting also approve the proposed law, it shall be presented to the governor-general for the royal assent.

APPENDIX B.

BIBLIOGRAPHICAL NOTES.

I confine these notes to the most accurate and available books and essays on the history of Canada.

For the French régime consult.—*Jacques Cartier's Voyages*, by Joseph Pope (Ottawa, 1889), Charlevoix's *History and General Description of New France*, translated by J. Gilmary Shea (New York, 1868); *Cours d'histoire du Canada*, by Abbé Ferland (Quebec, 1861); *Histoire du Canada*, by F.X. Garneau (4th ed., Montreal, 1882); F. Parkman's series of admirable histories of the French régime (Boston, 1865—1884), *The Story of Canada* (Nations' Series, London, New York and Toronto, 1896), by J.G. Bourinot, necessarily written in a light vein, is largely devoted to the days of French rule, and may profitably be read on that account in connection with this later book, chiefly devoted to British dominion.

For the history of Acadia, consult.—*Acadia*, by James Hannay (St. John, N.B., 1879); *History of Nova Scotia*, by Thomas C. Haliburton (Halifax, N.S., 1829). A valuable compilation of annals is *A History of Nova Scotia or Acadie*, by Beamish Murdoch (Halifax, 1867). *Builders of Nova Scotia*, by J.G. Bourinot (Toronto, and "Trans. Roy. Soc. Can.," 1900), contains many portraits of famous Nova Scotians down to confederation, and appendices of valuable historical documents.

Cape Breton and its Memorials of the French Régime ("Trans. Roy. Soc. Can.," vol. IX, and in separate form, Montreal, 1891) by J.G. Bourinot, gives a full bibliography of voyages of Northmen, the Cabots, Carrier, and Champlain, and of the Histories of the Seven Years' War. The same remarks apply to Winsor's *Narrative and Critical History of America* (Boston, 1886—89). The "Trans. Roy. Soc. Can.," since 1894, have several important papers by Archbishop O'Brien, Dr. S.E. Dawson, and others on the Cabot discovery.

British rule, 1760-1900:—Garneau's *History*, already mentioned, gives the French Canadian view of the political situation from 1760 until 1840; William Kingsford's *History of Canada* (Toronto, 1887-1898) has a fairly accurate account of events from 1760 until 1840, in vols. V-

X; *A History of Lower Canada*, by R. Christie, a member of the assembly of the province (Quebec, 1848-1854) is very useful for copies of public documents from 1774 until 1840.

The most important accounts of the U.E. Loyalists of the American Revolution by writers in the United States are:—L. Sabine's *Loyalists* (Boston, 1864), and Tyler's *Literary History of the American Revolution* (New York, 1897). Canadian accounts are to be found in Egerton Ryerson's *Loyalists of America* (Toronto, 1880)—remarkably prosaic—and Canniff's *History of Upper Canada* (Toronto, 1872). Consult also articles of J.G. Bourinot in the *Quarterly Review* for October, 1898, and the *Canadian Magazine* for April, 1898, in which names of prominent Canadian descendants of Loyalists are given.

Kingsford's *History*, vol. VIII, has the best Canadian account of the War of 1812-15. The most impartial American record of its causes and progress is Henry Adams's *History of the United States of America* (New York, 1860), vols VI and VII.

Garneau's *History* gives the most favourable estimate of Papineau and his party, who brought about the Rebellion in Lower Canada. Kingsford (vols. IX and X) writes impartially on the risings in the two Canadas.

Other works to be consulted are:—Lord Durham's *Report on the Affairs of British North America* (London, 1839); *Life of W. Lyon Mackenzie*, by Charles Lindsey, his son-in-law (Toronto, 1863); *The Upper Canadian Rebellion*, by J. Charles Dent (Toronto, 1885). The *Speeches and Letters* of the Hon. Joseph Howe (Boston, 1858) contain the ablest expositions of the principles of responsible government by its greatest advocate in British North America. See also Campbell's *History of Prince Edward Island* (Charlottetown, 1875). New Brunswick has not a single good history. *The Life and Times of Sir Leonard Tilley*, by James Hannay (St. John, N.B. 1897), can be read with advantage. See Prof. Ganong's valuable essays on the early history of New Brunswick in "Trans. Roy. Soc. Can," New Series, vols. I—v. Rev. Dr. Withrow's *History of Canada* (Toronto, 1888) has chapters on affairs of Prince Edward Island, New Brunswick and Nova Scotia, to date of publication.

For the history of Canada since 1840, consult.—*Canada since the Union* (1840—1880), by J. Charles Dent (Toronto, 1880—81); *Le Canada sous l'Union*, by Louis Turcotte (Quebec, 1871); *Memoirs of the Right Hon. Sir John A. Macdonald*, by Joseph Pope, his private secretary (London and Ottawa, 1894); *Debates on Confederation* (Quebec, 1865); *Confederation*, by Hon. J.H. Gray, M.P., a delegate to the Quebec Conference (Toronto, 1872).

For the constitutional development of Canada, consult.—*A Manual*, by J.G. Bourinot (Montreal, 1888, and included in latest edition of his *Parliamentary Procedure*, 1891); *How Canada is Governed*, by the same (Toronto, 1897—1900); *Parliamentary Government in the Colonies*, by Alpheus Todd (London, 1894); *Documents illustrative of the Canadian Constitution*, by W. Houston (Toronto, 1891). *Parliamentary Government in Canada*, by J.G. Bourinot (Amer. Hist. Association, Washington, 1892, and "Trans. Roy. Soc. Can.," 1892), contains a long list of books relating to the constitutional history of Canada. Also consult *How Canada is Governed* for works on constitutional, legal, municipal and educational history of the provinces of Canada.

For Manitoba and the North-west Territories the reader may consult:—*Manitoba. Its Infancy, Growth and Present Condition*, by Rev. Prof. Bryce (London, 1882); *History of the North-west*, by A. Begg (Toronto, 1894); *The Great Company*, by Beckles Wilson (Toronto and London, 1899); *Reminiscences of the North-west Rebellions*, by Major Boulton (Toronto, 1886). A remarkable *History of the Hudson's Bay Company*, by Rev. Prof. Bryce (London, New York and Toronto, 1900). For British Columbia:—A. Begg's *History* (Toronto, 1896).

For the literary progress of Canada, consult:—*The Intellectual Development of the Canadian People*, by J.G. Bourinot (Toronto, 1881); *Canada's Intellectual Strength and Weakness* ("Trans. Roy. Soc. Canada," vol. XI, also in separate form, Montreal, 1893), by the same, contains an elaborate list of Canadian literature, French and English, to date. The 17 volumes of the same Transactions contain numerous valuable essays on French Canadian literary progress.

Other valuable books to be consulted are:—*Canada and Newfoundland* in Stanford's *Compendium of Geography and Travel* (London, 1897), by Dr. S.E. Dawson, F.R.S.C.; *The Statistical Year Book of Canada*, a government publication issued annually at

Ottawa, and edited by Geo. Johnson, F.S.S.; *The Great Dominion* (London, 1895), by Dr. G.R. Parkin, C.M.G., LL.D., the eloquent advocate of imperial federation for many years, merits careful reading. *Canada and the United States*, in Papers of the Amer. Hist. Assoc. (Washington, July, 1891), and *Canada and the United States: their Past and Present Relations*, in the *Quarterly Review* for April, 1891, both by the present author, have been largely used in the preparation of the last chapter of this book.

With respect to the boundaries of Canada and the English colonies during the days of French dominion, and from 1763 until 1774 — *i.e.* from the Treaty of Paris until the Quebec Act — consult a valuable collection of early French and English maps, given in *A Report on the Boundaries of Ontario* (Toronto, 1873), by Hon. David Mills, now Minister of Justice in the Laurier government, who was an Ontario commissioner to collect evidence with respect to the western limits of the province. Consult also Prof. Hinsdale's *Old North-west* (New York, 1888); *Epochs of American History*, edited by Prof. Hart, of Harvard University (London and Boston, 1893); *Remarks on the French Memorials concerning the Limits of Acadia* (London, 1756) by T. Jefferys, who gives maps showing clearly French and English claims with respect to Nova Scotia or Acadia "according to its ancient limits" (Treaty of Utrecht). These and other maps are given in that invaluable compilation, Winsor's *Narrative and Critical History of America*. See also Mitchell's map of British and French possessions in North America, issued by the British Board of Plantations in 1758, and reprinted (in part) in the *Debates on the Quebec Act*, by Sir H. Cavendish (London, 1839). For text of Treaties of Utrecht (1612), of Paris (1763), of Quebec Act (1774), and other treaties and imperial acts relating to Canada, see Houston's *Documents*, cited above, p. 329. The maps of Canada and the disputed boundary in Alaska, which I give in this book, are taken from the small maps issued in 1899 by the Department of the Interior at Ottawa.

Canada Under British Rule 1760-1900

INDEX

Abbott, Sir John; prime minister of Canada, 257; death of, ib

Aberdeen, Earl of; governor-general of Canada, 265-267

Aberdeen, Lady, 267

Acadia College, N.S., founded, 163

Acadie or *La Cadie*; name of, 8; settled by France, 8, 9; ceded to Great Britain by Treaty of Utrecht (1713), 9; French inhabitants expelled from, 22, 23

Adams, President John; on the U.K. Loyalists, 76

Alaskan Boundary, 310-312; map of, 311

Alexander, Sir William (Lord Stirling); names Nova Scotia, 11

Allan, Sir Hugh; contributes funds to Conservative elections, 236; results of, 237

Allouez, Father; founds mission at La Pointe (Ashland), 17

Almon, M, B.; banker and politician of Nova Scotia, 178

American Revolution; causes of, 56-65; momentous events of, 63-67; its effects upon Canada and Maritime Provinces, 67-74, 81

Angers, lieutenant-governor; dismisses Mercier ministry in Quebec, 247

Anglican Church: first built in Upper Canada, 84

Annand, William; Nova Scotian journalist, and first minister of province after Confederation, 218

Annapolis (Port Royal) named, 9

Archibald, Sir Adams, delegate to Quebec Convention of 1864, 204; first lieutenant-governor of Manitoba, 230

Architecture in Canada, 288, 289

Art in Canada, 288

Assiniboia; name of Lord Selkirk's domain in North-west, 225

Australia, Commonwealth of; constitution of, 282, 283; comparisons between Canadian and Australian federal systems, 315-326 (Appendix A)

Baccalaos, or Newfoundland, 8

Bagot, Sir Charles, governor-general of Canada, 169

Baldwin, Robert, efforts of, for responsible government, 168, 169; joint leader with Lafontaine in Reform ministry, 170, 173; admirable character of, 184

Ballot, vote by; established, 239

Basques in Canada, 5

Batoche, N.W.T.; victory of loyal Canadian forces at, in second North-west rebellion of 1885, 253

Bay of Chaleurs Railway; scandal connected with, 247

Bering Sea dispute, 308, 309

Bibliographical notes, see App. B

Bidwell, Marshall Spring; reformer of Upper Canada, 146, 149, 151; unjust treatment of, by lieutenant-governor Head, 153

Big Bear, Indian Chief in N.W.T.; rebels against Canada and is punished, 253-254

Bishop's Palace; first parliament house of Lower Canada, 92, 160

Blair, Mr.; Canadian statesman, 265

Blake, Edward; Canadian statesman, 230, 231, 234, 241, 244, 255

Blanchard, Hiram; Nova Scotia, Unionist, defeated in 1867, 218

Botsford, Amos; first speaker of assembly of New Brunswick, 88

Boucherville, M. de; prime minister of Quebec, 245, 247

Bouchette, Joseph, Canadian general and author, 164

Boundary disputes; in North-west, 292; in Maine, 296-300; in Oregon, 300-302; in British Columbia (San Juan) 301, 302; in Alaska, 310-312. See *Maps*

Boundary of Ontario settled, 238

Bourgeoys, Sister, 34

Bowell, Sir Mackenzie; prime minister of Canada, 257

Brant, Joseph (Thayendanega), Mohawk Chief, 84; his loyalty to Great Britain, ib.

Brébeuf, Jean de, Jesuit martyr, 12

Bretons in Canada, 51

Briand, Bishop; consecrated after conquest, 43; loyal *mandement* of, in 1775, 58

British American League suggests federal union of provinces, 194

British Columbia, province of; its early history, 231, 232; enters Confederation, 232

British North America Act of 1867; passed to unite provinces, 215. See *Constitution of Canada*.

Brock, General; services of, during war of 1812-15, 114, 119; death of, ib.

Brown, George; Canadian journalist and reformer, suggests federal union, 196; advocates representation by population, 197; assists in bringing about Confederation, 197; joins the Taché-Macdonald government with other reformers, 198; leaves the coalition ministry, 217; unsuccessful mission to Washington to obtain reciprocity, 306; assassination of, 256; character of, 197, 202

Brown, Thomas Storrow; leads Canadian rebels at St. Charles in 1837, 134

By, Colonel, founder of Bytown (Ottawa), 158; engineer of Ruleau Canal, ib.

Cabot, John; voyages of, to North America, 4, 5

Caldwell, Receiver-General; defaulter to government, 126

Calvet, Pierre du; opponent of Governor Haldimand, 72; disloyalty of, 72, 73

Campbell, Sir Alexander; delegate to Quebec Convention of 1864, 203

Campbell, Sir Colin; governor of Nova Scotia, 173; opposes responsible government, ib.

Canada, name of, 6; discovery and settlement of, by France, 4-15; French exploration of, 15-21; conquered by Great Britain, 21-27; political, economic, and social conditions of, during French rule, 27-36; beginnings of British rule in, 37-45; influence of Quebec Act of 1774 upon, 45-48; during American Revolution, 67-74; United Empire Loyalists settle in, 81-86; political divisions of (in 1792), 91; effects of war of 1812-15 upon, 110-123; rebellion in, 134-156; social and economic condition of, in 1838, 156-164; union of, in 1840, 166; responsible government in, 167-173; social and economic conditions of, in 1866, 185-192; Confederation of, 215, 216; federal constitution of, 273-284, 315-326; first ministry of, under Confederation, 216, first parliament of, 218, 219; trade and revenue of, in 1899, 273; literature in, 284-287, art in, 288; sculpture in, ib.; architecture in, 288, 289; education in 289, 290; libraries in, ib.; relations with England and the United States, 390-314; bibliographical notes of, 327-330; maps of, see *Maps*

Canada's representation at "Diamond Jubilee" (1897), 35, 36, 270, 271

Canada Temperance Act. See *Temperance Legislation*

Canada and the United States, relations between (1783-1900), 290-313

Canadien, Le; established in French Canada, 95

Canadian Pacific Railway; history of 232, 233, 236, 242, 244

Canadian Trade Acts; respecting Upper and Lower Canada, 153

Canals of Canada, 273

Cape Breton, name of, 5

Carignan-Salières regiment settled in Canada 14

Carleton, Guy (Lord Dorchester); governor general of Canada, 44; his just treatment of French Canadians, ib.; his part in framing of the Quebec Act, 45; saves Canada during American revolution, 67; again governor-general, 89; his tribute to the U.E. Loyalists, ib.

Carleton, Colonel John; first governor of New Brunswick, 87

Carnarvon, Earl of; introduces British North America Act of 1867 in British Parliament, 215

Caroline steamer; seized by Canadians 295; international complications respecting 295, 296

Caron Father le; French missionary, 16

Caron, Sir Adolphe; minister of militia during North-west rebellion of 1885, 252; resists Riel agitation in French Canada, 254

Carter, Frederick B.T.; delegate to Quebec Convention of 1864, 206

Cartier, Sir George; a father of Confederation, 201; great public services of, ib.; death of, 233

Cartier, Jacques, discovers the St. Lawrence, 6, 7

Cartwright, Sir Richard; Canadian statesman, 94, 265

Casgrain, Abbé; Canadian author, 284

Cathcart, Lord; governor-general of Canada, 171, 172

Champlain, Samuel; founds Quebec, 9; career of, in Canada, 9-12, character of, ib.

Chandler, Edward Barron delegate to Quebec Convention of 1864, 205; public career of, 206

Chapais, J.C., delegate to Quebec Convention of 1864, 304

Chapleau, Sir Adolphe; resists popular clamour in French Canada for
Riel's pardon after rebellion of 1885, 254

Charlesbourg-Royal, 7

Charlevoix, Jesuit priest; historian of New France, 19

Chartier, Abbé; Canadian rebel of 1837, 135

Chartrand, murder of, in Lower Canadian rebellion of 1837, 135

Chateauguay, battle of; won by French Canadians, 116, 121

Château of St. Louis; founded at Quebec, 31; destroyed by fire, 160

Chauveau, Pierre O.J.; his services to education, 192; first prime minister of Quebec after Confederation, 217

Chenier, Dr.; Canadian rebel, 134; monument to, 135

Christie, Mr.; expelled from assembly of Lower Canada, 127;

Chrystler's Farm, battle at; won by British troops in 1813, 116

Civil Law of French Canada, 29; established under British rule, 46, 278

Clergy Reserves Question; origin of, 141; powerful factor in political controversy for years, ib.; settled, 186

Cockburn, James; delegate to Quebec Convention of 1864, 204; first speaker of commons' house of Dominion parliament, ib.

Code Napoléon in French Canada, 278

Colbert, French minister, 27

Colborne, Sir John (Lord Seaforth); represses rebellion in Lower Canada, 134, 138; governor-general of Canada, 138

Colebrooke, Sir William; lieutenant-governor of New Brunswick, 174

Coles, George; delegate to Quebec Convention of 1864, 206

Colonial Conference at Ottawa (1894), 200

Commissions, International, affecting Canada; Maine boundary, 296, Washington (1871), 302, 304-306; Washington (1887), 307, 308, Bering Sea, 309; joint high commission (Quebec and Washington, 1897-98), 309-313

Commonwealth of Australia. See *Australia*

Confederation of the British North American provinces; foreshadowed, 194; beginnings of, 195-198; initiated at Quebec Convention of 1864, 199; fathers of, 199-206, consummated, 206-215; birth of Dominion of Canada, 216; constitution of, 206-209, 273-284; first ministry under, 216; first parliament under, 217; results of, 272, 273

Congrégation de Notre-Dame established, 34

Constitutional Act of 1791; forms provinces of Upper and Lower Canada, 90, 91; general provisions of, 91, 92

Constitution of Canadian Dominion, 273-281; compared with that of Australian Commonwealth, 282-284, 315, 326 (App. A)

Cornwallis, Colonel, founds Halifax, 49

Corrupt elections: measures to restrain and punish, 239

Cortereal, Gaspar and Miguel; voyages of, to North America, 5

Coureurs-de-bois, 17, 18

Coutume de Paris established in French Canada, 29

Craig, Sir James; governor-general of Canada, 96; quarrels of, with leading French Canadians, character of, 96, 97

Crémazie, Canadian poet, 192

Crozier, Superintendent; defeated by half-breeds in North-west rebellion of 1885, 252

Cut Knife Greek, N.W.T.; Colonel Otter engages Indians at, in North-west rebellion of 1885, 253

Dalhousie College, Nova Scotia; founded, 163

Dalhousie, Lord, governor-general of Canada; quarrel of, with Papineau, 129

Daly, Sir Dominick; first minister of Canada under Lord Metcalfe, 170

Davies, Sir Louis; Canadian statesman, 265

Davies, English navigator; voyages of, to Canada, 7

Dawson, Sir William; Canadian scientist, 192, 286

Dickey, R.B.; delegate to Quebec Convention of 1864, 305

Dochet Island (St. Croix River); first settlement of French on, 8

Dominion of Canada; origin of name, 215; established, 215, 216; first ministry of, 216; first parliament of, 217; completed from Atlantic to Pacific, 227, 232, 234; history of, from 1873-1900, 236-272; map of, *at end.*

Dorchester, Lord; see *Carleton, Sir Guy*

Douglas, Sir James; governor of British Columbia, 232

Drew, Captain; seizes steamer Caroline on U.S. frontier, 154. See *Caroline.*

Drummond, Attorney-General; member of MacNab-Morin ministry, 186

Drummond, Dr., Canadian poet, 285

Drummond, General, services of, during war of 1812-15, 116, 117, 122

Duck Lake, N.W.T., defeat of government forces at, in Canadian rebellion of 1885, 252

Dumont Gabriel; takes part in Riel's North-west revolt of 1885, 252, 253

Dufferin, Lord; governor-general of Canada, 241, 243, 267

Durham, Earl of; high commissioner to Canada after rebellion of 1837, 136; his humanity and justice, 137; returns from Canada when rebuked in England, ib., his report on Canadian affairs, 165

Durham Terrace, constructed, 160

Education in Canada; state of, under French rule, 33, 34, in 1838, 162, 163; after union of 1840, 192; present condition of, 290; contributions by government and people, ib.

Elgin, Lord; governor-general of Canada, character of, 172, 173; established responsible government, 173; action of, on Rebellion Losses Bill in 1849, 188, 189

Falkland, Lord; governor of Nova Scotia, 176; quarrels with Joseph Howe and Liberal party, 177-179; returns to England, 179

Family Compact in Upper Canada; meaning of, 141; controls government, ib.

Fenian raids; in 1866, 213; in 1870-71, 230, 231, Canada never indemnified for, 305

Ferland, French Canadian historian, 192

Fielding, Mr., finance minister of Canada, 265, his budget of 1897, 209

Fish Creek, N.W.T.; General Middleton checked at, in engagement with rebels of 1885, 253

Fisher, Charles; delegate to Quebec Convention of 1864, 205

Fishery question between Canada and the United States, 293, 302, 304, 307, 308

Fitzgibbon, Lieutenant; successful strategy of, at Beaver Dams in 1813, 116

Franchise Act of Dominion, passed, 255, repealed, 268

Frechétte, French Canadian poet, 285

Free Trade policy of England; its early effects upon Canada, 172, 187, 189

French Acadians See *Neutrals*

French Canada; during French regime (1534-1760), 4-37; under military government after conquest by Great Britain, 37, 38; desire of British government to do justice to, 44, 45, provisions of Quebec Act affecting, 45, 48; political struggles and rebellion in, 124-138; influence of Union Act of 1840 upon, 170, 187; brought into confederation, 216; results of union upon, 273; literature in, 284, 285

French exploration in great valleys of North America, 15-21

French language; use of, restricted by Union Act of 1840, 187; restriction removed, ib.

Frobisher, English navigator; voyages of, to Canada, 8

Frog Lake, massacre at, in North-west rebellion of 1885, 252

Frontenac, Count de (Louis de La Buade); French governor of Canada, 13; eminent services of, ib.

Galloway, Thomas; his scheme for readjusting relations between Great
Britain and her old Colonies, 79

Galt, Sir Alexander; delegate to Quebec Convention of 1864, 20; public services of, ib.

Garneau, French Canadian historian, 192

German and Belgian Treaties; denunciation of, 261, 271

Gilbert, Sir Humphrey; takes possession of Newfoundland, 8

Glenelg, Lord; colonial secretary in 1838, 137

Gordon, Lt.-Governor; promotes federal union in New Brunswick, 212

Gosford, Lord; governor-general of Canada, 132, 134

Gourlay, Robert; misfortunes of, as a reformer in Upper Canada, 143-145

Grasett, Colonel; assists in repressing North-west rebellion of 1885, 253

Gray, Colonel; delegate to Quebec Convention of 1864, 206

Gray, John Hamilton, delegate to Quebec Convention of 1864, 205

Grey, Earl; colonial secretary, 172

Haldimand, general; governor-general of Canada, 71, 72

Haliburton, Judge, author of *Sam Sack*, etc., 164

Halifax, founded, 49

Harvey, Colonel; victory of, at Stoney Creek in 1813, 116. See *Harvey, Sir John*.

Harvey, Sir John; governor of Nova Scotia, of New Brunswick, establishes responsible government in the maritime provinces. See *Harvey, Colonel*.

Haviland, Thomas Heath; delegate to Quebec Convention of 1864, 206; public career of, ib.

Head, Sir Francis Bond; lieutenant-governor of Upper Canada, 148; his unjust treatment of reformers, 149-151; his rashness before rebellion, 152; represses rebellion, 153

Henry, William A.; delegate to Quebec Convention of 1864, 204

Hincks, Sir Francis; Canadian statesman, melancholy death of, 233

Historian of Canada, 192, 284

Hochelaga (Montreal); Indian village of, visited by Jacques Cartier, 6

Howe, Joseph; father of responsible government in Nova Scotia, 175, 176; his quarrel with Lord Falkland, 176-179; ability of, 183, 184; advocate of imperial federation, 195; opposes confederation from 1864-1868, 212, 219; his reasons for receding from his hostile position, 219; enters the Macdonald ministry, 220; lieutenant-governor of Nova Scotia, ib; sudden death of, ib; orator, poet, and statesman, 220, 221

Howland, Sir William P.; delegate to Westminster Palace Conference of 1866-67, 214; lieutenant-governor of Ontario, 217

Hudson's Bay Company; its great territorial privileges, 231-324; its claims purchased by the Canadian government, 227; map illustrating its charter, 222

Hull, General; defeat of, by Brock at Detroit, 114

Hundred Associates, Company of; established in Canada, 10

"Hunter's Lodges"; formed in United States to invade Canada, 154

Huntington, Lucius Seth; makes charges against Sir John Macdonald, 236

Huron Indians; massacre of, by the Iroquois, 12

Hutchinson, Governor Thomas (of Massachusetts); on relations between
Great Britain and her old Colonies, 98

Iberville, founder of Louisiana, 19

Immigration to Canada, 78, 79

Independence of old Thirteen Colonies acknowledged, by Great Britain, 74

Indians; British treatment of, 41, 42; Canadian relations with, 238, 239

Intellectual culture in Canada; under French rule, 35; under British rule, 164, 192, 284, 285

Intercolonial Railway; history of, 191, 215, 219

Iroquois Indians; ferocity of, 10-13

Jameson, Miss Anna, her "Winter Studies and Summer Rambles" in Upper
Canada in 1838, 157-159

Jesuit College at Quebec, 34

Jesuits' Estates, Act; political controversies respecting, 248

Jesuits in Canada, 11, 12; their estates confiscated by the British government, 38; restored in part, 248

Johnson, John; delegate to the Quebec Convention of 1864, 206

Johnston, James William; public career of, 175; eminence of, 185; early advocate of confederation, 194, 195

Joliet, Louis; discovers the Mississippi, 18

Journalism in Canada, 164, 287

Judiciary, independence of; political contests for, 128, 139

Keewatin, district of; established provisionally, 238

Kent, Duke of; commander of British forces in Canada, 193; gives name to P.E. Island, 53; letter to, from Chief Justice B.C. Sewell on union of provinces, 194

King, George E.; prime minister of New Brunswick after Confederation, 218

King's University, Nova Scotia; founded, 163

Kingsford, Dr.; Canadian historian, 284

Kingston, city of; first parliament of Canada meets at, in 1841, 167

Kirk, David; captures Quebec, 10, 11

Labrador, discovery of, 5; origin of name of, 7

Lafontaine-Baldwin Ministry, 170, 173; its successful administration of
Canadian affairs, 173

Lafontaine, Sir Louis Hippolyte; Canadian statesman and jurist, 170, 173, 184

La Gallissonière, French governor of Canada, 35

Lake of Woods, international boundary at, 292, 293; map of, 293

Lalemant, Gabriel; Jesuit martyr, 12

Land question; in Upper Canada, 143; in Prince Edward Island, 54, 234

Langevin, Sir Hector; Canadian statesman, delegate to Quebec Convention of 1864, 205; charges against, 258

Lansdowne, Marquess of; governor-general of Canada, 207

Lartigue, Bishop; *mandement* of, against French Canadian rebels, 135, 136

La Salle, Sieur de (Réné Robert Cavelier); at Lachine, 18; descends the
Mississippi, 18, 19; assassination of, 19

Laurier government; formation of, 265; measures of, 268-272

Laurier, Rt Hon. Sir Wilfrid; prime minister of Canada, 265; settles Manitoba school question, 266 267; represents Canada at celebration of
"Diamond Jubilee" (1897), 36, 270; his action on Canadian aid to England
in South African War, 372; his mastery of English, 267

Laval, Bishop; first Roman Catholic Bishop of Canada, 12; establishes tithes, 29

Laval University, Quebec, 290

La Valmière, a disloyal priest, 72

Lawrence, Governor; expels French Acadians from Nova Scotia, 23; encourages New England emigration, 51; opens first assembly in Halifax, 53

Lepine, Canadian rebel; punished, 241; his sentence commuted, *ib.*

Letellier de Saint-Just; lieutenant-governor of Quebec, 246; dismissed, 246, 247

Lévis, General; defeats Murray at St. Foye, 26

Liberal or Reform party; formed in Nova Scotia, 99; in Upper Canada, 141

Liberal Convention in Ottawa (1893), 259

Libraries in Canada, 290

Lisgar, Lord, governor-general of Canada, 267

Literature in Canada, during French régime, 35; before union of 1840, 164; after union, 192; since Confederation, 284-287

Londonderry in Nova Scotia; origin of name of, 51, 52

Lome, Marquess of; governor-general of Canada, 244; His services to Art,
Science, and Literature, 267

Louisiana, named by La Salle, 19

Louis XIV establishes royal government in Canada, 12, 27, 28

Lount, Samuel; Upper Canadian rebel of 1837, 148, 152-153; executed, 155

Loyalists. See *United Empire Loyalists*

Loyal and Patriotic Society of Upper Canada; usefulness of, during war of 1819-15, 121

Lundy's Lane, battle of; won by British in 1814, 117, 120

Lymburner, Adam; opposes separation of Upper from Lower Canada, 90

Macdonald, Andrew Archibald; delegate to Quebec Convention of 1864, 206

Macdonald, Baroness (of Earnscliffe), 257

Macdonald, Colonel George; at Ogdensburg in 1813, 115; at Chateauguay, 121

Macdonald, John Sanfield; first prime minister of Ontario after Confederation, 217

Macdonald, Rt. Hon. Sir John; enters public life, 173; member of government, ib.; settles Clergy Reserves question, 186; takes lead in establishing Confederation, 198, 199, 209; first prime minister of the Dominion, 216; resigns under unfortunate circumstances, 236; initiates the "National Policy" of Conservative party, 243; prime minister again, ib.; death of, 256; great ability, and patriotism of, 200, 256; mourned by all Canada, 257; monuments and tributes to his memory, ib.

Macdonell; Colonel John; first speaker of assembly of Upper Canada in 1792, 94

Macdonell, Vicar-General; first Roman Catholic Bishop of Upper Canada, 120

Mackenzie, Alexander; prime minister of Canada, 237; character of, ib., 243; his administration of public affairs (1873-78), 238-242; death of, 257

Mackenzie, Sir Alexander; North-west explorer, 224

Mackenzie, William Lyon; journalist and reformer, 146; enters Upper Canada legislature, 146; unjustly expelled, ib., first mayor of Toronto, 147; indiscretions of, ib.; moves for committee of grievances, 148, its report, ib.; defeat of, at elections of 1836, 150, resorts to rebellion, 152; defeat of, at Montgomery's and flight from Canada, 153; on Navy Island, 154; imprisoned in the United States, ib.; returns from exile, 182, exercises no influence in Canadian politics, ib.; poverty and death of, ib.; character of, 182, 183

MacLeod, international dispute respecting, 295

MacNab, Sir Allan; leads loyal "Men of Gore" against Canadian rebels in 1837, 153; orders seizure of steamer Caroline on. U.S. frontier, 154; prime minister of Canada, 186

Maine Boundary Dispute, 292, 296-300; map of, 296

Maisonneuve, Sieur de (Paul de Chomedey); founds Montreal, 12

Manitoba, first visited by French, 20; province of, established, 230

Manitoba school question, 262-265, 266, 267

Maps relating to Canada; of French, Spanish and British possessions in North America in 1756-1761, *at end*; of British possessions in 1763-1775, at end; of boundary established in 1783 between Canada and the United States, 75; of Hudson's Bay Co.'s territory, 222; of Northwest boundary in 1842, 293; of North-eastern boundary in 1842, 297; of Alaskan disputed boundary, 311; of the Dominion of Canada in 1900, at end.

Marquette, Father, founds mission of Sainte-Maria, 17; discovers the Mississippi, 18; death of, *ib.*;

Marriage laws in early Canada, 97

Masères, Attorney-general, 43

Matthews, Peter; Upper Canadian rebel, 148, 151, 153; executed, 155

McCully, Jonathan; delegate to Quebec Convention of 1864, 205

McDougall, William, delegate to Quebec Convention of 1864, 203; provisional lieutenant-governor of N.W.T., 227; Half-breed rebellion prevents him assuming office, ib.; disappears from public life, 230

McGee, Thomas D'Arcy; historian and orator, delegate to Quebec Convention of 1864, 203; his political career in Canada, ib.; assassinated, 221

McGill University, Montreal; founded, 163

McGreevy, Thomas, impeached for serious misdemeanors, 258; punishment of, ib.

McLane, executed for treason in 1793, 101, 102

McLure, General (United States General); burns Niagara in 1814, 116

Mercier, Honoré, prime minister of Quebec, 247; dismissed, ib.

Merritt, W. Hamilton; originator of Welland Canal, 159

Metcalfe, Lord; governor-general of Canada, 170; antagonism of, to responsible government, 171; retirement and death of, ib.

Métis or Half-breeds of the Canadian North-west, 225, 228, 249

Middleton, Major-general; commands Canadian forces on Riel's revolt of 1885 in North-west, 252-254

Military rule in Canada after 1760, 37, 38

Mills, David; Canadian statesman, 206

Minto, Earl of; governor-general of Canada, 268

Mitchell, Peter; delegate to Quebec Convention of 1864, 205; public career of, ib.

Mohawks, members of the Iroquois confederacy, 10; humbled by the Marquis de Tracy, 13. See *Brant Joseph, Iroquois.*

Monk, Lord; governor-general of Canada at Confederation, 216, 267

Montcalm, Marquis de; loses battle on Plains of Abraham, 26; death of ib.

Montgomery, Brigadier-General; invades Canada, 69, 70; death of, at Quebec, 70

Montreal founded, 12

Monts, Sieur de; founder of French *Acadie*, 8

Monts-Déserts named by Champlain, 9

Mowat, Sir Oliver; delegate to Quebec Convention of 1804, 203; public career of, 203, 265, 266

Municipal system of Canada; established, 185, 186; nature of, 278

Murray, General; in command at Quebec, 26; defeat of, at St. Foye, ib.; governor-general of Canada, 42; his just treatment of French Canadians, 43

Mutual or reciprocal preferential trade between Canada and England; advocacy of, 260, 271

Nation Canadienne, La; Papineau's dream of, 130, 133, 134

"National Policy," or Protective system; established by Conservative party (1879), 243, 244

Navigation Laws repealed, 187

Navy Island, see *Mackenzie, William Lyon*

Neilson, John; Canadian journalist and politician, 127, 131

Nelson, Robert; Canadian rebel of 1837-38, 138

Nelson, Dr. Wolfred; leader in Lower Canadian rebellion of 1837, 134

Neutrality of the Great Lakes, 294, 295

"Neutrals," on French Acadians; expulsion of from Nova Scotia, 22, 23

Newark (Niagara), meeting of first Upper Canadian legislature at, 93; seat of government removed from, to York, 101

New Brunswick; originally part of Acadie and Nova Scotia, 53; province of founded by Loyalists, 83; capital ib.; state of, in 1838, 162; political struggle for self-government in, 173, 174; takes part in Quebec Convention, 198, 205; brought into Confederation, 215, 216; boundary dispute with Maine, 296-300

New Brunswick school question, 201, 202

New Brunswick University; founded at Fredericton, 163

New Caledonia; old name of British Columbia, 232

Newfoundland; delegates from, to Quebec Convention of 1864, 206; refuses to join the Dominion, 235

Niagara, see *Newark*

Nicholson, General; captures Port Royal, 9

Norse voyages to Canada, 4

North-eastern Boundary question, 296-299; map of Boundary, 1842, 297

North-west Company; rival of the Hudson's Bay Company in North America, 224, 225

North-west Boundary dispute, 292, 293; map of, 293

North-west Territories, early history of, 221-227; annexation of, to Canada, 227, 230; first rebellion in, 227-230; government of, 277; second rebellion in, 249-255; districts of, 277

Canada Under British Rule 1760-1900

Nova Scotia (Acadie); first settled by France, 8, 9; foundation of Port Royal (Annapolis), 8; ceded to Great Britain by Treaty of Utrecht, 9; population of, at conquest, 15; first called Nova Scotia, 11; Halifax founded, 49; settlement by colonists of New England, 50, 51; expatriation of the Acadian French, 22, 23, 50, 51; population of, in 1767, 51; Irish immigration, ib.; Scotch immigration, 52; early government of, 52, 53, included New Brunswick, C. Breton, and St. John's Island (Pr. Edward I), 53; early courts of justice, 55; coming of Loyalists to, 82; state of in 1837-38, 162, political struggles in, for self-government, 174-180; take part in Quebec Convention of 1864, 198, 204; brought into Confederation, 215; people opposed to, 212, 218, 219; repeal movement gradually ceases in, 233

Novelists, Canadian, 164, 285, 286

O'Callaghan, Dr.; Canadian journalist and rebel, 130

O'Donohue, Canadian rebel, 231; amnesty to, 241

Ohio Valley, French in, 23

Oregon Boundary, dispute respecting, 300-302

Osgoode, Chief Justice; first speaker of legislative council of Upper Canada in 1792, 94

Ottawa, city of; founded, 158

Pacific Cable; action of Canadian government with respect to, 271

Palmer, Edward; delegate to Quebec Convention of 1864, 206

Panet, Joseph Antoine; first speaker of assembly of Lower Canada in 1792, 93

Papineau, Louis J.; leader of French Canadian malcontents in rebellion of 1837, 129-134; conduct of, on outbreak of rebellion, 134, 135; return of, from exile, 181; opposes responsible government, ib.; loses political influence, ib.; character of, 180-182

Pardon, prerogative of; instructions respecting exercise of, 241

Parishes established in French Canada, 29

Parker, Gilbert; Canadian novelist, 286

Parr Town, first name of St. John, New Brunswick, 83

Perry, Peter; founder of Upper Canadian Reform party, 141, 146, 150

Pictou Academy, Nova Scotia; founded, 163

Pitt, the elder (Lord Chatham); gives Canada to Great Britain, 25, 35, 36

Pitt, William (the younger); introduces Act separating Upper from Lower
Canada (Constitutional Act of 1791), 90, 91

Plains of Abraham; Wolfe's victory on, 26

Plattsburg, battle of, pusillanimity of General Prevost at, 117

Plessis, Bishop (Roman Catholic); patriotism of, in war of 1812-15, 120

Poets in Canada, 192, 284, 285

Pontiac's Conspiracy, 39

Pope, William H., delegate to Quebec Convention of 1864, 206

Portuguese discovery in Canada, 5

Post Office in Canada; under British management, 164; transferred to Canada, 187

Poundmaker, Indian chief in North-west; rebels against Canadian government, 253; punished, 254

Poutrincourt, Baron de; founder of Port Royal, 8

Powell, Chief Justice, his unjust treatment of Robert Gourlay, 145

Preferential trade with Great Britain, 200, 201, 269, 271

Prevost, Sir George (governor-general of Canada), retires from Sackett's Harbour 1813, 115; retreats from Plattsburg in 1814, 117; character of, 113

Prince, Colonel; orders execution of American raiders in 1838, 155

Prince Edward Island. See *St. John's Island*

Prince of Wales visits Canada, 193

Princess Louise, arrives in Canada with the Marquess of Lorne, 244; her support of Art, 288

Proclamation of 1764; for government of Canada, 40-42

Procter, General, defeats General Winchester in 1813, 115; beaten at Moraviantown in 1813, 116

Prohibitory Liquor Law; agitation for, 340; popular vote on, ib.

Protestantism unknown in French Canada, 28

Provincial governments established under Confederation, 217, 218

Provinces, constitution of, under Confederation, 275, 276

Puritan migration to Nova Scotia, 50

Put-in Bay (Lake Erie); British fleet defeated at, in 1813, 116

Quebec Act; origin of, 44, 45, its provisions, 45-47; how received in Canada, 46; unpopularity of, in old British colonies, 67

Quebec, Convention of, 1864; delegates to, 199-206; passes resolutions in favour of federal union, 206-209

Quebec founded, 9

Queenston Heights; battle of, in 1812, 114

Railways in Canada; in 1865, 191, in 1899, 273. See *Intercolonial R. Canadian Pacific R.*

Rebellion in Lower Canada; its origin, 124-133; Louis J. Papineau's part in, 129-134; outbreak of, 134; prompt action of authorities against, ib.; Dr. Nelson wins success at St. Denis, ib.; defeat of Brown at St. Charles, ib.; flight of Papineau and rebel leaders, ib.; fight at St. Eustache and death of Chenier, ib.; murder of Weir and Chartrand, 135; collapse of the rebellion of 1837, 135, 136; loyal action of Bishop Lartigue, 135; arrival of Lord Durham as British high-commissioner and governor-general, 136; his career in Canada, 137-138; Sir John Colborne; governor-general, 139; second outbreak of rebellion, 1838, ib.; promptly subdued, ib.; punishment of prominent insurgents, ib.; action of United States government during, 139; social and economic condition of Canada during, 159-162; remedial policy of British government, and new era of political development. See *Responsible Government in Canada.*

Rebellion in Upper Canada; effect of family compact on, 140, 141; of clergy reserves on, 141, 142; influence of Archdeacon, afterwards Bishop, Strachan in public affairs, 142; unjust treatment of Robert Gourlay, 143-145; persecution of William Lyon Mackenzie, 146-148; other prominent actors in, 148; indiscretions of the lieutenant-governor, Sir Francis Bond Head, 149-152; outbreak and repression of, 152, 153; flight of Mackenzie and other rebel leaders, 153; Mackenzie's seizure of Navy Island, 154; affair of the Caroline, ib.; filibustering expeditions against Canada from United States in 1838, 154, 155; prompt execution of filibusters by Colonel Prince, 155; action of U.S. authorities during, ib.; execution of Von Schoultz, Lount, Matthews, and other rebels, ib.; Sir George Arthur, harshness of, ib.; social and economic conditions of Upper Canada at time of, 156-159; rebellion leads to the enlargement of political privileges of people, See *Responsible Government in Canada.*

Rebellion Losses Bill (of 1849); its nature, 188; assented to by Lord Elgin, 189; consequent rioting and burning of parliament house at Montreal, 189, Lord Elgin's life in danger, ib.; his wise constitutional action, ib. Rebellions in North-west: See *North-western Territories,* and *Riel, Louis.*

Reciprocity of Trade between Canada and the United States; treaty of 1814, 190, 191; repeal of the same, 303; efforts to renew it, 304, 307; Canadians not now so favourable to, 310

Recollets, or Franciscans, in Canada, 11

Redistribution Acts of 1882 and 1897; measures to amend, rejected by Senate, 268

Representative institutions in Canada; established in Nova Scotia, 53; in New Brunswick, 88; in French or Lower Canada (Quebec), 91; in Upper
Canada (Ontario), ib.; in Prince Edward Island, 54; in Manitoba, 230; in
British Columbia, 232

Responsible government in Canada; beginnings of, 165-175; consummated by Lord Elgin, 173; struggle for, in New Brunswick, 173, 174; in Nova Scotia, 174-180; in Prince Edward Island, 180; prominent advocates of, 183-185; results of (1841-1867), 185-192

Revenue of Canada in 1899, 273

Riall, General; defeated by United States troops at Street's Creek in 1814, 117

Richardson, Major; Canadian author, 164

Richelieu, Cardinal; his effort to colonise Canada, 10

Rideau Canal, constructed, 158

Riel, Louis; leads revolt of French half-breeds in North-west, 228; murders Ross, 229; flies from the country, ib; elected to and expelled from the Canadian Commons, 241; reappears in North-west, and leads second revolt, 249-253; captured and executed, 253, 254; political complications concerning, 240, 254

Roberval, Sieur de (Jean François de la Rocque); attempts to settle Canada, 7

Robinson, Chief Justice; public career of, in Upper Canada, 145

Rocque, Jean François de la. See *Roberval*

Roebuck, Mr.; Canadian agent in England, 131

Rolph, Dr.; his part in Canadian rebellion of 1837, 151-153; character of, 183

Roman Catholic Church in Canada, 28, 29, 43, 46, 47

Rose, Sir John, effort of, to obtain reciprocity with United States, 304

Rosebery, Earl of, unveils Sir John Macdonald's bust in St. Paul's Cathedral, 256

Rouse's Point, boundary at, 302

Royal Society of Canada, 286

Rupert's Land; origin of name of, 224. See *North-west Territories of Canada*.

Russell, Administrator, 101

Russell, Lord John; introduces resolutions respecting Canada in British parliament in 1836, 132; also Act reuniting the Canadas in 1840, 166; lays basis of responsible government in Canada, 167. See *Responsible Government in Canada*.

Ryerson, Rev. Egerton; Loyalist, Methodist, and educationalist, 141, 147, 192

Sainte-Geneviève (Pillage Bay); named St. Laurens by Jacques Carrier, 7

Salaberry, Colonel de; defeats United States troops at Chateauguay, 121

Sanderson, Robert; first speaker of assembly of Nova Scotia, 53

San Juan Island; international dispute respecting, 301, 302

Sarrasin, Dr., French Canadian scientist, 35

Saskatchewan River (Poskoiac), discovery of, 20

Sculpture in Canada, 288

Seaforth, Lord. See *Colborne, Sir John*

Secord, Laura; heroic exploit of, in 1814, 120

Seigniorial tenure in French Canada, 14, 32; abolished under British rule, 186

Selkirk, Lord; attempts to colonise North-west, 225; death of, *ib.*

Seven Years' War; between France and Great Britain in America, 21-27

Sewell, Chief Justice (Loyalist); adviser of Sir James Craig, 96; suggests union of provinces, 194

Shea, Ambrose; delegate to Quebec Convention of 1864, 206

Sheaffe, General; services of, during war of 1812-15, 114

Shelburne, in Nova Scotia, founded by Loyalists, 82

Sherbrooke, Sir John, governor of Nova Scotia, 118; occupies Maine in war of 1812-15, ib.

Shirley, Governor; deep interest of, in Nova Scotia, 49

Simcoe, Colonel; first lieutenant-governor of Upper Canada, 93; public career of, 94

Simultaneous polling at elections established, 239

Slavery in Canada, 98

Smith, Chief Justice (Loyalist); first president of legislative council of Lower Canada in 1792, 92; suggests federal union of provinces, 194

Smith, Donald (Lord Strathcona); intervenes in North-west rebellion of 1870, 229

Social and economic conditions of the Canadian provinces; in 1838, 156-164; in 1866, 189-192; in 1900, 272-290

South African War; Canadians take part in, 271, 272

Square Gulf, or "golfo quadrado"; old name of St. Lawrence Gulf, 7

St. Charles; defeat of Canadian rebels in 1837 at, 134

St. Denis; Canadian rebels repulsed by British regulars in 1837 at, 134

St. Eustache; stand of Canadian rebels at, 134; death of Chenier, ib.

St. John, New Brunswick; founded, 83

St. John's, Island; named Prince Edward, 53; under government of Nova Scotia, *ib.*; survey of, ib.; separated from Nova Scotia, 54; public lands of, granted by lottery, ib.; political struggles in, for self-government, 180, 185; takes part in Quebec Convention of 1864, 206; enters Confederation, 234; settlement of its land question, ib.

St. Lawrence, River and Gulf of; origin of name of, 7

St. Lusson, Sieur; takes possession of the Sault, 18

St. Maurice forges founded, 30

Stadacona (Quebec), Indian village of, visited by Jacques Cartier, 6

Stanley, Lord, governor-general of Canada, 267

Steeves, William H.; delegate to Quebec Convention of 1864, 206

Strachan, Bishop (Anglican); patriotism of, during war of 1812-15, 121; his influence in Upper Canadian politics, 142

Strange, Lt.-Col.; engaged in repressing North-west rebellion of 1885, 253

Stuart, Andrew; prominent Canadian lawyer and politician, 127, 131

Sulpitians in Canada, 37

Superior Council of French Canada. See *Supreme Council*

Supreme Council, established by Louis XIV in French Canada, 28, 29

Supreme Court, established in Canada, 239

Sydenham, Lord (Poulett Thomson); governor-general of Canada, 166; carries out scheme of uniting the Canadas in 1840, 167; opinions of, on responsible government, 168; death of, 169

Taché, Sir Etienne Paschal; chairman of Quebec Convention of 1864, 199; character of, ib.

Talbot, Colonel, pioneer in Upper Canada, 157

Talon, Intendant, 13

Taite, Israel; accuses McGreevy of grave misdemeanours, 258; member of Laurier ministry, 206

Temperance Legislation; "Scott Act" passed, 239; *plèbiscite* on Prohibition, 240

Thompson, Sir John; prime minister of Canada, 257; sudden death of, ib; great ability of, ib.

Thomson, Poulett. See *Sydenham, Lord*

Tilley, Sir Leonard; delegate to Quebec Convention of 1864, 205; public career of, ib.; introduces scheme of "National Policy," 244

Timber trade in Canada, in early time, 162

Tithes established in French Canada, 29

Todd, Dr.; Constitutional writer, 286

Tonge, William Cottnam Tonge; Nova Scotian Liberal, 99; his controversy with Governor Wentworth, ib.

Trade of Canada in 1899, 273

Treaties, international, affecting Canada; of St. Germain-en-Laye (1632), 11; of Utrecht (1713), 9, 21, 22; of Paris (1763), 38; of Versailles, 292; of Ghent, 293; of 1818, 294; Ashburton (1842), 299; Oregon (1846), 301; reciprocity (1854), 303; of Washington (1871), 305, 306; Bering Sea, 308, 309, Anglo-Russian (Alaska), 310-312

Treaties with Indian tribes of Canada, 41, 238

Trutch, Sir Joseph; first lieutenant-governor of British Columbia under
Confederation, 232

Tupper, Sir Charles; prime minister of Nova Scotia, 192; services of, to education, ib.; delegate to Quebec Convention of 1864, 204; introduces legislation for construction of Canadian Pacific Railway, 244; high commissioner of Canada in London, 258; re-enters political life, ib.; action of, on Manitoba school question, 264; prime minister of Canada, 265; defeat of, at general elections of 1896, ib; difference with Lord Aberdeen, when governor-general, ib.; remarkable ability of, 204, 258; leader of Liberal Conservative party from 1896-1900, 258; policy of, on "preferential trade" with Great Britain, 271

Tyler, Professor, on U.E. Loyalists, 76

Uniacke, James Boyle; Nova Scotian statesman, 175; advocate of responsible government, 176; first minister of Nova Scotia, 180

Union of the Canadas in 1840, 166, 167

United Empire Loyalists; number of, during American Revolution, 76; justice done to, ib.; opinions of, on issues of revolution, 77, 78; suffering of, during revolution, 79; treatment of, after the peace of 1783, 80; compensation to, by British government, 81; settle in British America, ib; privations of, in Nova Scotia, 80; founders of New Brunswick, 83; of Upper Canada, 84; eminent descent of, 86; Canada's debt to, ib origin of name of, 89; representatives of, in first legislature of New Brunswick, 87, 88; of Upper Canada, 94; services of, during war of 1812-15, 188-120

Universities in Canada, 163, 289

University of Toronto, beginning of, 164

Upper Canada, founded by Loyalists, 84; first districts of, 89, 94; made separate province, 91, first government of, 93; Newark, first capital of, ib.; York (Toronto), second capital of, 94; rebellion in, see *Rebellion in Upper Canada*; state of, in 1838, 159; reunited with Lower Canada, 166; joins Confederation as Ontario, 216

Upper Canada College, Toronto, founded, 163

Ursulines at Quebec, 34

Vancouver Island; history of, 231, 232

Verendrye, Sieur de la (Pierre Gauthier de Varennes); discovers Manitoba and North-west of Canada, 19, 20

Verrazzano, Giovanni di; voyages of, to North America, 5

Victoria College, Upper Canada, founded, 164

Vincent, General; services of, in war of 1812-15, 115

Von Schoultz; leads filibusters into Canada, 155; executed, ib.

War of 1812-15; origin of, 103-110; population of Canada and United States during, 110-112; loyalty of Canadian people during, 113; services of General Brock during, 114; campaign of 1812 in Upper Canada, 114, 115; of 1813, 115, 116; of 1814, 117; maritime provinces during, 117, 118, close of, 118; services of Loyalists during, 118-120; Laura Secord, heroism of, 120; description of striking incidents of battles during, 121-123

Washington, George; eminent character of, 66

Washington Treaty of 1871, 304, 305

Weir, Lieutenant, murder of, in Lower Canadian rebellion of 1837, 135

Welland Canal commenced, 159; completed, 190

Wentworth, Sir John; Loyalist governor of Nova Scotia, 99

Westminster Palace Conference in London; Canadian delegates arrange final terms of federation at, 214, 215

Wetmore, Attorney-general; first minister of New Brunswick after Confederation, 218

Whelan, Edward; delegate to Quebec Convention of 1864, 206

White, Thomas; Canadian journalist and statesman, 256; sudden death of, ib.

William IV visits Canada as Prince William Henry, 193

Williams, Lt.-Col.; death of, in North-west rebellion of 1885, 254

Williams, Sir Fenwick ("hero of Kars"); lieutenant-governor of Nova Scotia, 213, 217

Wilmot, Lemuel A.; father of responsible government in New Brunswick, 174, 185; lieutenant-governor of the province, 217

Wolfe, General; at Quebec, 25; his bold ascent of heights, 25, 26; wins battle on Plains of Abraham, 26; death of, 26; a maker of Canada, 35

York (Toronto) made capital of Upper Canada, 101

Young, Sir William; Nova Scotian statesman and jurist, 185

Yukon, district of; gold discovery in, 209; administration of, ib, 277; boundaries of, 310-312

Copyright © 2023 Esprios Digital Publishing. All Rights Reserved.

Milton Keynes UK
Ingram Content Group UK Ltd.
UKHW050447280324
440101UK00016B/1249